Of Sympathy and Selfishness

I0808807

THE McDONALD
CENTER FOR
AMERICA'S FOUNDING
PRINCIPLES

MERCER
UNIVERSITY

The A. V. Elliott Conference Series

The Thomas C. and Ramona E. McDonald Center
for America's Founding Principles

Guided by James Madison's maxim that "a well-instructed people alone can be permanently a free people," the McDonald Center exists to promote the study of the great texts and ideas that have shaped our regime and fostered liberal learning.

Directors
Will R. Jordan
Charlotte C. S. Thomas

Published Volumes

Charlotte C. S. Thomas, ed., *No Greater Monster nor Miracle than Myself: The Political Philosophy of Michel de Montaigne*

Of Sympathy and Selfishness

The Moral and Political Philosophy of Adam Smith

Edited by | Charlotte C. S. Thomas

Mercer University Press | *Macon, Georgia*

MUP/ P506

Published by Mercer University Press, Macon, Georgia 31207

1400 Coleman Avenue
Macon, Georgia 31207

9 8 7 6 5 4 3 2 1

Books published by Mercer University Press are printed on acid-free paper that meets the requirements of the American National Standard for Information Sciences—Permanence of Paper for Printed Library Materials.

ISBN 978-0-88146-529-7
Cataloging-in-Publication Data is available from the Library of Congress

Contents

MERCER
UNIVERSITY PRESS

Endowed by
TOM WATSON BROWN
and
THE WATSON-BROWN FOUNDATION, INC.

Contributors

Jennifer Baker—Associate Professor of Philosophy, College of Charleston, Charleston, South Carolina

Scott Beaulier—Executive Director of the Center for Economic Liberty in the W. P. Carey School of Buisness at Arizona State University

Art Carden—Assistant Professor of Economics, Samford University, Birmingham, Alabama

Douglas Den Uyl—Vice President of Educational Programs, Liberty Fund, Indianapolis, Indiana

Ryan Patrick Hanley—Associate Professor of Political Science, Marquette University, Milwaukee, Wisconsin

Kevin S. Honeycutt—Assistant Professor of Philosophy, Mercer University, Macon, Georgia

Arielle John—Miller Upton Teaching Fellow, Beloit College, Beloit, Wisconsin

Joseph M. Knippenberg—Professor of Politics, Oglethorpe University, Atlanta, Georgia

Virgil Henry Storr—Senior Research Fellow and Director of Graduate Student Programs, Mercatus Center, George Mason University, Arlington, Virginia

Charlotte C. S. Thomas—Professor of Philosophy, Co-Director of the McDonald Center for America's Founding Principles, Director of the Philosophy, Politics, and Economics Program, Mercer University, Macon, Georgia

Eduardo Velasquez—Professor of Politics, Washington and Lee University, Lexington, Virginia

Stuart D. Warner—Professor of Philosophy, Roosevelt University, Chicago, Illinois

Acknowledgments

This collection of essays is based on the 2013 A.V. Elliott conference for Great Books and Ideas, the 6th annual conference sponsored by the Thomas C. and Ramona E. McDonald Center for America's Founding Principles.

The McDonald Center for America's Founding Principles began as a small conference in spring 2008. It secured initial funding that summer through Mercer University's Academic Initiatives Monetary (AIM) fund and has grown substantially each year. Neither this volume, nor the conference it is based upon, nor any of the other important work now done by the McDonald Center would have been possible without the foresight of Mercer President William D. Underwood, the confidence of the AIM committee, the support of College of Liberal Arts Dean Lake Lambert, and the entrepreneurial spirit of the center's founders.

In spring 2013, the McDonald Center received a generous endowment from Mr. A. V. Elliott, for whom our annual conference is now named. Also in 2013, Thomas and Ramona McDonald endowed all of the center's work, and with it they gave us their name. We are, and always will be, in deep debt to the Elliotts and McDonalds for their support.

Our conference on the moral philosophy and political economy of Adam Smith was a gathering of Smith scholars on Mercer's main campus in Macon, Georgia, and the culmination of a semester-long reading group made up of Mercer faculty and students. I am grateful to all of the participants in that group. Each of them contributed significantly to the excellent conversation that animated our conference and inspired this volume of essays. So, thank you, Will Jordan, Garland Crawford, Kathy Kloepper, Lori Johnson, Anna Weaver, John Dove, Lisa Bianco, Lauren Light, David Lockwood, Kimberly Lammers, Brandon Brock, Jackson Brown, Connor Cosenza, Ronnie Davis, Taylor

Garrett, Brianna Green, and David Wildes.

I'm sincerely thankful to Ryan Hanley, Douglas Den Uyl, Stuart Warner, Joseph Knippenberg, Eduardo Velasquez, Scott Beaulier, Art Carden, Kevin Honeycutt, and Jennifer Baker for presenting their scholarly work at the Elliott Conference, for interacting so thoughtfully with the students at the conference, and for submitting their revised essays for publication in this volume. It has been a great honor to learn about Smith from these brilliant, lovely people. I would also like to thank our undergraduate student panelists, who showed great ambition and courage by sharing their research on Smith with all of our visitors and their peers at Mercer who attended the Elliott conference: Brandon Brock, Jackson Brown, Connor Cosenza, and Ronnie Davis.

Many, many thanks are due to Marc Jolley and to the whole staff at Mercer University Press, who have been a pleasure to work with. I will be a better person if some tiny bit of their good spirit, thoughtfulness, and diplomacy has rubbed off on me during our collaboration on this volume.

Finally, it continues to be a great privilege to work as co-director of the McDonald Center with one of its founders, Will Jordan. For four years, I have enjoyed the remarkable and enviable task of fostering good conversations about great ideas among delightful people. Without Professor Jordan's energy and foresight, the McDonald Center would not exist. Without his thoughtfulness and good judgment, it would not be thriving. Without his friendship, my work for the Center would be much less fun. So, thanks, Will, for all you do, and for the grace with which you do it. Everyone who benefits from the good work of the McDonald Center is deeply in your debt.

Abbreviations

All citations are to the Glasgow edition of Smith's works published in paperback by Liberty Fund. The following abbreviations are used and follow the Glasgow edition's system of paragraph numbering (the sole exception is Smith's correspondence, which references letter number rather than paragraph number). Smith's original capitalization and punctuation have been retained, but his spelling has been modernized in places where needed.

CAS—*Correspondence of Adam Smith*, ed. E. C. Mossner and I. S. Ross (Indianapolis: Liberty Fund, 1987).

EPS—*Essays on Philosophical Subjects*, ed. W. P. D. Wightman and J. C. Bryce (Indianapolis: Liberty Fund, 1982).

HA—"The Principles Which Lead and Direct Philosophical Enquiries: Illustrated by the History of Astronomy," in *EPS*.

LJ—*Lectures on Jurisprudence*, ed. R. L. Meek, D. D. Raphael, and P. G. Stein (Indianapolis: Liberty Fund, 1982). "A" and "B" refer to the Reports of 1762–1762 and 1766, respectively.

LRBL—*Lectures on Rhetoric and Belles Lettres*, ed. J. C. Bryce (Indianapolis: Liberty Fund, 1985).

TMS—*The Theory of Moral Sentiments*, ed. D. D. Raphael and A. L. Macfie (Indianapolis: Liberty Fund, 1982).

WN—*An Inquiry into the Nature and Causes of the Wealth of Nations*, ed. R. H. Campbell, A. S. Skinner, and W. B. Todd (Indianapolis: Liberty Fund, 1981).

Introduction

Charlotte C. S. Thomas

During a recent visit to Mercer University to deliver a talk on religious liberty, former United States ambassador to the United Nations and prominent philosopher, theologian, and political theorist, Michael Novak made an interesting offhand remark about Adam Smith. He said, in effect, that Smith's work on the causes of the wealth of nations had been proven over and over again in the last two hundred years and that questions concerning the causes of poverty were no longer the important questions. If we understand what causes wealth, he said, then those who come to the international bargaining table cannot appeal to the poverty of their people without also admitting that someone is doing something wrong.

This is a remarkable and, no doubt, controversial claim, but it highlights the relevance of Adam Smith and the other architects of the new science of man for contemporary debate and policy design. Smith's great work of political economy, *An Inquiry into the Nature and Causes of the Wealth of Nations*, lays out principles of wealth creation that have been continuously tested theoretically and practically since its publication, and they have been shown sound. There is little serious debate whether individual rights, private property, stable institutions, and the rule of law are important to the development of nations. Instead, debate rages regarding how to negotiate the cultural and spiritual costs of wealth, how to establish and maintain a legal and institutional context that promotes liberty and equal opportunities for all, and how to manage the inequalities that inevitably emerge from those equal opportunities.

Readers of Smith know, however, that these were Smith's questions, too. He set the intellectual agenda not only for an economic theory but also for a political theory that takes seriously the institutional complexities of wealth creation and a moral theory that takes seriously the spiritual costs of living in commercial society. There is no better example of this than the story of "The Poor Man's Son" from Smith's first great work, *The Theory of Moral Sentiments* (hereafter, *TMS*).[1] As Smith tells it, a young man with great energy and a stable subsistence, but without significant resources, becomes drawn to the "frivolous utilities" available to the wealthy. He imagines that were he to acquire a "machine" to carry him about and thus avoid the inconvenience and fatigue of walking or riding, he would be more "content." If he were to live in a palace, rather than his father's cottage, he would be "more at ease." His "natural indolence" suggests to him that if he had a retinue of servants, he would be saved from "a great deal of trouble." "He thinks if he had attained all these, he would sit still contentedly, and be quiet, enjoying himself in the thought of the happiness and tranquility of his situation."[2]

Of course, the poor man's son does not find tranquility either in the pursuit or the attainment of these objects. Instead, he exhausts his life in their pursuit, denying himself the pleasures and satisfactions already in his reach. And, in their attainment, he realizes that they do not bring the contentment that he had imagined they would. Through the whole of his life he pursues the idea of a certain artificial and elegant repose he may never attain, for which he sacrifices a real tranquility that is at all times in his power, and which, if in the extremity of old age he should at last reach, he will find to be in no respect preferable to that humble security and contentment he had abandoned for it.

On his deathbed, the poor man's son finally recognizes the futility of looking for contentment in increased conveniences or in the beautifully efficient machines and systems that promise them. He recognizes that fancy things do not offer tranquilities that are not already available through simple things. In short, Smith anticipates the plot of *Citizen Kane* and every other work of literature or theory that explores the siren song of consumerism.

[1] *The Theory of Moral Sentiments*, ed. D. D. Raphael and A. L. Macfie (Indianapolis: Liberty Fund, 1982).

[2] Ibid., 181.

Consumerism and life in commercial society are not the same. The poor man's son is caught up in consumerism as it is generally understood in the contemporary world. He believes that things will make him happy, so he organizes his life in order to acquire more and more and better and better things. Either he recognizes that he is on an emotional "hamster wheel" and jumps off at some point, or he keeps plugging away without ever realizing that he is no closer to happiness than before. Consumerism thrives within commercial society, but so do many other ways of being in the world. The poor man's son, like many others, falls for the false promises of frivolous utilities. It is in our nature, according Smith, for us to be weak to their appeal, but we can do otherwise, and many in commercial society do. We can "live well," pursuing those activities and situations and things that bring genuine satisfactions and recognizing that very different activities and situations and things will offer those satisfactions to different people. Individual rights, private property, rule of law, and stable institutions provide a context in which we can direct our own lives, and in which we can create countless opportunities for others to direct their own.

One of the most compelling contemporary voices for the variety of good lives that commercial society (i.e., capitalism) not only allows but also, in fact, promotes, is economic historian Deirdre McCloskey. She puts it this way,

> People have purposes. A capitalist economy gives them scope to try them out. Go to an American Kennel Club show, or an antique show, or a square-dancing convention, or to a gathering of the many millions of American bird watchers, and you'll find people of no social pretentions passionately engaged. Yes, some people watch more than four hours of TV a day. Yes, some people engage in corrupting purchases. But, they are no worse than their ancestors, and on average better.[3]

That's the key. Some people, like the poor man's son, make corrupting choices when they find themselves within a social and

[3] Dierdre N. McCloskey, *Bourgeois Virtue: Ethics for an Age of Commerce* (Chicago: University of Chicago Press, 2010), 24.

political context where they may choose their own path. But, others make good choices out of the same context. And, importantly, it is only when one makes one's choices for oneself that one has the opportunity to be fully free, self-determining, and virtuous. So, it is possible to live poorly in commercial society, but throughout human history it has been possible, even likely, that one would live poorly. What is new and unprecedented about commercial society is that there are more opportunities than ever for people to live well.

For those of us who are interested in moral theory and who find Smith's account compelling, questions abound regarding the best ways to live one's life in the heady context of wealth and freedom. For those whose interests lean toward political and economic questions, Smith offers many insights to deepen our understanding of the institutional implications of the explosion of the world's wealth. Smith's basic insights are persuasive, but there is much work to be done to understand them in their original context, adapt them to our current circumstances, and keep a close eye on how to keep reconciled the moral, political, and economic ideas that he presented as so inextricably connected.

This volume offers readers a broad range of perspectives on Adam Smith's political economy, moral theory, and contemporary relevance. It is made up of revised versions of papers presented at the 2013 A. V. Elliott Conference on Great Books and Ideas sponsored by Mercer University's McDonald Center for America's Western Foundations. Scholars of philosophy, political science, and economics from all over the country came together for a few days that spring to discuss Smith's moral and political philosophies. Our particular task was to think about the relationship between Smith's moral theory and political economy, and to consider the relevance of the Smithian corpus, taken whole, for contemporary American society.

Our keynote speakers for the conference were Douglas Den Uyl (Liberty Fund) and Ryan Patrick Hanley (Marquette University). Den Uyl, who is well know for his work on neo-Aristotelian virtue ethics, gives us a "note" in this volume on prudence and commerce in Smith. In contemporary parlance, he argues, prudence has lost its meaning as a virtue, but such meaning is retained by Smith, especially in Part VI of the *Theory of Moral Sentiments*. The self-regarding nature of prudence does not, by his account, rule out a simultaneous other-regarding aspect, which Smith retains. Such a reading of this section of the *TMS* is particularly interesting, given that it was written after the publication of the *Nature and Causes of the Wealth of Nations* and thus seems to reflect back on the way prudence should be understood in Smith's political economy.

In "On Vernon's Smith," Ryan Hanley explores Nobel laureate Vernon Smith's debts and disagreements with Adam Smith's moral theory and political economy. In the history of economics, very little precedes Adam Smith's theoretical framework, and very little has come more recently than Vernon Smith's breakthroughs in experimental economics. So, Hanley's essay draws together for consideration some of the oldest and newest ideas in the tradition. He calls explicitly for a "renewed engagement between students of the past and students of the present" for what a deepened understanding of the tradition can offer to contemporary experimental economists and for how contemporary research can push towards new ways of interrogating Adam Smith's fundamental insights regarding commercial society.

Stuart Warner, in "Grounded in Nature," pushes toward an understanding of the deepest metaphysical context for Smith's moral theory and political economy, asking what his comportment to the transcendental realm might be, and how one should understand his frame of reference for attempting to understand the human condition. Nature plays a central role in Smith's *TMS* and is, indeed, personified in Smith's text, but what is the nature of Nature for Smith? What are Smith's purposes—rhetorically, morally, and religiously—for his presentation of Nature as an entity with intentions? And, given a clearer view of what Nature is for Smith, what light does it shine on human nature, reason, and our moral agency?

Virgil Storr and Arielle John offer a different perspective on Smith, but one that, like Warner's, promises to change the way much of Smithian moral theory should be read. Rather than pushing toward a deeper understanding of one of Smith's foundational ideas, Storr and John illuminate the influence of Smith's cultural context for his arguments regarding "the impartial spectator" and ask whether this fundamental idea can function meaningfully without the cultural assumptions within which it was framed. What comes into focus when we aren't looking through "The Impartial Spectator's Moral Spectacles"?

Kevin Honeycutt's essay "Adam Smith's Philosophical History" takes up Smith's understanding of history and its relevance for his moral theory and political economy. Specifically, Honeycutt explores Smith's *Lectures on Rhetoric and Belle Lettres* to consider the function of history in Smith's thought. Notably, the idea of sympathy emerges as central to Smith's account of history and thus serves as a bridge to *TMS* where sympathy is also central. Particularly in the "History of Historians," Smith presents ancient figures such as Tacitus and Livy, whose writing demonstrates how history distinguishes itself from poetry in its emphasis on the instruction of the reader, particularly through the cultivation of sympathy.

In her essay "Visible Hands: Ethics and the Market," Jennifer Baker seeks a norm for market behavior, a justification "that helps us assess why market behavior is acceptable and when it is." Contemporary accounts of the moral normativity of commercial activity tend to be incoherent or to present a false dilemma: i.e., one is either operating with a market or is operating virtuously. It is clear that markets have contributed substantially to the improvement of our material conditions, so some market activities should be understood as a part of a set of activities that could enact, for example, generosity and thus be a part of virtue. It is equally obvious that not all market activities can be characterized in those terms. So, what divides these two kinds of commerce? What are the criteria for a norm that could guide a meaningful assessment of the morality of market activities? Baker offers a list of such criteria and speculates on a norm that might satisfy them.

Art Carden brings Smith's insights on the natural human attraction to system to bear on one of the most pressing contemporary issues: the desire of wealthy individuals and nations to contribute to those who are less wealthy and in need of economic development. Smith probably would not have been able to comprehend the wealth of the contemporary developed world or the gap between that wealth and the poverty of much of the developing world. But, Smith's account of human nature holds, as do his cautions against presumption, foolish systematicity, and an unconstrained vision of the human condition. Carden traces Smith's influence through the work of Friedrich Hayek and contemporary theorists such as Thomas Sowell, Deirdre McCloskey, and Christopher Coyne in order to show Smith's relevance to these very present and pressing questions.

Scott Beaulier, like Carden, takes up a pressing contemporary question and considers how Adam Smith might help us develop a response, but for Beaulier the question is what to do about an oppressive national debt. As current as this question is, Smith has a direct and detailed response based on his experiences with the sovereign's management of the national debt of his day. Smith details the machinations of a state that needs to declare itself bankrupt but that resorts to "juggling tricks" to avoid bankruptcy, and he lays out the deleterious consequences of such actions. Beaulier takes Smith's account of the "juggler" and examines the ways the United States juggles its debt instead of facing it in a fair, open, and honorable way. He concludes his essay with an attempt to adapt Smith's advice for dealing with an oppressive national debt to current policy recommendations.

Joseph Knippenberg, who regularly teaches Adam Smith's *Wealth of Nations* in a sophomore level core course at Oglethorpe University, presents his thoughts on how Smith's ideas function within the context of a contemporary liberal arts curriculum, as well as what Smith's philosophy seems to recommend for liberal education. He begins with the insight that all American liberal arts colleges exist within a market context, a commercial society, and that such a context makes the "unproductive work" of teaching in a liberal arts college tense, controversial, and extremely important. Knippenberg also considers what advice Smith might have for those within the academy who deal with this tension by complaining about the vulnerability of liberal arts education to the market or what advice he might have for politicians who find themselves tempted to build grand systems to "fix" liberal education, rather than allowing institutions to develop within their own organic contexts and in light of the local knowledge that only their stakeholders are likely to possess.

Finally, Eduardo Velasquez asks the provocative question "Was Adam Smith a Buddhist?" By emphasizing the anecdotal, phenomenological character of the *TMS*, Velasquez begins with an account of what it might look like to "practice" thought within the *TMS*, rather than to engage its arguments as objects to be consumed or appropriated. Velasquez goes on to consider Smith as a contemplative philosopher and to explore the insights into Smith's philosophy that might follow from approaching him through the framework of contemporary contemplative theory.

All in all, the essays in this volume span the disciplines of philosophy, economics, politics, history, and literature, with nods to everything else from the creative arts to natural science. They also range broadly through the history of political economy, exploring Adam Smith's researches into ancient philosophy as well as his relevance to some of the most pressing policy questions of our day. It is, I think a fitting testament to the breadth, strength, and relevance of Smith's thought for today, and a trailhead to paths forward for meaningful and relevant interdisciplinary Smithian research.

1 | Grounded in Nature

An Essay on Adam Smith's *Theory of Moral Sentiments*

Stuart D. Warner

> The good order or the rational is the result of forces which do not themselves tend toward the good order or the rational.
>
> —Leo Strauss, *Natural Right and History*

Our temptation is to turn to the final part of *The Theory of Moral Sentiments* in an attempt to discover the thematic unity of the book. In the second paragraph of Part VII, Smith articulates two questions, the answers to which can be thought to provide the warp and weft of the book: What is virtue? What is the human faculty by which virtue is recommended to us? Since Smith does not begin *TMS* by directly announcing the subject matter of the work—indeed, he seems to begin *in medias res*—and since he does indeed contemplate these two questions during the course of his inquiry, there is a certain plausibility in this approach.

If we are, however, to seek guidance from Part VII, we might be better served to direct our attention to its opening paragraph, for there Smith points to what is perhaps the deepest and most profound theme of the book—the role of nature in moral matters. He remarks, "If we examine the most celebrated and remarkable of the different theories which have been given concerning the nature and origin of the moral sentiments, we shall find that almost all of them coincide with some part or other of that which I have been endeavouring to give an account of; and that if every thing which has already been said be fully considered, we shall be at no loss to explain what was the view or aspect of *nature* which led each particular author to form his particular system" (*TMS*, VII.i.1; my emphasis). What Smith indicates here, and what he takes great pains to exhibit if only by his own example throughout *TMS*, is that a conception of human nature provides the foundation of, and building force for, his theory of moral sentiments. Furthermore, since any careful inquiry into human nature is inextricably woven into an inquiry into nature generally, we should be aware of the possibility that Smith's theory of moral sentiments is part of this larger tapestry.

The extraordinary density of references in the work to "nature" and its cognates testifies that articulating a conception of nature is central to Smith's intention in *TMS*. Such terms appear no fewer than six hundred times. Although word counting is not definitive in and of itself that something important is at work in a book, it clearly can on occasion be suggestive and illuminating. And in the present case, given the scarcely to be exaggerated importance of the concept of nature in the history of philosophy—ancient, medieval, and modern alike—it is difficult not to conclude that Smith's almost continuous engagement with and appeal to nature is critical to understanding his thought in *TMS*.

The reader does not have to wait long to observe Smith's interest. In the very opening line of *TMS*, Smith writes, "How selfish soever man may be supposed, there are evidently some principles in his *nature*, which interest him in the fortune of others, and render their happiness necessary to him, though he derives nothing from it except the pleasure of seeing it" (*TMS*, I.i.1.3; my emphasis). Distancing himself at the outset from the view that all human action revolves exclusively around self-interest, Smith proclaims that individuals have by nature a concern for the fortune and happiness of others. The claim is artfully formulated. It leads us at the same time to recognize that human beings are by nature self-interested and also to suppose the self-interested conduct of individuals as the given, the concern for others needing to be affirmed against that backdrop.

Human beings, then, possess by nature two orientations—one that directs them to be concerned with themselves, and one that directs them to be concerned with others. The recognition of this immediately suggests a host of questions to the reader, all of which bear on the relationship between these twin orientations. How pronounced is the concern for others relative to our concern for ourselves? If our concern for ourselves is vastly more pronounced, how is social order possible? Is it indeed in virtue of our concern for others that social order arises among human beings? All of these questions implicate one another, a process animating most nearly everything in *TMS*: How are the self-interested actions of individuals to be reconciled with each other in such a manner that individuals can live satisfactory lives?

The rarely noticed subtitle of *TMS* signals the order that the book will initially follow: *An ESSAY towards an Analysis of the Principles by which Men naturally judge concerning the Conduct and Character, first of their Neighbors, and afterwards of themselves*. So, the first two parts of the book consider an individual judging other individuals, while the third part considers an individual judging himself. Given Smith's understanding that it is only after individuals reach the point of judging others that they can come to judge themselves, a matter with which Part III begins, this arrangement is surely appropriate, and it thus places a certain premium on those first two parts. Their significance is further magnified by the recognition that it is at the outset of the book that Smith most fully sets forth his conception of human nature, a conception to which we now turn. Ironically enough, though, when Smith narrows his scope to an individual's judgment of himself, he also widens it to a conception of nature more broadly conceived.

Smith's elucidation of human nature begins with a claim to which we have already alluded, namely, that human beings by nature are concerned with others. The concern to which he points is not, however, that of a general benevolence, a capacity of which he is quite suspicious. Instead, it is a concern or an interest in the joy of another individual—or sorrow, or grief, or pleasure, or pain, or anger, or resentment, or gratitude. Nevertheless, because we do not have a direct, immediate experience of the sentiments of others, achieving an understanding of how they are affected by the conditions in which they find themselves is particularly problematic. Smith suggests in the opening pages of *TMS* that it is the action of the imagination that allows us to overcome this difficulty: "As we have no immediate experience of what other men feel, we can form no idea of the manner in which they are affected, but by conceiving what we ourselves should feel in the like situation" (*TMS*, I.i.1.2). We imaginatively place ourselves in the circumstances of the other, and our imagination represents to us what we would feel were we in those circumstances. This action is the ground of what Smith calls "fellow-feeling" or sympathy, and it is thus through the imagination that we come to feel something like the sorrow, pity, grief, joy, etc., of the other, which thereby leads us to feel for the other. It is also part of Smith's contention that with some passions (e.g., joy and grief), the very expression of them can give rise to sympathy, but only because they immediately suggest some fortune, good or bad, that has affected the individual.

An important example for Smith of the imagination situating us elsewhere involves death. We imagine our souls in the inanimate bodies of others, bodies that are decaying and being eaten away at every moment: "the idea of those circumstances, which undoubtedly can give us no pain when we are dead, makes us miserable while we are alive." This leads to a supremely important principle for Smith, the dread of death, a principle that indeed serves as a "great restraint upon the injustice of mankind." Thinking we are alive while in a dead body is, Smith states, "an illusion of the imagination" (*TMS*, I.i.1.13). This illusion has, however, the salutary end of aiding the cause of justice—and it turns out that this is not the last time in *TMS* where salutary ends are instigated by such illusions.

What is striking about this account of imaginatively entering into the circumstances of another is that we never really come to know what that other would feel in those circumstances—we only come to know what we would, but do not actually, feel. Now, Smith does enrich his account toward the end of *TMS*, of which more shortly, but pertinent here is Smith's understanding that it is an imaginative act of transference that allows us to feel for others and thereby form some kind of attachment to them.

However pivotal a role the imagination plays within Smith's understanding of human nature, the passions perform an even greater one. For him, the passions are the core of human nature, and this is particularly revealed in the detailed way in which he canvasses the subject in Part I of *TMS*. It is also revealed in his frequent use of the expressions "the passions of human nature" and "the original passions of human nature," a use that underscores the essential association of the two. It is quite apparent that more than any other capacity of human beings, it is the passions that interest him the most.

Smith begins his discussion of the passions through an analysis of what he terms the correspondence (or harmony) of sentiments. This correspondence is a factual state in which the sentiment of a spectator more or less matches that of the actor. Thus, an actor experiences joy, and a spectator, through an act of the imagination, places himself in the position of the actor and experiences that joy as well. We seek this correspondence because, "nothing pleases us more than to observe in other men a fellow-feeling with all the emotions of our own breast" (*TMS*, I.i.2.1). The pleasure is thus derived not from the correspondence itself, but from an observation of that correspondence—and this pleasure is sought not only by the actor, but by the spectator, also: both receive pleasure from the concord of sentiments. This pleasure is somewhat difficult to come by, because the correspondence of sentiments is a hard-won achievement. The intensity of the passion of the actor is naturally greater than that of the spectator, and thus what is required is for the actor to lower the pitch of his passion and the spectator to elevate his. The desired correspondence can come about only by this mutual effort.

The analysis we have presented so far cannot be the whole of Smith's account of the correspondence of sentiments. If the spectator cannot directly experience the sentiments of the actor and can only approximate them by imaginatively placing himself in the actor's circumstances, the actor also cannot directly experience the imaginatively created sentiments of the spectator. To put the matter simply, how can the actor and spectator know that some degree of correspondence has been achieved? Smith offers his most explicit answer to this problem toward the end of *TMS*:

> The great pleasure of conversation and society...arises from a certain correspondence of sentiments and opinions, from a certain harmony of

> minds, which like so many musical instruments coincide and keep time with one another. *But this most delightful harmony cannot be obtained unless there is a free communication of sentiments and opinions.* We all desire, upon this account, to feel how each other is affected, to penetrate into each other's bosoms, and to observe the sentiments and affections which really subsist there. The man who indulges us in this natural passion, who invites us into his heart...seems to exercise a species of hospitality more delightful than any other. (*TMS*, VII.iv.28; my emphasis)

The question now facing Smith's reader is, if speech is the instrument for discovering the sentiments of another, then why is an act of the imagination needed at all? An individual can *ex hypothesi* honestly express his joy or grief concerning some situation to another, and he can feel pleasure or sorrow about that situation in such a way that it leads to a correspondence of the sentiments of both. However, being pleased that someone else is joyful does not mean that one thinks he should be joyful. Simply to take pleasure in another's joy is not to judge that the circumstances that gave rise to that joy are appropriate to it. The key role of the imagination here is that by allowing us to place ourselves in the other's situation, and thus ascertaining how we would feel, we are in a position to judge the *propriety* of the other's sentiments; we are able to approve or disapprove of those sentiments; we can engage in acts of approbation or disapprobation. The moral world of propriety and impropriety is opened up to us by the imagination. Moreover, the true pleasure involved in the correspondence of sentiments comes from our fellow-feeling with the other, and this sympathetic response stems from a prior imaginative act. Therefore, the imagination is necessary to a correspondence of sentiments, however, it is not sufficient: knowledge of the correspondence comes about only through speech. Speech is necessary to a correspondence of sentiments, but it too is not sufficient: an act of the imagination on the part of the spectator is necessary in the first place to produce the sentiments that make up one part of the correspondence.

Smith's discussion of the diversity of human passions in Part I employs a complicated typology that categorizes passions in terms of those that take their origin from the body, those that take their origin from the imagination, and the unsocial passions, the social passions, and the selfish passions. And while Smith's carefully crafted disquisition covers the broadest range of passions, from hunger and thirst, to the passion uniting the sexes, physical pain, love, serenity, hatred, resentment, joy, grief, admiration, devotion, generosity, humanity, kindness, compassion, friendship, jealousy, and envy, as they bear upon the interests of the actor alone, the discussion never strays far from the question as to whether it is easy or difficult for the spectator to go along with the passion, thus possibly allowing for and facilitating a correspondence of sentiments. Here, Smith's analysis of resentment or hatred is illustrative of the approach he takes. According to him, hatred or resentment is a passion with which it is difficult for the spectator to sympathize. The primary reason is that the spectator's sympathy is divided between the actor who feels the passion and the person against whom the passion is directed, and this latter concern mitigates and diminishes the former. Thus, "Before resentment…can become graceful and agreeable, it must be more humbled and brought down below that pitch to which it would *naturally* rise, than almost any other passion" (*TMS*, I.ii.3; my emphasis). Hatred and resentment are rough and unfriendly passions that force individuals away from each other, and thus it is good, Smith avers, that they are shared less easily than others (*TMS*, I.ii.3.1). Nevertheless, the passion of resentment is, in Smith's estimation, one of the guardians of justice. Thus, the tension that is inherent to resentment is imparted to questions of sociality and justice. For Smith, all of the passions can be rightly characterized as principles of motion: the passions impel human beings to act. Given that the locus of Smith's reflections on the passions is how they facilitate the bonds of fellow-feeling, we can say that his analysis points the way to an understanding of how the different trajectories of human motion or action lead to the possibility of a unified social order, for which some elements of justice are a prerequisite.

Two other passions that figure prominently throughout Part I of *TMS* are joy and sorrow. Smith observes that it is easier to sympathize with the former, and thus it is easier for the spectator's sentiment born of the imagination to match, more or less, that of the actor. Actively seeking the sympathy of the other, we are disposed, Smith says, to make a show of our joy—and this leads us, while hiding our poverty, to make our riches and greatness visible. The rich revel in their success because they believe they "naturally draw" the attention of the world upon themselves; the poor, on the other hand, feel ashamed of their condition. "It is chiefly from this regard of mankind," Smith remarks, "that we pursue riches and avoid poverty." Smith elaborates upon this thought when he comments that the pursuit of "that great purpose of human life which we call bettering our condition" is motivated by the desire for the approbation and sympathy of others, that is, the "purpose of human life" is motivated by *vanity*, for that is the form that approbation and sympathy take here; vanity, the desire to be noticed and approved of, is "the most ardent desire…of human nature" (*TMS*, I.iii.2). Under its sway, the imagination enters the room and paints the condition of the rich in "delusive colors" (*TMS*, I.iii.2.1), and in such a manner that we attend to the approbation to which the rich are subject, and we neglect the toil and trouble that is their lot. Thus, "wealth and greatness are often regarded with the respect and admiration which are due only to wisdom and virtue… (*TMS*, I.iii.3.1). Perhaps, then, it should be no surprise that Smith comes to argue that it is the desire to admire the rich that is a fundamental source of the corruption of our moral sentiments.

My focus has principally been on Part I of *TMS*—and in so doing I've set aside Smith's important discussion of merit and demerit: judging the ends that individuals are led by their passions to seek, which is the principal subject of Part II—because it is here that Smith most fully elaborates upon his understanding of the imagination and the passions, as well as vanity—that is, that he most fully sets down the sub-rational elements of human nature. We can further elaborate upon Smith's understanding of these matters by turning away from questions involved in judging others to those involved in judging oneself, and thus turn to Part III of *TMS*, and Smith's staccato presentation of the impartial spectator.

Smith begins by commenting that, "We can never survey our own sentiments and motives, we can never form any judgment concerning them; unless we remove ourselves, as it were, from our own natural station, and endeavour to view them as at a certain distance from us" (*TMS*, III.1.2). It is our partiality to our own interests that gets in the way of judging ourselves properly, and thus some other perspective must be found that will provide a more accurate judge of our conduct and character. To shed light on this provision, Smith first turns to others who are spectators, indeed, impartial spectators, of our conduct: "We endeavour to examine our own conduct as we imagine any other fair and impartial spectator would examine it" (*TMS*, III.1.2). This is not the first time in *TMS* that Smith invokes this suggestive standard, for it occurs at least eight times in parts I and II, especially as relates to the passion of resentment. And although the issue in the present case concerns judging one's own conduct or character, like the earlier ones, the appeal to the impartial spectator is to a perspective external to oneself. Following the above passage, Smith postulates that it was only by first observing others—and ultimately making moral judgments about them—that we were led to observe and make moral judgments about ourselves. We were directed to pursue the latter by considering how our actions would appear to ourselves if we were in the position of a person either observing or being affected by our conduct. In so doing, "We *suppose* ourselves the spectators of our own behaviour, and endeavour to *imagine* what effect it would...produce upon us" (*TMS*, III.1.5; my emphasis). Looming over Smith's analysis here is his understanding that our interest in the approval and disapproval of others is driven by our desire for praise. However, we powerfully gravitate toward something more, namely, being praiseworthy—and this, Smith contends, rests on our own judgments about ourselves. A jurisdiction other than the man without—that is, an external spectator, however impartial he might be—is required, and toward this end Smith articulates a conception of a divided self, wherein an individual is both actor and spectator of himself *qua* actor: "When I endeavour to examine my own conduct...I divide myself, as it were, into two persons; and that I, the examiner and judge, represent a different character from that other I, the person whose conduct is examined into and judged of" (*TMS*, III.1.6). The idea of the impartial spectator as reconceptualized in Part III—in which the jurisdiction of this "man within the breast" is established and authorized—is, then, that of an internalized figure, and despite the obvious fact that the individual remains (within) himself, one part of him, somehow apparently phenomenologically detached from his "natural station" (*TMS*, III.1.2), judges the other.

Having brought this internalized impartial spectator onto center stage in the first chapter of Part III, Smith implicates him in some kind of tragedy in the next:

> The supposed impartial spectator of our conduct seems to give his opinion in our favour with fear and hesitation; when that of all the real spectators...is unanimously and violently against us. In such cases, this demigod within the breast appears, like the demigods of the poets, though partly of immortal, yet partly too of mortal extraction. (*TMS*.III.2.32)

Smith presents a marked tug of war between the judgment of external judges and the impartial spectator within, for the former can issue disapproving judgments of us, while the judge within sees the matter quite otherwise—and thus a traumatic tension between our desire for praise and our longing to be praiseworthy begins to assert itself. When the impartial spectator judges steadily, he is true to his divine element; when confounded and vexed by the opposition to him, he "discovers his connexion with mortality" (*TMS*.III.2.32) and in inclining to the human part of his origin, allows himself to suffer greatly. In this poetic portrayal, the impartial spectator fails to provide sufficient consolation to allow one to ward off the disapproval of others, but Smith proffers that our nature provides a solution for this failure in the form of a disposition—"a hope and expectation deeply rooted in human nature"—to appeal to a higher authority, "the all-seeing Judge of the world," who is there at the scene to support an infirmed and morose mind with a promissory note that one's virtue will ultimately be rewarded, thereby facilitating one's "happiness in this life" (*TMS*, III.2.33).

However, the impartial spectator to whom Smith returns in the very next chapter appears newly fortified and relatively unscathed by the turmoil above, and "the all-seeing judge of the world" no longer is part of the cast of characters:

> Though the testimony of the supposed impartial spectator…cannot always alone support him; yet the influence and authority of this principle is, upon all occasions, very great; and it is only by consulting this judge within, that we can ever see what relates to ourselves in its proper shape and dimensions; or that we can ever make any proper comparison between our own interests and those of other people. (*TMS*, III.3.1)

It is under the horizon of these comments that Smith radicalizes the tension between an attachment to one's own interests and a concern for the interests of others. So powerful is the former, and so weak is the latter, that even a small loss or gain to our own interests dwarfs in importance to an immense loss or gain to those with whom we have no connection. Smith magnifies his point with his famous example involving a comparison of the loss of one's own little finger to the bulk of China being swallowed up by an immense earthquake. The former would trouble us greatly, and we would lose sleep; the latter would occupy our thoughts, and we would feel some sorrow, but "provided he never saw them, he [would] snore with the most profound security over the ruin of a hundred millions of his brethren" (*TMS*, III.3.4). Nature, however, has provided a counterweight to recalibrate the skewed scales of interest, but Smith does not locate it in the domain of a humanitarian or benevolent impulse. Instead, the source for a greater equilibrium of interest is to be found in a reconfigured conception of the impartial spectator, one in which reason figures prominently:

> It is reason, principle, conscience, the inhabitant of the breast, the man within, the great judge and arbiter of our conduct. It is he who, whenever we are about to act so as to affect the happiness of others, calls to us, with a voice capable of astonishing the most presumptuous of our passions, that we are but one of the multitude, in no respect better than any other

> in it; and that when we prefer ourselves so shamefully and so blindly to others, we become the proper objects of resentment, abhorrence, and execration. It is from him only that we learn the real littleness of ourselves, and of whatever relates to ourselves, and the *natural* misrepresentations of self-love can be corrected only by the eye of this impartial spectator. (*TMS*, III.3.4)

The passion of self-love, of human partiality, is so powerful that the corrective to this passion cannot be located within the bowels of the passions themselves. Here, for the first time in *TMS* reason asserts itself, and it does so as a countermeasure to self-love. Only reason can realign our perspective so that we are able to resign our own interests to those of others when matters of generosity and injustice are at stake. And reason is able to engender a stronger love, Smith declares, a passion or a love of "what is honourable and noble, of the grandeur, and dignity, and superiority of our own characters" (*TMS*, III.3.4). Indeed, though he might suffer from the heaviest burdens of misfortune, the man of constancy, of self-command, the wise and just man, is able to listen to the voice of the impartial spectator within and conduct himself by his dictates: the habit of so acting "has become perfectly familiar" (*TMS*, III.3.25) to such a person.

By the time we reach the end of the third chapter of Part III, Smith has instilled confidence in us about the impartial spectator's capacity to contain and mitigate the partiality of self-love. Nonetheless, as the scene changes and we enter the next chapter, Smith rends that confidence asunder. The title of that chapter, "Of the Nature of Self-deceit, and of the Origin and Use of General Rules," indicates its twin themes, and not surprisingly they are inexorably connected.

Broadly speaking, there are two occasions in which an individual might attempt to discover how "the impartial spectator would view" his actions: in deliberating about an action to be undertaken, and in reflecting upon that action in the aftermath. In both instances, Smith tells us, our judgments are more than apt to be partial, especially in the most important instance, namely, the first: "When we are about to act, the eagerness of passion will seldom allow us to consider what we are doing, with the candour of an indifferent person." Even if we try to assume the stance of another, "the fury of our own passions constantly calls us back to our own place, where everything appears magnified and misrepresented by self-love" (*TMS*, III.4.3). The deceitful misrepresentations of self-love afflict us much less after we have acted, and when we try to reflect upon what we have done, we can identify with the impartial spectator, the man within the breast. After the fact, though, such judgments carry little significance compared to those that preceded our actions, the deed having already been done. Nevertheless, even here our judgments are less than frank and fail to inoculate us in the future against the self-deceit that infects our judgment: "This self-deceit, this fatal weakness of mankind, is the source of half the disorders of human life. If we saw ourselves in the light in which others see us...a reformation would generally be unavoidable. We could not otherwise endure this sight" (*TMS*, III.4.6).

It is, Smith suggests, mighty difficult to mobilize the impartial or indifferent spectator—the latter expression one Smith invokes eight times in *TMS*, half of which appear in this section of text—against the self-deceit born of self-love, however, "Nature...has not left this weakness...altogether without a remedy; nor has she abandoned us entirely to the delusions of self-love" (*TMS*, III.4.7). That remedy takes the form of general rules of conduct. These rules are formed, and evolve over time, by our observations of the conduct of others, and these particular cases lead us insensibly to arrive at general rules, which we then apply not only to others, but also to ourselves, both in terms of disapprobation and approbation. Smith's position is that it is principally by resting our judgments on such rules that we are able to combat the misrepresentations of self-love concerning what it is proper for us to do. *TMS* is a masterwork of examples, and Smith's illustration in this context is instructive. Consider someone in the throes of furious resentment, moved by his passion to take violent action in response to what another has done to him. Unless his education has been most singular, he will fall back on a general rule that prohibits a violent response. However, his fury may have been such that had he been contemplating this kind of action for the very first time, and therefore absent any consideration of a general rule to guide his conduct, "he would undoubtedly have determined it to be quite just and proper, and what every impartial spectator would approve of." What checks his action, though, is his recognition of and "reverence for" (*TMS*, III.4.12) a general rule prescribing against the action—that is, without being educated in certain general rules of conduct, he not only would have no guard against his own improper act of violence but also would be supported in his endeavor by the impartial spectator himself. And this train of thought leads Smith to lay bare an inner nerve of *TMS*, the importance of which cannot be overestimated, that a regard for general rules of conduct is "the only principle by which the bulk of mankind are capable of directing their lives" (*TMS*, III.5.1). But with this, Smith's tacit admission appears to be that there are those few—the man of self-command, the man of constancy, the just and wise man—for whom the appeal to the impartial spectator is a possible, pivotal, and uplifting element in their moral lives, and Part VI of *TMS*, added in the sixth and final edition in 1790, with its fuller articulation of the man of self-command, seems to confirm and amplify this account. Thus for Smith, the endemic dangers posed by the partiality of human passion are checked by two somewhat divergent principles of rational governance: reason, with respect to the few; and general rules of conduct, which regulate the lives of the many.

Now, not surprisingly, the most important—and the most precise in terms of articulation and application—of these general rules of conduct are the rules of justice, a subject Smith develops most fully in Part II of *TMS*. For a number of reasons, Smith pays special attention to these, and he suggests so too does Nature. Indeed, Nature, for example, treats beneficence and justice differently. Although Nature "exhorts mankind to acts of beneficence" (*TMS*, II.ii.3), it does not provide for a sanction to enforce the performance of such acts in the form of some passion. There is such a passion as regards justice, namely, resentment, whereby we feel the impulse to punish those who do not act justly; along with this passion, "Nature has implanted…that consciousness of ill-desert, those terrors." That Nature does this signals the greater importance of justice as compared to beneficence. The latter is an "ornament which embellishes, not the foundation which supports the building." To the contrary, justice "is the main pillar that upholds the whole edifice. If it is removed, the great immense fabric of human society, that fabric which to raise and support seems in this world...to have been the peculiar and darling care of Nature, must in a moment crumble into atoms" (*TMS*, II.ii.3). The efforts of Nature have secured an enabling condition required if civilized life is to exist and flourish. The stinginess of our natural inclinations generated by self-love and self-deceit are mitigated by a bounty facilitated by Nature.

In touching upon certain features of Smith's conception of general rules of conduct as we have now done with respect to justice and beneficence, we have encountered a conception of nature that goes far beyond human nature, a sense of nature that is integral to Smith's intention in *TMS*. This conception of Nature—capitalized in almost every case—is of Nature personified.

In addition to cases silently alluded to above, here are a myriad of others in *TMS* to which Smith appeals: "Nature teaches us" (*TMS*, II.ii.3.12); "the intention of Nature" (*TMS*, I.ii.3.6); "Nature loads us with sorrows" (*TMS*, I.iii.1.12); "Nature compels them" (*TMS*, I.iii.2.2); "the doctrine of Nature" (*TMS*, I.iii.2.4); "Nature does not seem to have dealt with us so kindly" (*TMS*, II.1.5n); "the great ends which Nature seems to have proposed" (*TMS*, II.i.5n); "retaliation seems to be the great law dictated to us by Nature" (*TMS*, II.ii.1.10); "Nature exhorts mankind" (*TMS*, II.ii.3.4); "Nature implants the irregularity of the sentiments in the human breast" (*TMS*, II.ii.3.2); "Nature...formed man for society [and] endowed him with an original desire to please" (*TMS*, III.2.6; III.2.7); "That we should be but little interested...in the fortune of those whom we can neither serve nor hurt...seems wisely ordered by Nature" (*TMS*, III.3.9); "Nature for the wisest purposes" (*TMS*, III.3.13); "Nature had sufficiently prepared us" (*TMS*, III.3.13); "Nature has established" (*TMS*, III.3.21; III.5.10); "The reward which Nature bestows upon good behaviour under misfortune" (*TMS*, III.3.27); "Nature from her parental care" (*TMS*, III.3.28); "Man is by Nature directed to correct, in some measure, that distribution of things which she herself would otherwise have made" (*TMS*, III.5.9); "Nature seems to have happily adjusted our sentiments" (*TMS*, IV.2.3); "the voice of Nature herself"; "The preservation and healthful state of the body seem to be the objects which Nature first recommends to the care of every individual" (*TMS*, VI.i.1); "Nature has wisely judged"; "the benevolent wisdom of nature" (*TMS*, VI.ii.1.20), etc.

Central to most of the examples of Nature personified in *TMS* is a *teleological* conception of nature, a conception so germane to Smith's intention in *TMS* that it merits close scrutiny. Smith's contention here is that Nature not only endows human beings with ends worthy of pursuit, but she also endows them with the means required to achieve them. These ends are so important that nothing can be left to chance. Smith writes,

> With respect to all those ends, which upon account of their peculiar importance, may be regarded, if such an expression is allowable, as the favourite ends of nature, she has constantly in this manner not only endowed mankind with an appetite for the end which she proposes, but likewise with an appetite for the means by which alone this end can be brought about.... Thus self-preservation, and the propagation of the species, are the great ends which Nature seems to have proposed in the formation of animals.... [And] though we are...endowed with a very strong desire of those ends, it has not been intrusted to the slow and uncertain determinations of our reason, to find out the proper means of bringing them about. Nature has directed us to the greater part of these.... (*TMS*, II.i.5n)

That self-preservation and the propagation of the species are the great ends that Nature has proposed, does not, of course, mean that they are the highest ends for human beings. Their importance instead appears to be that absent the achievement of these two ends, an individual could not achieve any other, and a nation, say, would be hard pressed to achieve greatness without an ever-increasing population. The most salient feature of this passage, however, is its view of reason. Smith's claim appears to be that were reason not, shall we say, relatively feeble, Nature would not have to endow us with the internal motion directing us in the pursuit of these ends, as well as the means to achieve them. The appeal to the ends of Nature stems, therefore, from a certain incapacity of reason. This theme—although curiously enough most fully developed in Part II of *TMS*—of the incapacity of reason to effect certain ends, is pervasive, both unannounced and explicit, throughout the entire book; it surely has to be read in connection to what we have already canvassed, namely, Smith's discussion of the impartial spectator.

Smith develops this theme further in the only passage in *TMS* in which he explicitly considers the problem of final causality:

> In every part of the universe we observe means adjusted with the nicest artifice to the ends which they are intended to produce; and in the mechanism of a plant, or animal body, admire how every thing is contrived for advancing the two great purposes of nature, the support of the individual, and the propagation of the species. But in these, and in all such objects, we still distinguish the efficient from the final cause of their several motions and organizations. The digestion of the food, the circulation of the blood, and the secretion of the several juices which are drawn from it, are operations all of them necessary for the great purposes of animal life. Yet we never endeavour to account for them from those purposes as from their efficient causes, nor imagine that the blood circulates, or that the food digests of its own accord, and with a view or intention to the purposes of circulation or digestion. The wheels of the watch are all admirably adjusted to the end for which it was made, the pointing of the hour. All their various motions conspire in the nicest manner to produce this effect. If they were endowed with a desire and intention to produce it, they could not do it better. Yet we never ascribe any such desire or intention to them, but to the watch-maker, and we know that they are put into motion by a spring, which intends the effect it produces as little as they do. *But though, in accounting for the operations of bodies, we never fail to distinguish in this manner the efficient from the final cause, in accounting for those of the mind we are very apt to confound these two different things with one another. When by natural principles we are led to advance those ends, which a refined and enlightened reason would recommend to us, we are very apt to impute to that reason, as to their efficient cause, the sentiments and actions by which we advance those ends, and to imagine that to be the wisdom of man, which in reality is the wisdom of God.* Upon a superficial view, this cause seems sufficient to produce the effects

> which are ascribed to it; and the system of human nature seems to be more simple and agreeable when all its different operations are in this manner deduced from a single principle. (*TMS*, II.ii.3.5; my emphasis)

The world of nature, both animate and inanimate is infused with ends, above all the preservation and propagation of life. But in such cases, we do not ascribe intent to the digestive process or the sexual reproductive process, any more than we would the movement of the parts of the watch that allow it to indicate the time for us: we do not, in cases like this, conflate what is indeed efficient causality with final causality. However, we are apt to conflate these two forms of causality, Smith claims, when it comes to a variety of human ends. Even when it is "natural principles" that lead to those certain ends—in which case efficient causality would be at work—if a "refined and enlightened reason" would recommend those same ends to us—in which case final causality would be at work—we would be tempted to conclude that the end was sought as the result of reason. It is of considerable importance that natural principles and enlightened reason can coincide with respect to the ends that would be achieved, although there is nothing in what Smith writes that would suggest that enlightened reason (or wisdom) could also coincide with respect to the means necessary for the achievement of those ends. Furthermore, we can say that Smith seems to be pointing to the idea that not only can enlightened reason arrive at an understanding of certain ends, but it can also arrive at an understanding of the unintended means that can achieve those ends. Smith's appeal to God is of considerable importance as well. Our reflections on this appeal is deepened by considering it in a somewhat different context.

There are several moments in *TMS* where a claim comes to rest on the idea of "the Author of nature," and "the great Director of the universe." When Smith does this, it is always to implicate the realm of things human within something that looks very much like a theodicy. We can best understand and appreciate this by working our way through Part III, chapter five, "Of the influence and authority of the general Rules of Morality, and that they are justly regarded as the Laws of the Deity."

Throughout Parts II and III of *TMS*, Smith repeatedly adverts to the "sacred" character of the rules of morality, and in almost every instance the rules in question are the rules of justice. Smith gives no explicit argument why he ascribes the sacred to the rules of morality and justice, but he makes the centrality of its role clear: "Without this sacred regard to general rules, there is no man whose conduct can be much depended upon" (*TMS*, III.5.2). It is in the context of underwriting the sacred character of the rules of morality that Smith invokes the Deity. Reverence for these rules is "enhanced by an opinion which is first impressed by nature, and afterwards confirmed by reasoning and philosophy, that those important rules of morality are the commands and laws of the Deity, who will finally reward the obedient, and punish the transgressors..." (*TMS*, III.5.3). Smith proceeds to offer a brief conjectural history of religion—in which Jupiter figures prominently—elucidating how religion was able to provide a sanction to morality. Shortly thereafter, he turns to the relationship between following the rules of morality and the achievement of happiness:

> The happiness of mankind, as well as of other rational creatures, seems to have been the original purpose intended by the Author of nature, when he brought them into existence. No other end seems worthy of that supreme wisdom and divine benignity which we necessarily ascribe to him; and this opinion, which we are led to by the abstract consideration of his infinite perfections, is still more confirmed by the examination of all the works of nature, which seem *all* intended to promote happiness, and to guard against misery. (*TMS*, III.5.7; my emphasis)

Following this remark, Smith fleshes out the character of these theodical elements contained therein. Despite "the disorder in which all things appear to be in the world...every virtue naturally meets with its proper reward, with the recompense which is most fit to encourage and promote it" (*TMS*, III.5.8). Only an extraordinary set of circumstances can get in the way of this remarkable coincidence of virtue and reward. Thus, success in commerce comes from hard work, prudence, and ambition; the virtues of truth, justice, and humanity give rise to being beloved; and only accidents stand in the way of these achievements. The

Author of nature, or the Deity, thus more or less vouchsafes that morality will be rewarded, that the good will prosper, and that the evil will not.

Smith carries out this argument with great rhetorical flourish—indeed, almost bombast—and this should give us some pause. But before we even have time for that, Smith begins to chip away at the position he has portrayed:

> But though the general rules by which prosperity and adversity are commonly distributed, when considered in this cool and philosophical light, appear to be perfectly suited to the situation of mankind in this life, yet they are by no means suited to some of our natural sentiments. Our natural love and admiration for some virtues is such, that we should wish to bestow on them all sorts of honours and rewards, even those which we must acknowledge to be the proper recompenses of other qualities, with which those virtues are not always accompanied. (*TMS*, III.5)

Thus, our natural sentiments are disposed to seeing various virtues rewarded in ways that Nature herself does not prescribe. Although Nature prescribes that prudence and industry be rewarded with wealth, our natural sentiments want to see magnanimity and justice so rewarded. It should be noted that Smith's way of articulating this conflict involving Nature is more slippery than it appears at first sight, as he himself slips into referring to Nature as "the natural course of things," and understanding it in terms of "natural consequences" and "natural events" (*TMS*, III.5.9). This suggests, we believe, that the distributions granted to various virtues result simply from the various complicated interactions among men. And we should also take notice here of the use to which Smith puts philosophy. There is no evidence, despite Smith's apparent promissory note, of philosophy's sustaining the argument that the laws of morality are the commands of the Deity. Instead, philosophy is brought on stage in support of the position that there is a valuable correspondence between certain actions and certain rewards.

What also begins to slip away through the course of Smith's argument is one of the reasons why he appeals to the Deity as the Author of nature in the first place, namely, that the Author has so arranged nature that virtue will be rewarded and vice punished, and particular virtues will be rewarded in appropriate ways *in this life*—and it is this that marks this part of *TMS* as a theodicy. In a series of examples, Smith points to instances in which the natural sentiments of man will judge that some injustice in the distribution of the goods of the world has taken place, and has taken place in a manner in which we have no power to rectify it. Smith then states,

> When we thus despair of finding any force upon earth which can check the triumph of injustice, we naturally appeal to heaven, and hope, that the great Author of our nature will himself execute hereafter, what all the principles which he has given us for the direction of our conduct, prompt us to attempt even here; that he will complete the plan which he himself has thus taught us to begin; and will, in a life to come, render to every one according to the works which he has performed in this world. And thus we are led to the belief of a future state, not only by the weaknesses, by the hopes and fears of human nature, but by the noblest and best principles which belong to it, by the love of virtue, and by the abhorrence of vice and injustice. (*TMS*, III.5.10)

We must highlight two things that Smith is putting forth here. First, since the Author of nature is unable to effectuate a condition of justice in this lifetime, individuals look to its accomplishment in a hereafter; that is, the Author of nature has been rendered nugatory in this world and anchored instead to some future state. Second, an astonishing reversal has been made. Earlier in the argument, the natural sentiments were engaged against the order established by the Author of nature; by the end of the argument, the natural sentiments are appealing to that Author.

To see more fully what Smith is doing with his invocation of the Author of nature, we must revisit the end of that crucially important passage about final and efficient causality that we quoted earlier:

> When by natural principles we are led to advance those ends, which a refined and enlightened reason would recommend to us, we are very apt to impute to that reason, as to their efficient cause, the sentiments and actions by which we advance those ends, and to imagine that to be the wisdom of man, which in reality is the wisdom of God. Upon a *superficial*

> *view*, this cause seems sufficient to produce the effects which are ascribed to it; and the system of human nature seems to be more simple and agreeable when *all its different operations* are in this manner deduced from a single principle. (*TMS*, II.ii.3; my emphasis)

Upon reflection, these remarks are as curious as those that anchored the Author of nature to a future state. The point of the *whole* of the passage was to indicate that efficient causes *sans* intention are responsible for a variety of human phenomena, but human beings are inclined to ignore this and posit some intention in their stead. However, this is exactly what Smith himself does, the intention's being God's and not man's! Moreover, Smith concludes the passage with this marvelously ambiguous comment about the "superficial view." We need to ask exactly which is the superficial view—that is, to what does "this cause" refer, enlightened reason or God? However one answers this question, the response, by the very argument Smith makes, is no substitute for the natural principles of the world.

We would have to go through many more examples of Smith's appeals to the Author of nature, God, and the Deity to establish our case firmly, but the direction our argument points is this—such appeals are rhetorical in character and made with two ends in mind: they are meant to cover up Smith's skepticism about a transcendent realm, simultaneously providing a frame of reference whereby Smith's predominantly religious readers, especially his students, can accept and indeed embrace a variety of arguments in *TMS* about our moral lives.

The issue that now needs to be considered is how we are to understand Smith's repeated references to Nature personified, especially in the light of his remarks about final causality upon which we have focused. We would surely be challenged, after all, to credit Smith with the view that Nature actually has intentions. What we must take cognizance of is the finely tuned tension that threads its way along the warp and weft of *TMS* between reason and nature. We would not be exaggerating much, if at all, to claim that *TMS* is a book devoted to deflating some of the possibilities of the exercise of reason with respect to human conduct. In particular, as Smith's famous example in Part IV of

TMS of the poor boy who wants to become rich reveals, many of the achievements of human beings are not the result of ends that are part of anyone's intention. We have within us principles of motion that lead us to take certain actions, which intersect and coincide with the actions of others, thereby producing an end or a result that was no part of anyone's design. By acting in the slipstream of vanity, self-love, the imagination, and the natural sentiments, individuals are able collectively to achieve something of significant value, something beyond the pale of the intention of any individual, beyond the pale of the reason of any individual, and beyond the pale of the efforts of anyone. It is thus within this context that we should consider Smith's Newtonian remark that, "All general rules are commonly denominated laws; thus general rules which bodies observe in the communication of motion, are called the laws of motion. But those general rules which our moral faculties observe in approving or condemning whatever sentiment or action is subjected to their examination, may much more justly be denominated such" (*TMS*, III.5.6).

Smith's many appeals to Nature personified, then, turn out below the surface to be appeals to human nature; to principles of action other than reason that lead individuals to an array of unintended ends. Sometimes the achievement of these ends is salutary to these individuals, and sometimes not. However this may be, we must be careful not to go so far as to believe that Smith's understanding is that we have little use for reason. For in the world of action, prudence has no small role to play, which is underscored by Smith's addition of Part VI to *TMS* in the final edition. And in the world of things intellectual, we need only to offer *TMS* as evidence of reason's power and sway. Indeed, Smith thought he had reconstructed by reason the sub-rational forces at work in human nature that lead to the ends that he always has in view. High on the list of Smith's insights is the recognition that although reason can understand these forces of nature that aid in the human enterprise, and thus can afford us some considerable self-understanding, it cannot adequately and intelligently present itself as a substitute for them.

2 | The Impartial Spectator's Cultural Spectacles

Virgil Henry Storr and Arielle John

Introduction

The impartial spectator plays a central role in Adam Smith's theory of moral sentiments.[1] Acting as a stand-in for the judgments of our behavior that others in society would render if they were unencumbered by their own particular biases and were fully aware of our motivations and the circumstances under which we acted, the impartial spectator is an imaginary construction that individuals call upon to evaluate their conduct and to guide their actions (*TMS*, 110). Though we care about the opinions of others, we are aware that they are likely to misunderstand our sentiments because they tend to be partial and lack the knowledge of our motivations and circumstances. As such, we do not view the opinions of others as an adequate guide for our behavior. Instead, we learn to care much more about the opinions of the impartial spectator (*TMS*, 130). Above all, we wish to seem proper in his eyes. We seek his approbation and hope to avoid his disapprobation. We also develop the habit of adopting the gaze of the impartial spectator when evaluating the behavior of others.

For Smith, the man in the breast is the internal representation of the impartial spectator; he is impartial in the sense that he is neither a party to our dealings nor affected by our actions. He is also not predisposed to take our side in our dealings with others nor is he biased against us. As Smith describes, the impartial spectator is "a person quite

[1] James Otteson (*Adam Smith's Marketplace of Life* [Cambridge: Cambridge University Press, 2002] 45), for instance, has described the impartial spectator as "one of the most important contributions Adam Smith made to ethics." See David Raphael (*The Impartial Spectator: Adam Smith's Moral Philosophy* [Oxford: Oxford University Press, 1975] 2007) and Martin Leroch ("Adam Smith's Intuition Pump: The Impartial Spectator," *Homo Oeconomius* 25/1 [2008]: 5–26) for useful expositions of this concept.

candid and equitable...one who has no particular relation either to ourselves, or to those whose interests are affected by our conduct" (*TMS*, iii.3.2). He does not view our burdens as being necessarily more onerous than others. He does not see our aspirations as being necessarily nobler than those of others. Instead, he sees us as disinterested observers who were in possession of the relevant facts of the matter would see us.

Although there is wide agreement in the literature on Smith's theory of moral sentiments that Smith conceived of the impartial spectator as a non-partisan disinterested observer of our actions, there is wide disagreement on how universal the moral judgments offered by the impartial spectator are likely to be. There remains a debate about whether Smith's impartial spectator is meant to be a better version of ourselves (i.e., one with our personality but without our biases), a representative of the particular societies where we are from or live (i.e., one that judges us according to a particular set of social mores), or a representative of the deity or of all of mankind (i.e., one with perhaps imperfect access to universal morality). Unfortunately, Smith adds to rather than clarifies the confusion here because at times he has seemed to advance all three views of the impartial spectator.[2] Arguably, appealing to how the impartial spectator comes to be formed rather than appeals to the various and competing descriptions of the impartial spectator that Smith advances might help to resolve this confusion.

If we focus on Smith's description of how the impartial spectator is developed, there is reason to believe that he potentially could be quite a parochial figure. It seems likely that what he thinks of as right and wrong, which sentiments he views as praiseworthy and blameworthy, are going to be conditioned by the context in which he developed. In fact, based on Smith's account, it appears that the process of enculturation that we all go through as we grow into adulthood and the process through which the impartial spectator develops are parallel processes and might be the same process.

[2] Leroch, "Adam Smith's Intuition Pump," 6.

As such, though the impartial spectator is a universal character (in that we all reference him regardless of where we are from), the content of his character is potentially culturally specific (in that what he tells us to do might differ across cultures). Others have, of course, stressed the cultural plurality of the impartial spectator. As Forman-Barzilai argued, "Smith's theory of moral sentiments was ultimately a description of how moral culture develops and sustains itself."[3] And, "Smith's account of the origins of our moral criteria culminates in a culturally insular portrait of our moral life."[4] Although we agree with Forman-Barzilai's stressing of the cultural plurality of moral judgment, we disagree with her that, for Smith, the absence of deep cultural diversity regarding the core of our morality offers the only and best hope that individuals will escape their "entanglement" within cultural space.[5] Unlike Forman-Barzilai, who sees appeals to "negative justice as a candidate for universal normativity" as the only/best way beyond our cultural bias that Smith offers,[6] we see greater intercultural engagement (perhaps of the sort that occurs within markets) as being consistent with Smith's project and critical for escaping our tendency toward moral parochialism.[7] Although Forman-Barzilai

[3] Fonna Forman-Barzilai, "Smith on 'connexion', culture and judgment," in *New Voices on Adam Smith*, ed. Leonidas Montes and Eric Scliesser (London: Routledge, 2006) 94.

[4] Ibid., 95.

[5] Ibid.

[6] Ibid., 91, 100.

[7] Forman-Barzilai advances the claim that "Smith developed a theory of commercial cosmopolitanism in good measure to soothe his troubled realism" (*Adam Smith and the Circles of Sympathy: Cosmopolitanism and Moral Theory* [Cambridge: Cambridge University Press, 2010] 214). Recognizing the likelihood that our moral sentiments would be parochial and the dangers of parochialism, on this view, Smith's commercial cosmopolitanism explains why one group might come to value the welfare of another group. As she put it elsewhere, Smith believed "free commercial intercourse among nations was a new mode of cosmopolitanism that promised to mitigate conflict among spatially disparate entities, and to generate a tolerable peace in the absence of better motives" (393). While correct, this view underestimates the potential of the market to transform our moral sentiments by promoting a process of intercultural engagement.

faithfully represents the path beyond cultural insularity that Smith adopts in *TMS* and is, rightfully, skeptical that justice does the "universalizing work" that Smith believed it did, we believe that Smith offers an additional path beyond cultural insularity.[8]

This chapter argues that Smith's impartial spectator is likely to be wearing cultural spectacles and explores the implications of adopting this view. Section II, thus, describes the process by which the impartial spectator is formed. Smith clearly viewed this as a social process. Though he did not emphasize the potential parochialism of the man in the breast, there is reason to believe that he was aware of this possibility. Section III, then, briefly describes those aspects of the impartial spectator that are likely to be universal (i.e., shared by all instantiations of the impartial spectator) and those aspects that are likely to be culturally specific (i.e., unique to specific cultures or sub-cultures). To preview, we argue that the moral categories the impartial spectator relies on are likely to be universal but the moral content that he espouses is culturally conditioned. Next, Section IV teases out some of the implications of adopting this view of a spectacled spectator. In particular, we focus on how well the impartial spectator serves us in our dealings with individuals from different cultures and how he is affected by our engagement with those from other cultures. Finally, Section V offers concluding remarks.

The cultural development of the man in the breast

Smith notes in the beginning of *TMS* that we are concerned with the wellbeing of others as well as the sympathy that others have for us. We are pleased when, recognizing our circumstances, others feel our joy or pain. We are disappointed when others cannot or do not sympathize with us. We wish to receive their approbation and to avoid their disapprobation. As Smith explains,

> …if you have either no fellow-feeling for the misfortunes I have met with, or none that bears any proportion to the grief which distracts me;

[8] Forman-Barzilai, "Smith on 'connexion', culture and judgment," 94.

> or if you have either no indignation at the injuries I have suffered, or none that bears any proportion to the resentment which transports me, we can no longer converse upon these subjects. We become intolerable to one another. I can neither support your company, nor you mine. (*TMS*, 21)

Absent a mutual sympathy between us, it is difficult, if not impossible for us to connect with each other. If you are not able to be aroused by my passions or distressed by my pains, only a limited level of rapport is possible between us.[9]

Because sympathy requires our being able to imagine how we would feel if we were confronted with the other person's situation (i.e., the happiness or sorrow they would feel at some event), we expect more sympathy from those who know us better because they are better positioned to imagine how a certain event will make us feel. As Smith explains,

> We expect less sympathy from a common acquaintance than from a friend…we assume, therefore, more tranquility before him, and endeavor to fix our thoughts upon those general outlines of our situation he is willing to consider. We expect still less sympathy from an assembly of strangers, and we assume, therefore, still more tranquility before them, and always endeavor to bring down our passions to that pitch, which the particular company we are in may be expected to go along with.

The social distance between an individual and a stranger will cause each of them to moderate their passions when they are around each other.[10] According to Smith, this tranquility is not "only an assumed appearance: for if we are at all masters of ourselves, the presence of a mere acquaintance will really compose us, still more than that of a friend;

[9] As Smith describes, "the too indulgent mother, the too indulgent father, the too generous and affectionate friend, may sometimes perhaps…be looked upon with a species of pity" (*TMS*, 40).

[10] Maria P. Pagnelli, "The Moralizing Role of Distance in Adam Smith: The Theory of Moral Sentiments as Possible Praise of Commerce," *History of Political Economy* 42/3 (2010): 425–41.

and that of an assembly of strangers still more than that of an acquaintance" (*TMS*, 23). Our desire for mutual sympathy will not cause us merely to *pretend* to be less overwrought or less overjoyed than we actually are but will actually cause us to *be* less excited.[11] It is through this process of continually matching the pitch of our passions in the presence of others, whom we cannot expect to mirror our natural sentiments, that we learn what the appropriate sentiments are for certain situations.[12]

Although we desire their approbation and hope to avoid their disapprobation, we are not content with the approval of others. According to Smith,

> Nature, when she formed man for society, endowed him with an original desire to please, and an original aversion to offend his brethren.... But this desire of the approbation, and this aversion to the disapprobation of his brethren, would not alone have rendered him fit for that society for which he was made. Nature, accordingly, has endowed him, not only with a desire of being approved of, but with a desire of being what ought to be approved of; or of being what he himself approves of in other men. (*TMS*, 116)

[11] The reverse of this is also likely to be true and, as such, might explain riots and mob violence. If, for instance, surrounded by a group of strangers who are enflamed, matching your sentiments with theirs might not require a flattening of your emotions but a rising of your temper. Just as an assembly of strangers should not be expected to understand why you are excited by something that does not excite them, they cannot be expected to understand your standing there unaffected in the face of a situation that excites public sentiment.

[12] Smith uses the examples of laughter and death to explain this point. On laughter, he says, "We have learned...from experience, what sort of pleasantry is upon most occasions capable of making us laugh" (*TMS*, 17). As a result, "we approve...of the laughter of the company, and feel that it is natural and suitable to its object; because, though in our present mood we cannot easily enter into it, we are sensible that upon most occasions we should very heartily join in it" (*TMS*, 17). Regarding news of the death of a stranger's relative, Smith remarks, "We have learned...from experience, that such a misfortune naturally excites such a degree of sorrow, and we know that if we took time to consider his situation, fully and in all its parts, we should, without doubt, most sincerely sympathize with him" (*TMS*, 18).

We do wish to receive praise but we also wish to be worthy of the praise that we receive. It is not enough that we escape the blame of others; we wish to not be blameworthy.

Because others may be unwilling to give us the praise we deserve or may excuse our behavior though it should inspire blame, Smith has argued that we require an independent tribunal to judge our behavior (*TMS*, 116). For Smith, the man in the breast, the internal representation of impartial spectator, is an imaginary construction that individuals call upon to evaluate their conduct and to guide their actions. As Smith explains,

> ...though man has...been rendered the immediate judge of mankind, he has been rendered so only in the first instance; and an appeal lies from his sentence to a much higher tribunal, to the tribunal of their own consciences, to that of the supposed impartial and well–informed spectator, to that of the man within the breast, the great judge and arbiter of their conduct. The jurisdictions of those two tribunals are founded upon principles which, though in some respects resembling and akin, are, however, in reality different and distinct. The jurisdiction of the man without, is founded altogether in the desire of actual praise, and in the aversion to actual blame. The jurisdiction of the man within, is founded altogether in the desire of praise-worthiness, and in the aversion to blame–worthiness; in the desire of possessing those qualities, and performing those actions, which we love and admire in other people; and in the dread of possessing those qualities, and performing those actions, which we hate and despise in other people. (*TMS*, 130)

The impartial spectator acts as a stand-in for the judgments of our behavior that others in society would render if they were not biased and were fully cognizant of our motivations and the circumstances under which we acted (*TMS*, 110).[13] Although we continue to want the

[13] As Smith explained, we "endeavor to examine our own conduct as we imagine any other fair and impartial spectator would examine it" (*TMS*, 110). And, "When I endeavor to examine my own conduct, when I endeavor to pass sentence upon it, and either to approve or condemn it, it is evident that, in all such cases, I divide myself, as it

approval of others, we want most of all to gain the approval of the impartial spectator.[14]

Although Smith believes that the impartial spectator is a universal figure (i.e., everyone is able to reference him), he nonetheless appears to have believed that our impartial spectators were shaped by our experiences. Smith, for instance, uses the example of a man being raised outside of society to make this point (*TMS*, 110).[15] As he writes,

> Were it possible that a human creature could grow up to manhood in some solitary place, without any communication with his own species, he could no more think of his own character, of the propriety or demerit of his own sentiments and conduct, of the beauty or deformity of his own mind, than of the beauty or deformity of his own face.... Bring him into society, and he is immediately provided with the mirror which he wanted before. It is placed in the countenance and behaviour of those he lives with, which always mark when they enter into, and when they disapprove of his sentiments; and it is here that he first views the propriety and impropriety of his own passions, the beauty and deformity of his own mind.[16]

---

were, into two persons; and that I, the examiner and judge, represent a different character from that other I, the person whose conduct is examined into and judged of. The first is the spectator, whose sentiments with regard to my own conduct I endeavour to enter into, by placing myself in his situation, and by considering how it would appear to me, when seen from that particular point of view. The second is the agent, the person whom I properly call myself, and of whose conduct, under the character as a spectator, I was endeavouring to form some opinion. The first is the judge; the second the person judged of" (113).

[14] Note that Smith does talk about how difficult it is to listen to the man in the breast when all of society disagrees.

[15] As others have pointed out, it is an unfortunate thought experiment because no one is ever really raised outside of society.

[16] Clifford Geertz (*The Interpretation of Cultures* [New York: Basic Books, 1973]) invokes a similar thought experiment and hence makes a very similar point, when he says culture equips us with blueprints that we would not have had in a vacuum: "Our first ideas of personal beauty and deformity, are drawn from the shape and appearance of others, not from our own" (111). "Undirected by culture patterns," Geertz reiterates, "man's behavior would be virtually ungovernable, a mere chaos of pointless acts and

The people who we interact with as we mature are, thus, likely to shape our impartial spectators; that is, we are likely to adopt the moral judgments of the people around us. Indeed, for Smith, the man within the breast is both a guide as we experience the world and is affected by our experiences in the world, becoming increasingly refined throughout our lives.

The impartial spectator is, thus, likely to be wearing cultural spectacles. Our impartial spectators are bound to reflect the ethical systems of our cultures.[17] Indeed, this process through which we form our moral sentiments resembles the process of enculturation through which children are raised to into their respective cultures.[18]

---

exploding emotions, his experience virtually shapeless" (46). Both Smith and Geertz conduct the thought experiment of man without society, without culture. Geertz concludes that culture "is not just an ornament of human existence but...an essential condition for it" (ibid.).

[17] The definition of culture used in this chapter relies heavily on Geertz. Geertz defined culture as "an historically transmitted pattern of meanings...a system of inherited conceptions...by means of which men communicate, perpetuate, and develop their knowledge about and attitudes toward life" (*The Interpretation of Cultures*, 89). According to Geertz "our ideas, values, our acts, even our emotions, are, like our nervous system itself, cultural products—products manufactured, indeed, out of tendencies, capacities, and dispositions with which we were born, but manufactured nonetheless" (50). To cite a trivial example, it would be strange indeed for Mary to grow up in a culture where announcements of the marital engagement of two people are systematically met with happiness and congratulations and yet Mary systematically expresses sorrow upon hearing such news. This is because Mary, if she were raised within that culture, would have had to ascribe a certain cultural significance to the act of two people making a lifelong commitment to each other. She may experience sorrow for personal reasons, but she will know that it is appropriate to express happiness and congratulations toward to the engaged couple.

[18] Forman-Barzilai, "Smith on 'connexion', culture and judgment," 95.

The Universal and Culturally Specific Character of the Impartial Spectator

Smith seemed to be aware of the possibility that our men in the breast could be affected by our cultures. As Smith confesses, "since our sentiments concerning beauty of every kind, are so much influenced by custom and fashion, it cannot be expected, that those, concerning the beauty of conduct, should be entirely exempted from the dominion of those principles" (*TMS*, 200). And, as Smith explains,

> The different situations of different ages and countries are apt, in the same manner, to give different characters to the generality of those who live in them, and their sentiments concerning the particular degree of each quality, that is either blamable or praise–worthy, vary, according to that degree which is usual in their own country, and in their own times. That degree of politeness, which would be highly esteemed, perhaps would be thought effeminate adulation, in Russia, would be regarded as rudeness and barbarism at the court of France. That degree of order and frugality, which, in a Polish nobleman, would be considered as excessive parsimony, would be regarded as extravagance in a citizen of Amsterdam. Every age and country look upon that degree of each quality, which is commonly to be met with in those who are esteemed among themselves, as the golden mean of that particular talent or virtue. And as this varies, according as their different circumstances render different qualities more or less habitual to them, their sentiments concerning the exact propriety of character and behaviour vary accordingly. (*TMS*, 204)

Indeed, it would be strange if customs did not affect our moral sentiments.

As noted above, others have, of course, stressed the cultural plurality of the impartial spectator. Forman-Barzilai for instance, argued that "Smith's account of the origins of our moral criteria culminates in a culturally insular portrait of our moral life."[19] Similarly, Gibbard writes, "if Smith's…story supports his detached observer theory, it supports the theory in a relativized form. The proper feelings for a person, Smith

[19] Ibid.

must say, are those of a detached observer who belongs to that person's own culture.... If his fellows, the ones who matter, are of his own culture, the detached observer should be too."[20]

Smith, nonetheless, believed that the effect of custom on our moral sentiments was not all that significant. First, Smith believed that custom was less likely to affect our moral sentiments than it was likely to color other aspects of our lives (e.g., our tastes). As Smith explains, "the influence of custom and fashion upon moral sentiments is not altogether so great" and "their influence here, however, seems to be much less than it is every where else" (*TMS*, 200). Also, "the sentiments of moral approbation and disapprobation, are founded on the strongest and most vigorous passions of human nature; and though they may be somewhat warpt, cannot be entirely perverted" (ibid.). Second, Smith believed that there tended to be cross-cultural agreement regarding the core of our moral sentiments. As Smith writes, "the different manners which custom teachers us to approve of in the different professions and states of life, do not concern things of the greatest importance" (*TMS*, 209). And, "it is not...in the general style of conduct or behavior that custom authorizes the widest departure from what is the natural propriety of action" (ibid.).

Culture, for Smith, leads to a diversity of "manners" across cultures but does not lead to diversity in the "general style of conduct or behavior." Stated another way, Smith believes that culture will color how our impartial spectators look and sound but will not affect the core of what they have say. As Otteson explains, "Smith's argument is that custom and fashion only influence the less important, marginal concerns of the moral judgment, but not the central concerns."[21] Similarly, Forman-Barzilai suggests that Smith believed that his theory of negative justice would do the "universalizing work" and, as such, allow individuals

[20] Allan Gibbard, "Moral Concepts: Substance and Sentiment," *Philosophical Perspectives* vol. 6, Ethics (1992) 199–221.

[21] James R. Otteson, *Adam Smith's Marketplace of Life* (Cambridge: Cambridge University Press, 2002).

to escape their cultural bias.[22] Likewise, Griswold has explained that for Smith "moral criticism is attentive to context, presupposes custom, and engages understanding from within a specifiable temporal context, but ... moral criticism is not ... blinded by custom."[23] As Griswold remarks, Smith believed that there were "natural principles of right and wrong" that could not be reduced to custom.[24]

Arguably, Smith exaggerates the range of our moral sentiments that would fall within a universal moral core (to the extent that there is one).[25] Moreover, Smith underestimates the cultural diversity that we observe in

[22] Forman-Barzilai, "Smith on 'connexion', culture and judgment," 91.

[23] Charles L. Griswold Jr., *Adam Smith and the Virtues of Enlightenment* (New York: Cambridge University Press, 1999) 51.

[24] Ibid.

[25] Recall that for Smith, there are certain behaviors among human beings that we sympathize without knowing much about their situation. He first gives the example of a smile and frown. "A smiling face is," he says, "to everybody that sees it, a cheerful object; as a sorrowful countenance, on the other hand, is a melancholy one" (*TMS*, 11) While this may be true, we contend that it is somewhat simplistic and devoid of the details that underlie seemingly simple behaviors like smiling. For example, it may be that in one culture, too much smiling is the mark of a foolish person or a flirtatious person, whereas a serious countenance is the mark of wit and more sophisticated humor. In such a culture, seeing a smiling face may not automatically rouse happiness in the observer—the observer may think she is being flirted with, and she may try to avoid the smiling person. On smiling, Geertz explains, "Smiling at pleasing stimuli and frowning at unpleasing ones are surely in some degree genetically determined (even apes screw up their faces at noxious odors) but sardonic smiling and burlesque frowning are equally surely predominantly cultural, as is perhaps demonstrated by the Balinese definition of a madman as someone who, like an American, smiles when there is nothing to smile at" (*The Interpretation of Cultures*, 50). Geertz also reminds us that even something as insignificant as wink can have different meanings – it can represent different things depending on the case: "an involuntary twitch," "a conspiratorial signal to a friend," even "a parody" (6). One simple human act like smiling or winking can have multiple meanings within a culture. Across cultures, the number of meanings must therefore increase. Removing an individual from one culture and placing her within another culture may make it difficult or even impossible for her to sympathize completely with the passions of the persons in the alien culture. This is because expressions of those passions by the foreigners may signify to her altogether different passions.

the world regarding what would have to, for him, constitute that universal moral core.[26]

While it is likely that the impartial spectator is a universal figure and the categories that he relies on as he makes moral pronouncements are also universal, the content of his character is likely to be culturally conditioned. For instance, a notion of justice is a moral value that people all over the world seem to have. Broadly speaking, justice occurs whenever a person is granted her "just desserts." So, for example, in all societies some form of "dessert" awaits a person who commits a crime. An injustice, on the other hand, occurs whenever some fate befalls a person that she did nothing to deserve. So we behave unjustly when we punish someone for a crime she did not commit or when we fail to punish a criminal.

[26] Geertz laments the "consensus gentium" in anthropology—"the notion that there are some things that all men will be found to agree upon as right, real, just, or attractive and that these things are, therefore, in fact right, real just, or attractive," a notion he claims has been pervasive since the Enlightenment. In this view, part of the things we do are universal as they come from within us, and this explains the existence of universal cultural patterns, even if other things we do emanate solely from copying other people. Geertz disagrees with this approach. He insists that there is nothing universal in religion, marriage, and property, because we cannot universally define them. As Geertz argues, "there is a logical conflict between asserting that, say, 'religion,' 'marriage,' or 'property' are empirical universals and giving them much in the way of specific content, for to say that they are empirical universals is to say that they have the same content, and to say that they have the same content is to fly in the face of the undeniable fact they do not" (*The Interpretation of Cultures*, 39). Thus, like tragedy and romance, there is too much in the details of things like religion and marriage that vary from culture to culture to describe them as universal human traits. As Geertz continues, "To make the generalization about an afterlife stand up alike for the Confucians and the Calvinists, the Zen Buddhists and the Tibetan Buddhists, one has to define it in most general terms, indeed—so general, in fact, that whatever force it seems to have virtually evaporates" (40). Finally, as he suggests, "That everywhere people mate and produce children, have some sense of mine and thine, and protect themselves in one fashion or another from rain and sun are neither false nor, from some points of view, unimportant, but they are hardly very much help in drawing a portrait of man that will be a true and honest likeness and not an untainted 'John Q. Public' sort of cartoon" (ibid.)

The particulars of justice differ substantively across cultures. In one culture, adulterers might be punished with execution by stoning. In another culture, adultery may be discouraged but not seen as a crime; perhaps only certain classes of murderers are viewed as punishable with execution, and stoning might be viscerally opposed and viewed as a form of torture. Similarly, the bigamist may be condemned in one culture and admired in another. These differences in the application of justice are not trivial. Although the categories of offense and punishment are certainly universal, they differ widely across cultures. There is no universal, objective way to designate a crime or a punishment.

An additional example demonstrates the point that the impartial spectator wears cultural spectacles. Like justice, a general notion of honor can also be found in many societies, but the definition of honorable action is highly variable across cultures. Honorable action might loosely be defined as action that is considered respectable, righteous, and deserving of widespread esteem and emulation. McCloskey argues that prior to the sixteenth century, a person in northwestern Europe was considered honorably occupied only if he was a member of the military, the priesthood, or the nobility.[27] Gradually, however, a cultural change occurred such that "an old class of town dwellers, formerly despised by the clergy and the aristocracy and the peasantry, began to acquire a more dignified standing, in the way people thought and talked about it, in European rhetoric about middle-class activities."[28] These town dwellers were merchants. Only when enough people came to see honor in being a merchant, and they found it respectable "to invent a machine for making screws or to venture in trade to Cathay," as McCloskey puts it, commerce began to flourish in Europe and people's lives materially improved.[29]

[27] Deirdre N. McCloskey, *The Bourgeois Dignity: Why Economics Can't Explain the Modern World* (Chicago: University of Chicago Press, 2010).

[28] Ibid., 10.

[29] Ibid., 12.

Arguably, the notion that business activity is a respectable and admirable way to earn a living persists in Western society today, but this value is not the same across all cultures. Although our impartial spectators encourage us to be honorable, their judgments of our actions are colored by what our various cultures deem honorable. What is considered honorable can significantly differ across cultures.

Smith, in fact, seems to concede as much (*TMS*, 210). Recall his discussion of infanticide and the sanction given to this practice in an ancient and civilized culture such as Athens as well as in the savage nations of his day. As Smith explains,

> Can there be greater barbarity, for example, than to hurt an infant? Its helplessness, its innocence, its amiableness, call forth the compassion, even of an enemy, and not to spare that tender age is regarded as the most furious effort of an enraged and cruel conqueror.... Yet the exposition, that is, the murder of new–born infants, was a practice allowed of in almost all the states of Greece, even among the polite and civilized Athenians; and whenever the circumstances of the parent rendered it inconvenient to bring up the child, to abandon it to hunger, or to wild beasts, was regarded without blame or censure.... We find, at this day, that this practice prevails among all savage nations. (*TMS*, 209–210)

This would seem to suggest that there is not universal agreement on the "natural principles" of negative justice that Smith recommends. Note also that, as Smith admits, "when custom can give sanction to so dreadful a violation of humanity, we may well imagine that there is scarce any particular practice so gross which it cannot authorize" (*TMS*, 210). Consequently, we have every reason to believe that our impartial spectators will nonetheless view us through cultural spectacles.

To preview one of the arguments that we will advance in the next section, Smith ultimately rests his hopes for an impartial spectator who can escape its tendency toward parochialism on the process of acculturation that occurs during a process of intercultural engagement. The more and more diverse our actual spectators the less likely our imagined spectators are to be parochial.

The Implications of a Spectacled Spectator

Several implications flow from accepting that the man in the breast is likely to be a spectacled spectator. First, within groups, our impartial spectators promote group harmony but not necessarily moral advancement. Second, when interacting across groups, we may be ill-served or misled by our impartial spectators (i.e., we may censure what we should praise and vice versa). Third, as hinted at above, when we interact with a greater variety of people, we become more tolerant of differences and our impartial spectators are likely to be less culturally bound.

Recall that, for Smith, mutual sympathy was a precondition for comity. As Smith explains, if you cannot sympathize with my passions in a certain sphere, you and I cannot even converse on the subject. Consequently, each of us learns to match the pitch of our passions with those that we would expect those around us to accept. Although Smith tends to stress the ability of our impartial spectators to help us to escape our partisanship, it is its ability to help us to behave in a way that those in our community would want us to behave if they knew all of the facts of the matter that makes group harmony possible.

Consider, for instance, the practice of female genital mutilation (FGM). This practice, common in African countries such as Egypt, Mali, and Sudan, entails partially or completely removing external female genitalia and otherwise damaging female genital organs. By many accounts, the procedure is coercive, traumatically painful, and life threatening, yet older women who have themselves undergone FGM are typically the ones doing it to young girls. UNICEF (2005) estimates that three million girls and women receive FGM per year, and some African immigrants living in Europe and North America continue to practice FGM in spite of Western laws and taboos against it.[30]

[30] UNICEF, "Female Genital Mutilation/Female Genital Cutting: A Statistical Exploration" (New York: UNICEF, 2005).

How can such a seemingly abhorrent practice persist among a group of people and be practiced by women? According to Yoder et al., a majority of women who reside in these cultural groups regard FGM as "part of their commonsense understanding of what parents should do for their daughters."[31] These women therefore find the practice to be appropriate.[32] They (as parents) often engage in FGM voluntarily for the group benefits they perceive that it will bring. Stated another way, a Sudanese mother's impartial spectator may approve of her parenting only if she allows her seven-year-old daughter to undergo the procedure. A mother who rejects the mutilation for her child is rejecting the group identity. She stands to lose rapport with other mothers and will face ostracism for threatening the group's harmony. These could very well be sufficient reasons for a mother to agree to a practice such as FGM. Thus, the impartial spectator can encourage the replication of certain extraordinary practices within groups (promoting group harmony) as opposed to discouraging group insularity.

Additionally, appeal to the impartial spectator may not be helpful in our dealings with someone from another culture. In fact, we might offend when we mean to flatter, or we might take offense when others mean to compliment us. Note that this difficulty would still exist even if Smith were correct that only our manners—but not our core principles—were affected by custom.

Imagine, for instance, the English-speaking Eastern Caribbean native who comes to the United States without a deep understanding of American culture, history, and politics. That person may, in casual conversation, refer to African Americans as "Negroes." He or she is unaware that many Americans find the word "Negro" to be offensive. Whereas, in the United States, the terms "black" and "African American"

[31] Stanley P. Yoder, Noureddine Abderrahim, and Arlinda Zhuzhuni, "Female Genital Cutting in the Demographic and Health Surveys: A Critical and Comparative Analysis," *DHS Comparative Report* 7 (Maryland: ORC Macro, 2004) 43.

[32] See Christopher Coyne and Rachel Coyne, "The Identity Economics of Female Genital Mutilation," *Journal of Developing Areas* 48/2 (Spring 2014).

replaced "Negro" (which, in turn, replaced "colored"), the term "Negro" remains in use in countries such as Guyana, Trinidad, and Tobago, particularly among older people. An American's impartial spectator will therefore likely judge the Caribbean person's use of the word to be a racial slur. It will advise the American to feel and act insulted. Or, the American impartial spectator will judge the Caribbean person's use of the word as antiquated and advise the American to respond with pity. Either way, the American is likely unaware that the Caribbean person's impartial spectator judges her use of the term "Negro" as neutral and appropriate. In this and similar situations, relying on our own impartial spectators' judgments of what is acceptable can lead us to misinterpret other people's behavior.

Finally, our men in the breast will have greater cultural awareness if we engage with a greater variety of cultures. Recall that Smith stressed that absent others serving as mirrors, we would not be fit for society. The more mirrors we encounter during our lives, the more varied those mirrors will be and the less narrow and particular we should expect our impartial spectator to be.

Consider, for instance, the character Stephen Dedalus in James Joyce's *The Portrait of the Artist as a Young Man*. Stephen, the main character, starts his life in a poor, Irish Catholic household. He is looked down upon in school for his family's low social rank and is vilified for wanting to marry a Protestant girl. He eventually moves with his family to Dublin, where he goes from debauched and gluttonous, enjoying the company of several prostitutes, to utterly pious. In his journey he encounters and befriends people like Aubrey Mills, Father Arnall, Davin, Cranly, and Emma, who each influence and challenge his ideals. We also see Stephen change as he reads the works of Dumas, Dante, Aquinas, and Aristotle. Stephen eventually relinquishes all the constraints of nation, religion, and family. He devotes his life to writing, as he is finally able to make peace with his love of art and beauty. Stephen's transformation would not have been possible had he not been exposed to the different viewpoints and philosophies offered by the people he met, the locations he visited, and the books he read.

Similarly, as Storr argued elsewhere, "the market is likely to have a positive impact on our impartial spectators in several ways."[33] In the market, we come into contact with an expanding and potentially varied group of others. Indeed, as the scope of the market and the extent of the division of labor expands, the number and the diversity of people with whom we interact on a regular basis increase dramatically. As Storr writes, "the market, thus, enlarges our spheres of sympathy/intimacy i.e. we come to care about the opinions and wellbeing of more people than we otherwise would as a result of our dealings in the market."[34] Stated another way, it encourages the kind of meaningful intercultural engagement that might allow our impartial spectators to remove their cultural spectacles.

Conclusion

The impartial spectator, that imaginary figure within each of us that judges our behavior and thus regulates our actions, is at the center of Smith's *Theory of Moral Sentiments*. We consider a judge to be impartial because she judges not by her own whims or wishes but according to an established and given body of law. Likewise, our impartial spectators pass judgment on our thoughts, beliefs, and actions, not from positions that are biased in our favor but according to the fairest and most unbiased standards it can conceive of (i.e., the standards of behavior that independent others in our community would hold us to if they knew all of the relevant details of our circumstances).

Something like the impartial spectator is certainly at work as we decide right and wrong, when we feel pride or shame, when we attribute praise or blame. When we look at other people's actions and judge those actions as being right or wrong, or worthy of approval or disapproval, however, we are using a framework of meaning imparted to us, to a

[33] Virgil H. Storr, "The Impartial Spectator and the Moral Teachings of Markets," in *Oxford Handbook of Freedom*, ed. David Schmidtz (Oxford: Oxford University Press, forthcoming).

[34] Ibid.

degree, by others. The impartial spectator evolves through a process of enculturation, and, as such, the impartial spectator will look very different in different cultural contexts. The impartial spectator is, like all of us, a cultural creature.

In this chapter, we have argued that the impartial spectator comes to develop its spectacles, and hence its character, through a process of enculturation. Wanting to receive praise and to avoid blame, we simply try to act as others around us act. However, since other people can be biased, we realize that other people's feelings toward us are not always the best barometer of our actions. Thus, the impartial spectator within us becomes our judge as we seek to become people who are "objectively" worthy of praise and innocent of blame. To judge us at all, the impartial spectator needs a lens to help it discern the right and wrong in our actions, and that lens is our culture.

Furthermore, we contend that the spectator's judgments are culturally specific. While Smith posited that all impartial spectators would have a fundamentally similar morality, we believe it is important to distinguish similar moral categories from the diverse content of those categories. Thus, while persons from two different cultures may find it moral to be loyal, fair, or hardworking, what constitutes loyalty, fairness, and hard work can differ substantially between cultures. As such, the impartial spectator levies truly different judgments on individuals from different cultures, leading to very different types of behavior.

These differences in behavior matter. Because the impartial spectator attempts to align our actions with actions considered worthy of approval in our culture, we have a tendency to perpetuate cultural behaviors that may be damaging to some. The fact that the spectator wears these cultural spectacles may explain why practices like female genital mutilation and the ill treatment of minority groups persist. Furthermore, the impartial spectator's judgment of us may be at odds with how people from other cultures judge us, and the resulting misunderstandings may cause antagonism between people of different cultures. On a more positive note, however, we should expect that the more we encounter people different from ourselves, the more our passions are moderated, and more cultured our spectator becomes. Thus, the more cosmopolitan our lives, the more understanding, tolerant, and cosmopolitan our views become.

3 | Adam Smith's Philosophical History

Kevin S. Honeycutt

When he interpreted Rousseau, Bertrand de Jouvenel insisted that he wrote not as an expert, but merely as a familiar reader. The same spirit animates this essay. In what follows, I will explore Smith's understanding of history and of the task of the historian, especially as it is set forth in the *Lectures on Rhetoric and Belle Lettres*, which were delivered c. 1762.

Smith died on 17 July 1790. Almost a year later, an interview between Smith and his purported friend, "Amicus," was published in the 11 May 1791 edition of *The Bee*.[1] The stated aim of the interview was to relate "Anecdotes tending to throw light on the character and opinions of the late Adam Smith." As far as I am aware, the identity of Amicus remains unknown, and so it is impossible to resolve whether we should trust his testimony. Nonetheless, his remarks afford us a starting point of inquiry. Amicus relates that Smith had "some singular opinions," including a preference for Livy "to all other historians, ancient and modern," and he goes on to say that Smith "knew of no other who had even a pretense to rival him, if David Hume could not claim that honor."[2] Amicus's claim is that Smith preferred Livy among the ancient historians and Hume among the moderns. Is there textual evidence to support this claim? That is our question.

[1] This interview is included as Appendix I (pp. 227–31) in *LRBL*.

[2] Here is Amicus's full remark: "The Doctor [Smith] had some singular opinions. I was surprised at hearing him prefer Livy to all other historians, ancient and modern. He knew of no other who had even a pretense to rival him, if David Hume could not claim that honor. He regretted, in particular, the loss of his account of the civil wars in the age of Julius Caesar; and when I attempted to comfort him by the library at Fez, he cut me short. I would have expected Polybius to stand much higher in his esteem than Livy, as having a much nearer resemblance to Dr. Smith's own manner of writing. Besides his miracles, Livy contains an immense number of the most obvious and gross falsehoods."

Philosophy and History

In his 1 November 1785 letter to the Duc de la Rochefoucauld, Smith notes his plans for two future works:

> I have not forgot what I promised to your Grace in an edition of the "Theory of Moral Sentiments," which I hope to execute before the end of the ensuing winter. I have likewise two other great works upon the anvil; the one is a sort of Philosophical History of all the different branches of Literature, Poetry, and Eloquence; the other is a sort of theory and History of Law and Government. The materials of both are in a great measure collected, and some Part of both is put into tolerable good order. But the indolence of old age, though I struggle violently against it, I feel coming fast upon me, and whether I shall ever be able to finish either is extremely uncertain. (*CAS*, 248)

Smith never finished either of the works that he mentions in the letter. However, the rough outlines of each are to be found in the *Lectures on Rhetoric and Belle Lettres* and the *Lectures on Jurisprudence*, respectively.[3] And it is noteworthy that Smith uses the term "History" to describe each project, with the first labeled "a sort of Philosophical History." A philosophical history might simply be a history of philosophies or philosophical systems. For instance, in the so-called "History of Astronomy," Smith speaks of finding a "clue that is most capable of conducting us through all the labyrinths of philosophical history," and the context is an investigation of "all the different systems

[3] Though I will not hesitate to ascribe statements in the *LRBL* to Smith himself, Smith did not write the published manuscript. His own manuscript of this lecture course was destroyed in the week before his death according to his instructions. Rather, as the editors of *LRBL* point out, "[o]ur manuscript is the result of a continuous collaboration between two students intent on making the notes as full and accurate a record of Smith's words as their combined resources can produce" (p. 4 of the Editors' Introduction in *LRBL*). We must therefore take the exact wording, though perhaps not the substance, of the *LRBL* with qualification. In Dugald Stewart's "Account of the Life and Writings of Adam Smith, LL.D.," John Millar reports that Smith's original lecture course "discovered strong marks of taste and original genius." See Stewart I.17 in *EPS*, 274.

of nature" known to the west (*HA* II.12). But this use of the adjective "philosophical" does not appear to be Smith's sense in the letter above. Rather, "philosophical" appears to be doing a different kind of work there; it appears to suggest that one can give a history that is itself philosophical.

It is important here to distinguish two senses of "history." Smith was aware of progressive, speculative theories of history; Turgot published his famous essay on progress in 1750, and Diderot published the first volume of the *Encyclopédie* in 1751. But there is no sense that Smith held this progressive view; rather, he understood the historical process to be the result of human action but not of human design, as Adam Ferguson would later put it.[4] Thus, when Smith speaks of "history," he means the critical study of historical facts and the historical process. In other words, he means something more akin to the task of the historian than to the task of the speculative philosopher of history (e.g., Hegel).

Smith says that philosophy "is the science of the connecting principles of nature"; that it "*endeavors* to introduce order into this chaos of jarring and discordant appearances" by "*representing* the invisible chains which bind together all these disjointed objects" (emphasis added); that it "may be regarded as one of those arts which address themselves to the imagination"; that it is the "science which *pretends* to lay open the concealed connections that unite the various appearances of nature" (emphasis added); that it begins in wonder and is done for its own sake; and that its "ultimate end" is the "the repose and tranquility of the imagination."[5] Furthermore, Smith says that a philosophical system

[4] Adam Ferguson, *An Essay on the History of Civil Society* (London: 1767), 187. Cited by Friedrich A. Hayek, *Law, Liberty, and Legislation, Volume I: Rules and Order* (Chicago: University of Chicago Press, 1973), 20.

[5] The first three quotations are from *HA*, II.12; the third and fourth are from *HA*, III.3; and the fifth is from *HA*, IV.13. On Smith's use of "principle," at least two of his examples elsewhere are instructive. The second chapter of the *WN* purports to treat "Of the Principle which gives occasion to the Division of Labor." Though Smith asserts that this is self–interest, he does not call it a principle. He does, however, call its contrast, "the

"is an imaginary machine invented to connect together in the fancy those different movements and effects which are already in reality performed" (*HA*, IV.19).[6] In other words, philosophical accounts endeavor to soothe the imagination by representing or describing causes in ways that we find orderly. There is a pretense of explanation, but it is not fulfilled, nor need it be for our imagination to be satisfied. The standard for philosophical explanation is not a rational account of causation but what Smith elsewhere calls propriety, that is, the suitability of an affection to a cause (*TMS*, I.i.4.1).[7]

By contrast, Smith says that "[t]he chief purpose of History" is to "relate Events and connect them with their causes without becoming a party on either side" (*LRBL*, ii.70). Smith has confidence that the

---

charity of well–disposed people," a principle explicitly (*WN*, I.ii.2). Secondly, Smith begins *TMS* by asserting that, however selfish we suppose man, "there are evidently some principles in his nature" which interest him in the fortune of others (*TMS*, I.i.I.1). He shortly declares that the "dread of death" is "one of the most important principles in human nature" (I.i.1.13). On Smith's use of "nature," several of his examples elsewhere are instructive. He speaks of "the natural system of perfect liberty and justice" (*WN*, IV.vii.c.44), "the obvious and simple system of natural liberty" (*WN*, IV.ix.51; see also *WN*, I.x.a.1–2, I.vii.6, I.vii.30, and IV.ix.17), the "natural price" of a good that flows from this system of liberty (*WN*, I.vii.4) and the "propensity to truck, barter, and exchange one thing for another," which is a "certain propensity in human nature" (*WN*, I.ii.1). Smith declines in *WN* to investigate whether this propensity is "one of those original principles in human nature, of which no further account can be given" or whether it is a "necessary consequence of the faculties of reason and speech" (*WN*, I.ii.2). However, in the *Lectures on Jurisprudence*, Smith claims that the foundational "principle" of the propensity is "clearly the natural inclination everyone has to persuade" (*LJA*, vi.56) and that "the real foundation" of the propensity is "that principle to persuade which so much prevails in human nature" (*LJB*, 221).

[6] Smith says that the Newtonian theory of gravitation is "the most happy, and, we may now say, the greatest and most admirable improvement that was ever made in philosophy (*HA*, IV.67; see also *HA*, IV.76). This is because it has "completely removed all the difficulties the imagination" had previously had in conceiving the attraction and motion of objects (*HA*, IV.67). However, Smith is clear that even this theory is a hypothetical description rather than a causal explanation (*HA*, IV.76).

[7] See also *TMS*, I.i.3.1.

historian, rather than the philosopher, is the one who actually penetrates to real causes. But the historian's task is complicated in that human affections can take on the status of causes. When discussing history as opposed to philosophy, then, Smith distinguishes between internal and external causes. External causes are the causes that directly produce an event. Internal causes are those that "though they no way affected the event yet had an influence on the minds of the chief actors so as to alter their conduct from what it would otherwise have been" (*LRBL*, ii.v.20). This looks at first glance to be a straightforward contradiction. How can internal causes "in no way" affect an event while at the same time influence the "chief actors" in an event so that they act "otherwise" than they would have? One charitable interpretation is that Smith's point here is that internal causes at first do not *appear* to be causes in the philosophical sense. However, Smith says that the "causes of human actions are motives," and it is certain that "no one ever acts without a motive" (*LRBL*, ii.192). Thus, it is part of the task of the historian, as opposed to the philosopher, to reckon with the psychology of historical actors. Though Smith says that "[t]he *describing* of characters is no essential part of a historical narration" (emphasis added), the historian must still reckon with the character of the historical actors when giving an *explanation* (*LRBL*, ii.24).[8] In the end, internal causes fall within the aegis of causation that the historian treats. This is one of the reasons why one might claim that the historian offers a superior or, at any rate, more complete causal account than that of the philosopher.

[8] Smith says, "Xenophon is almost the only ancient Historian who professedly draws characters...Herodotus and Thucydides hardly describe any characters" (*LRBL*, ii.24). Smith also says elsewhere that directly describing a character is rarely done by the ancients, since to do it "with any tolerable degree of perfection requires great skill, deep penetration, an accurate observation and almost perfect knowledge of men" (*LRBL*, i.189). The "great fault" we are apt to make when describing characters is "making them so General that they Exhibit no Idea at all" (*LRBL*, i.99). Contrast the modern historian, Clarendon, who spends all his time describing characters "such that "there is hardly a footman brings a message but what he gives us an account of his character" (*LRBL*, ii.72).

The historian's subject matter is similarly multi-faceted and expansive. The historian's business is to "narrate facts" (*LRBL*, ii.39). As he does with causes, Smith distinguishes between external and internal facts. External facts consist of the "transactions that pass without us," but internal facts are "the thoughts, sentiments, or designs of men, which pass in their minds" (*LRBL*, i.151). What's more, Smith says that the historian's "facts must be real" lest the "end proposed by history" remain unfulfilled (*LRBL*, ii.18). Because they are real, we can and do have opinions about them. As a result, we run the risk of loving our opinions of the facts more than the facts themselves; we run the risk of becoming partisans. In contrast to the ancient histories, Smith says, "it has been the fate of all modern histories to be written in a party spirit" (*LRBL*, ii.72–73).[9]

In short, Smith distinguishes between the philosophical task of *imagining* connections (which may be hypothetical) in the natural world and the historical task of *narrating* the real connections in the human world, including the thoughts, sentiments, and designs of human beings (*LRBL*, ii.19). It is true that philosophy can also choose to adopt the narrative mode as it is understood on Smith's account.[10] But historical narration must deal with actual events, not hypothetical scenarios or models, and actual events are things that we view affectively. Because we view them affectively, they tempt us away from the disinterested stance of the historian. In other words, since history is not the narration of all causes but only of the causes that excite human beings, there is a tension between the disinterested stance of the historian and the historical product itself, which must be of interest to its readers. Smith says that a historian is to "expose the causes of every thing only in proportion to the impression it makes" (*LRBL*, ii.v.19). Though our curiosity to know a cause becomes greater as a phenomenon makes a greater impression on

[9] Smith offers Clarendon and Burnet as prime examples of this mistake and others.

[10] Indeed, in the work of some twentieth century philosophers (e.g., Paul Ricouer), Smith's distinction between philosophy and history becomes blurred.

us, we are not "greatly interest[ed]" by the changes or accidents in "inanimate or irrational beings" (*LRBL*, ii.v.18 and ii.15, respectively). It is a remarkable statement and one that appears to greatly deflate the prestige of philosophy in comparison to history. By contrast, "[a]s it is mankind we are chiefly connected with it must be their actions which chiefly interest our attention" (*LRBL*, ii.1). Smith elaborates:

> It is to be observed that no action however affecting in itself, can be represented in such a manner as to be very interesting to those who had not been present at it, by a bare narration where it is described without taking notice of any of the effects it had on those who were either actors or spectators of the whole affair. (*LRBL*, ii.5)

History is concerned not only with how actors or spectators cause an event but how they are affected by it. Smith says that the accidents "which affect the human Species interest us greatly by the Sympathetical affections they raise in us" (*LRBL*, ii.16).

Sympathy, one of the central ideas of *The Theory of Moral Sentiments*, is thus also one of the central ideas of the *Lectures on Rhetoric and Belles Lettres*, at least with respect to the study of history. This is why "the facts which are most commonly narrated and will be most adapted to the taste of the generality of men" by historians are not the facts that pertain to the natural world. Rather, they are facts that pertain to "the actions of men," specifically the "more complex and important actions of men" (*LRBL*, ii.15 and ii.1, respectively). Smith says that a history of earthquakes might be of interest to a naturalist; nonetheless, it would be "very dull and uninteresting to the generality of mankind" (*LRBL*, ii.15–16).[11] The issue is not whether earthquakes are interesting as such but whether they *appear* interesting to the generality of mankind. It is "Design and Contrivance" that "chiefly interests us," and we can see intention in the actions of human beings. As a result, human events interest us the more we are able to ascertain their design. It is worth emphasizing that Smith believes that we are in fact able to ascertain their

[11] Contrast *LRBL*, ii.v.19.

design, i.e., penetrate to the actual causes of human actions. Smith suggests that we are granted deeper access to the human world than the natural world by virtue of the human world being something that we have made.

Human events also interest us when their subject matter is such that we are affected in unusual or extraordinary ways. Smith says that "the Design of History" is to relate both external and internal facts "so far as they are necessary to explain the great changes and revolutions of States which it is intended to relate" (*LRBL*, i.151). In other words, Smith suggests that we are particularly interested in a specific subset of the "actions of men," i.e., political actions, and that we are particularly affected by wars, revolutions, upheavals, and conflicts. Since Smith says elsewhere that "the art of war…is certainly the noblest of all arts" and that "[n]othing tends so much to promote public spirit as the study of politics…," it looks as if most, if not all, histories should be political or military histories (*WN*, V.i.a.14 and *TMS*, IV.1.11, respectively).

Now, this at first appears to be a curious result given Smith's emphasis on sympathy. Smith says that "[t]he actions and perceptions which chiefly affect us and make the deepest impression on our minds are those that are of the misfortunate kind and give us in the perception a considerable degree of Uneasiness" (*LRBL*, ii.1). One would think that sympathy would guide us to care the most about the misfortune of the people closest to us, and indeed Smith says just this in many places of *The Theory of Moral Sentiments*. However, when it comes to history, there is a wrinkle, for Smith says that we are accustomed to the misfortunes of people like ourselves. We are not interested in reading a chronicle of the suffering of our neighbors; we have already heard it at the fencepost many times. To read about or see the suffering or striving of the great, however, is unusual, which is why "Kings and Nobles make the best characters in a Tragedy" (*LRBL*, i.90). As opposed to philosophical connections that must soothe the imagination, historical connections must somehow animate it. And although it is possible for a historian to focus excessively on "the private affairs of the monarchs" so that his history is merely an "account of the Lives of the princes," nonetheless we tend as human beings to be affected the most by the change in fortunes of those superior to us (*LRBL*, ii.73).[12] Smith says that this is because "[t]here is in human Nature a servility which inclines us to adore our Superiors and an inhumanity which disposes us to contempt and trample under foot our inferiors" (*LRBL*, ii.90). The historical preferences of the generality of mankind, strikingly enough, flow from human nature; in this sense, these preferences are not subjective. Taste for Smith has an objective component that flows from the nature of human beings.

This leads us to another difference between philosophy and history. Part of our interest in history is indeed due to the subject matter of history. But our interest also flows from the style of the historian, i.e., of the author of the historical work. We must feel drawn into a historical work not only by its subject matter but by what Smith calls "style," which is the correlate in the *Lectures on Rhetoric and Belle Lettres* to sympathy (e.g., in *TMS*) and the imagination (e.g., in *HA*). The historian "can only excite our affection by the narration of the facts and setting them in as interesting a view as he possibly can" (*LRBL*, ii.38). Smith thus distinguishes the historical or narrative style from that of the didactic, as well as from what he variously calls the rhetorical or the oratorical.[13] The historical style is first and foremost the narration of the relevant facts, though a historian, like a philosopher, "should never leave any chasm or Gap in the thread of the narration even though there are no remarkable events to fill up that space."[14] But the manner of this smooth narration may differ. "Few historians have trespassed" against the rule that events should be listed in the order in which they occurred, since "the mind naturally conceives that the facts happened in the order they are related." And indeed Smith insists that "[t]here is no connection with which we

[12] Smith's example of an historian who excessively treats princes is Paul de Rapin Thoyras. See also *LRBL*, ii.34.

[13] For these distinctions, see *LRBL*, ii.13 and ii.37–40.

[14] Regarding the historical style, see *LRBL*, i.149 and ii.74. Regarding the lack of gaps in historical narration, see *LRBL*, ii.36 and ii.133. See also *HA*, II.2–3, II.8, and II.11.

are so much interested" as cause and effect. However, when events happen simultaneously, the historian can choose a causal connection of place rather than one of time, running through all the events at one place before returning to the beginning and exploring the events at another place (*LRBL*, ii.31 and ii.32, respectively).[15] The historian has a narrative flexibility that the philosopher lacks; he can appeal to the taste of the generality of mankind in various ways.

The best history for Smith, as opposed to a mere chronicle, may be called a "philosophical history" for two reasons. First, it considers causes as part of its subject matter. Second, it animates the imagination by structuring its narration causally, i.e., in a manner that excites us, and with no causal gaps. But history, even philosophical history, differs from philosophy as such in that the former focuses on the things most important to us rather than any causal connection whatsoever. Insofar as it offers an account of great events (e.g., wars and revolutions) and superior beings (e.g., heroes and kings), history speaks to our human nature, or at least that part of it that is servile and inhuman. It is almost as if Smith were suggesting, in a perhaps playful inversion of Aristotle, that history is at once higher and more universal than philosophy and that it does not elevate us but rather speaks to the dark places in our souls.

The Ancient Historians

Though Smith may have intended the polished version of the *Lectures on Rhetoric and Belle Lettres* to be a philosophical history of all the different branches of literature, poetry, and eloquence, it does not take that form in its current state. However, nested within it is such a philosophical history, which Smith calls "*the History of Historians*"

[15] Smith defends Thucydides against the charge, made by Dionysus of *Helicarnassus*, that the he excessively adheres to a narrative connection of time such that "it is impossible to form a distinct notion of what passed in any one place" (*LRBL*, ii.33). Smith notes that it is a fair criticism in principle but is "perhaps not altogether just with regard to Thucydides," since his subject matter is a war that spans a long period of time.

(*LRBL*, ii.44).[16] As Smith's "History of Astronomy" is at once a narrative and a case study that reveals philosophical principles, the "History of Historians" is at once a narrative and a case study that reveals historical principles. It is a causal account of the rise and development of history as an intellectual endeavor and a critical examination of what historians do when they write historical accounts.

History begins as poetry. Smith says the first historians, like the first poets, chose the "marvelous for their subject" (*LRBL*, ii.60). The poets were "the first Historians of any" in that they "recorded those accounts that were most apt to surprise and strike the imagination." These accounts concerned "military exploits," since "of the actions of men" they are the ones that are "most fraught with adventures that are fit to amaze and gratify the desire men have especially in the early periods for what is marvelous" (*LRBL*, ii.44 and ii.45, respectively). Smith implies that Homer was thus the first historian, and later says that there is no "essential difference" between a "historical poem" and a "history" except that one is in prose and the other in verse. Indeed, it is "needless to prove the superiority of Poetry over prose," Smith says; everyone already knows it (*LRBL*, ii.74 and ii.76, respectively).

Why, then, does history arise from poetry to take on a life of its own? How does history differ from poetry? The fundamental difference is one of aim. The chief design of poetry is amusement and entertainment; as a result, the poet does not have to tell the truth.[17] By

[16] The italics are Smith's.

[17] Regarding poetry and entertainment, see *LRBL*, ii.76. Regarding poetry and truth, see *LRBL*, ii.79. It is worth noting in this context that Smith says that the design of romance, like that of poetry, is strictly to entertain (*LRBL*, ii.19) and that Descartes' *Discourse on Method* is "justly esteem[ed] one of the most entertaining Romances that has ever been written" (*LRBL*, ii.134). In the *Discourse*, Descartes says that he is offering it as a history or, if the reader prefers, a fable. Shortly thereafter, he describes the dangers of histories and fables and warns that attempting to regulate one's morals based on them is likely to cause us to fall into the extravagances of the paladins of our romances (*tomber dans les extravagances des paladins de nos romans*) and to conceive purposes that surpass our powers. See *Oeuvres de Descartes*, ed. Charles Adam and Paul Tannery, rev. ed. (Paris:

contrast, the "design of historical writing is not merely to entertain" (*LRBL*, ii.16). Though the historian is not supposed to be didactic, he must still keep in view "the instruction of the reader."[18] History arises from poetry because the historians recognize the need to learn from the great actions of the past in order to offer us some manner of guidance about the future.[19] It is important to recognize that this is a claim about the self-understanding of the participants, not about how those participants are viewed by others. Though Homer may very well have been treated as a credible historical and military source even into the 5th century BC, it is far from clear that he viewed himself in this way.[20]

Who are the historians who emerge to offer us this guidance? For the most part, Smith offers high praise for the work of the ancient historians, going so far as to praise the study of antiquity in general:

> Antiquity is necessary to give any thing a very high reputation as a matter of Deep knowledge. One who reads a number of modern books although they be very excellent will not get thereby the Character of a Learned

---

Vrin, 1964–1976) 6:4, 6–7. Though *les paladins* were originally legendary knights, it is worth noting that Cervantes published the two volumes of *Don Quixote* in 1605 and 1615 (Descartes published the *Discourse* in 1637). Smith says that the *Discourse* "does not perhaps contain a word of truth" (*LRBL*, ii.134).

[18] Regarding the historian and didacticism, see *LRBL*, ii.39–40. The quotation is from *LRBL*, ii.16. See also *LRBL*, ii.62.

[19] Thucydides makes this point explicit in his statement concerning his design at 1.23. See also the preface to Livy's *History*, as well as 6.1, 21.1, and 31.1.

[20] Indeed, as late as Eusebius (4th C. AD), the historicity of the *Iliad* could be accepted. Compare Pascal, *Pensées*, IX, §628 (New York: E. P. Dutton & Co., 1958): "These fabulous historians are not contemporaneous with the facts about which they write. Homer composes a romance, which he gives out as such, and which is received as such; for nobody doubted that Troy and Agamemnon no more existed than did the golden apple. Accordingly he did not think of making a history, but solely a book to amuse; he is the only writer of his time; the beauty of the work has made it last, every one learns it and talks of it, it is necessary to know it, and each one knows it by heart. Four hundred years afterwards the witnesses of these facts are no longer alive, no one knows of his own knowledge if it be a fable or a history; one has only learnt it from his ancestors, and this can pass for truth."

man; The acquaintance of the ancients will alone procure him that name. (*LRBL*, ii.215)

It is thus no surprise that Smith offers a philosophical history of the five great ancient historians—Herodotus, Thucydides, Xenophon, Livy, and Tacitus.[21]

Smith says that Herodotus was "[t]he first author who formed the Design of expanding the plan of history" (*LRBL*, ii.47). And he is indeed doing something new: *historia* in Greek means "inquiry," and *histor* means "witness." His history is innovative and lays the foundation for future work, both in terms of subject matter and style: he begins his history 240 years before his time; treats both Greek and barbarian polities; and does so in a "graceful and easy" style that connects his subject matter "in such an easy and natural manner as to leave no gap nor chasm in his narration." Nonetheless, because Herodotus's predecessors were poets, his history is close to poetry, both in time and in technique; although he does not include as many fabulous and marvelous examples as the poets, his "design indeed seems to have been rather to amuse than to instruct" (*LRBL*, ii.47-48 and ii.48, respectively).

Smith says that history continued in the state in which Herodotus left it until Thucydides wrote his own history, suggesting that Thucydides reshapes Herodotean history as Herodotus reshaped poetic history (*LRBL*, ii.49). Though Thucydides fought in most of the battles he describes, he is the first historian who "who pays any attention at all to Civil History," with all previous historians, as far back as Homer, "attach[ing] themselves merely to the military."[22] Thucydides innovates

[21] Smith also offers brief remarks on more minor historians such as Polybius (*LRBL*, ii.v.20, ii.25, and ii.54–55), Pliny (*LRBL*, ii.39), Julius Caesar (*LRBL*, ii.v.20 and ii.52–54), and Dionysus of Helicarnassus (*LRBL*, ii.46 and ii.57). However, the heart of his account is his treatment of Herodotus, Thucydides, Xenophon, Livy, and Tacitus. It is worth noting that historical accounts today would generally exclude Xenophon from such a list.

[22] Regarding Thucydides' combat experience, see *LRBL*, ii.v.20. Regarding his difference from the previous historians with respect to civil history, see *LRBL*, ii.51.

not only with respect to his subject matter but also his design; Smith says that Thucydides held "the proper design of historical writing," with the implication being that Herodotus did not (*LRBL*, ii.49). Indeed, Smith suggests that Thucydides is the first historian who attempts a complete separation from poetry. Smith continues:

> He [Thucydides] tells us that he undertook that work that by recording in the truest manner the various incidents of that war and the causes that produced it, posterity may learn how to produce the like events or shun others, and know what is to be expected from such and such circumstances. In this design he has succeeded better perhaps than any preceding or succeeding writer. (*LRBL*, ii.49)[23]

Thucydides is thus not only an innovator in that he departed from the custom of Herodotus; he is an exemplar in that his work remains *the* historical standard, at least in terms of causal narration. Smith says that "[t]here is no author who has more distinctly explained the causes of events than Thucydides" (*LRBL*, ii.25). Furthermore, Thucydides "never introduces any circumstances that do not [in] some way contribute to the producing some remarkable change in the affairs of the two contending states" (*LRBL*, ii.50).[24] His narration is "crowded with the most important events"—i.e., the events that are "of consequence to the narration"—and accounts for every event by the external causes which produced it (*LRBL*, ii.49 and ii.51, respectively). Even the orations he inserted into his history are "excellently adapted" to his end, and Smith strangely does not seem to find any poetic resonance in the fact that Thucydides admits that he contrived some of them (*LRBL*, ii.173–74).[25] In contrast to modern historians, Thucydides excels at indirect discourse,

[23] See also *LRBL*, ii.173.

[24] See also *LRBL*, ii.181.

[25] See also *LRBL*, ii.176. See Thucydides 1.22.1 for Thucydides's admission that he made certain speeches fit the necessary sense of the occasion. Though Smith puts the number at "about 48 Orations" (*LRBL*, ii.74), there are 141 speeches in Thucydides if one includes both direct and indirect discourse.

a technique that Smith recommends "when we mean to affect the reader deeply."[26]

However, Smith criticizes Thucydides on stylistic grounds. Smith says that Thucydides pleases those "who desire to know the truth and the causes of the different successes of the war" but that nonetheless he is less "amusing" than Herodotus. In contrast to Herodotus' aforementioned "easy and graceful" style, Thucydides's style is "Strong and Nervous" (*LRBL*, ii.173–74). Furthermore, Smith says that Thucydides "never observes any sort of connection in the circumstances he brings in," noting repeatedly that the circumstances mentioned in "the battle in the night" would do equally well in whatever order they were placed.[27] Though Thucydides offers a vastly superior causal account than that of Herodotus, his style is less amusing, and thus less interesting, than that of Herodotus. There is room, then, to improve upon the work of Thucydides—to improve the style that strikes the imagination.

This improvement is made in Xenophon, who for Smith appears as something of a culmination of Greek historical writing. Smith says that Xenophon's style is "easy and agreeable, not so strong as that of Thucydides but perhaps more pleasant" (*LRBL*, ii.51). Being a general, Xenophon understands war, but he writes of it and of his involvement in it "without the least ostentation" (*LRBL*, ii.52). Smith lauds the "plainness…ingenuity, and openness of heart" of Xenophon's writings while noting how difficult it is to offer any particular passage as support of this claim:

> It is not easy to convey a notion of Xenophon's beauties, [as] there are no passages which taken by themselves could show his manner and his

[26] Regarding Thucydides's excelling at indirect discourse, see *LRBL*, ii.28. Regarding Smith's claim that this technique affects the reader deeply, see *LRBL*, ii.7.

[27] *LRBL*, ii.36. See also *LRBL*, ii.56. Regarding the ordering of "the battle in the night," see *LRBL*, ii.23, ii.36, ii.51, ii.58, and ii.66. Smith refers to Demosthenes's night attack on Epipolae. See Thucydides, 7.43–45.

> peculiar excellencies.... He must be read through to perceive his beauties and enter into his manner.[28]

Xenophon "draws us gradually" into his histories, and in doing so "becomes one of the most engaging, though not one of the most passionate[,] and interesting of authors." He does not "raise those violent emotions that Thucydides does but he pleases and engages fully as much." Smith strikingly compares Xenophon's historical writing to painting, saying that "though neither the Lines nor the Coloring or expression be very strong yet the ordonnance of the piece is such that it is on the whole very engaging and attractive."[29] Perhaps Xenophon is not simply the best Greek historian as such, then, but somehow he conveys what that excellence would feel like.

Livy is able to make explicit the aesthetic impression that Xenophon can only show and suggest, making the stylistic improvement over Thucydides complete. But somehow this is at once an achievement and a failure, as we will see. Smith says that Livy "supports the dignity of his narration by the interesting manner in which he relates the several events," calling this the "Poetical method" and thus suggesting that Livy's manner of writing history is much closer to that of Herodotus than that of Thucydides (*LRBL*, ii.27 and ii.36, respectively). Smith says,

> Of all the Latin historians Livy is without doubt the best; and if to be agreeable were the chief view of an author he would merit the chief rank amongst the whole number. He does not indeed enter deeply into the causes of things, in the same manner as the Greek historians do; but on the other hand he renders his descriptions extremely interesting by the great number of affecting circumstances he has thrown together, and that not without any connection, as is the method of Thucydides, but in an order natural to the times in which they happened and the circumstances themselves. (*LRBL*, ii.56)

[28] Both quotations are from *LRBL*, ii.52. See also *LRBL*, ii.53.

[29] The previous three quotations are from *LRBL*, ii.53.

Smith speaks further of the "peculiar excellency of Livy's style," which is the "grandeur and majesty which he maintains through the whole of his works and in which he excels all other historians though perhaps he is inferior in many other respects" (*LRBL*, ii.56). Livy is "much more ornate" than Herodotus and Thucydides, and he does not make a habit of holding the reader in suspense (*LRBL*, ii.170).[30] Rather, he "seems almost with Design to give warning of the Event of his battles as of Thrasymene and Cannae" (*LRBL*, ii.29). Furthermore, Smith says that Livy excels at indirect discourse and that he often uses speeches to offer observations and reflections that would not be so "properly made" in the guise of author.[31] Smith suggests that there is in Livy's writing a consummate mastery of rhetoric; it is not hard to see why he would prefer such a style, and in this sense Amicus may well have been right.

However, this achievement of style and return to Herodotean technique is not achieved without cost. Smith does not agree with the general accusation that Livy is "very inaccurate" in his account of military affairs, but the defense is backhanded; Smith merely says that Livy is "not so faulty in this respect as common fame reports" (*LRBL*, ii.56). But the real problem does not concern subject matter but rather historical aim: Livy does not enter deeply into the causes of things and seldom endeavors to account for events either by external or internal causes (*LRBL*, ii.56 and ii.27). It is almost as if Livy is simply the Roman recapitulation of Herodotus and that the art of the historian has at once progressed and regressed; Smith says that "Livy without question far excels Herodotus and Sallust [but] on the other hand falls no less short of Thucydides" (*LRBL*, ii.57). The price of Livy's eloquence is a loss of explanatory power.

This problem remains unresolved in Smith's narrative of the ancient historians, which ends effectively with Tacitus. As Livy is something of a return to Herodotus, Tacitus is something of a return to Thucydides;

[30] In this context, Smith groups Tacitus with Livy.

[31] Regarding Livy excelling at indirect discourse, see *LRBL*, ii.5–7. Regarding Livy speaking through the speeches of characters rather than his own voice, see *LRBL*, ii.43.

Smith compares Tacitus's long and precise sentences to those of Thucydides and ranks Tacitus alongside Xenophon and just after Thucydides as historians who distinctly explain causes.[32] However, Tacitus does not simply return to the Thucydidean ideal of causal explanation; he refashions it. Smith says that Tacitus "departed altogether from the plan of former historians," which was to explain the causes of "great revolutions" and to "instruct their readers in what manner such events might be brought about or avoided" (*LRBL*, ii.62). On the contrary, Tacitus formed a very different plan for his own writings, which was to use only internal causes and internal facts (*LRBL*, ii.67). According to Smith, Tacitus noticed that the most interesting parts of previous histories were those that accounted for the effects upon the minds of both historical actors and spectators. Thus, he imagined writing a history entirely in this mode (*LRBL*, ii.62–63).[33] This effort was largely successful; we are told that Tacitus "executed his works in a manner most suitable to this design" and that he "leads us so far into the sentiments and mind of the actors" that he offers us "some of the most striking and interesting passages to be met with in any history" (*LRBL*, ii.65 and ii.67, respectively). Though the "Deliberative orations of Tacitus are considerably different from those of Thucydides or Livy," Smith claims that they are "very consistent with that Idea of Historical writing which Tacitus entertained" (*LRBL*, ii.186).[34] And though Tacitus's method "perhaps will not tend so much to instruct us in the knowledge of the causes of events," Smith claims that "it will be more interesting and lead us into a science no less useful, to wit, the knowledge of the motives by which men act" (*LRBL*, ii.67). In other words, Tacitus offers the foundations of a science of internal causes and in doing so

[32] Regarding the similarity of the sentences of Tacitus and Thucydides, see *LRBL*, i.13. Regarding Tacitus and causation, see *LRBL*, ii.26.

[33] See also *LRBL*, ii.23 and ii.186.

[34] With respect to deliberative and judicial orations, Smith says that "[a]s Livy is a sort of Medium betwixt Tacitus and Thucydides, so is Xenophon betwixt Thucydides and Livy" (*LRBL*, ii.187; see also *LRBL*, ii.181 and ii.185–86).

finally enables history to set itself apart from both poetry and philosophy. Smith praises Tacitus's *Annals* as the work in which "the character of Tacitus chiefly appears" and in which "he kept in view entirely the notion he had conceived of the beauty of writing History" (*LRBL*, ii.65). It would thus appear to be a work that would rank alongside all other historical writings.

Here we return to a familiar motif: this depth and attractiveness are not purchased without cost. Smith says that Tacitus focuses on internal causes because he "seems to have been but little versant in Military or indeed public affairs of any sort" (*LRBL*, ii.23).[35] Since Smith speaks of the "ingenuous temper" of Tacitus, one might assume that Tacitus knew this about himself and chose to focus on his strengths (*LRBL*, ii.26). However, even with respect to internal causes, Smith says that Tacitus seems "too often to have had recourse to Causes too minute and too trivial, in order to account for the conduct of the person" he is describing (*LRBL*, i.191–92). Furthermore, though Smith praises the fact that Tacitus's own observations "do not stand out from narration but often appear to make a part of it," he admits that Tacitus is "often guilty" of leaving gaps in his narrations (*LRBL*, ii.42 and ii.37, respectively). Finally, unlike Thucydides (but like most other historians), Tacitus often introduces circumstances that do not contribute to a causal account but instead give him "an opportunity of displaying [his] Eloquence" (*LRBL*, ii.50). In the end, Tacitus embodies the great innovating spirit but also the rhetorical missteps of ancient history.

The overall arc of Smith's views on the ancient historians appears to be as follows: Herodotus creates history; Thucydides refines its explanatory power at the expense of style; Livy refines its style at the expense of its explanatory power; and Tacitus expands its explanatory power at the expense of its previous design. Xenophon occupies a curiously ambiguous central place in the narrative in that he somewhat improves upon the style of Thucydides while retaining Thucydides's

[35] See also *LRBL*, ii.26–27.

understanding of history.[36] In this sense, he is not a watershed figure like the other four although one might argue that he is as a result the most excellent combination of causal explanation and style. Is Xenophon, then, curiously enough, Smith's model historian? And might there be a modern historian in the vein of Xenophon?

Machiavelli

The primary curiosity concerning Smith's treatment of modern historians is that he passes over many of the greatest candidates in complete silence. Amicus mentions Hume as a possible rival to Livy's excellence. But Hume never appears in the *Lectures on Rhetoric and Belle Lettres*.[37] All of Hume's major writings were available to the public by the time Smith gave his lectures; additionally, Hume and Smith were friends, had extensive correspondence, and shared mentors such as the Irish philosopher Francis Hutcheson.[38] There is no doubt whatsoever that Smith was intimately familiar with Hume's writings, including his writings on history. But it is a simple fact that he is never mentioned. Similarly, Voltaire is never mentioned even though his "Essay on the

[36] This is most clearly seen in Xenophon's *Hellenica*, which is a direct sequel to Thucydides's *History* and which Smith calls Xenophon's "treatise of the Grecian affairs" (*LRBL*, ii.54).

[37] The editors of *LRBL* propose an allusion to Hume's *History* in the marginal note to ii.73, but this suggestion is entirely speculative (p. 116 n. 9 in *LRBL*).

[38] Hume published *A Treatise of Human Nature* in 1739 (Book III was published in 1740) and his two *Enquiries* in 1748 and 1751. He published the first volume of the *History of England* in 1754 and the complete edition, spanning six volumes, in 1762. His *Natural History of Religion* was published in 1757 and the majority of his moral, political, and literary essays were published between 1741 and 1758. *An Enquiry Concerning Human Understanding* appeared for the first time under that title in the 1758 edition of *Essays and Treatises on Several Subjects*. It had been published several times, beginning in 1748, under an earlier title, *Philosophical Essays Concerning Human Understanding*. The *Dialogues Concerning Natural Religion* were not published in Hume's lifetime, although Hume originally intended for Smith to publish them upon Hume's death. See the foreword to David Hume, *Essays Moral, Political, and Literary*, ed. Eugene Miller (Indianapolis: Liberty Fund, 1985), xi n. 1 and n. 2.

Customs and Spirit of the Nations," a landmark work, was published in 1756; and even though Smith elsewhere deems Voltaire "the most universal genius perhaps which France has ever produced" and says that he "is acknowledged to be, in almost every species of writing, nearly upon a level with the greatest authors of the last age, who applied themselves chiefly to one" (*EPS*, 254).[39] Nor is Montesquieu ever mentioned even though his history of the decline of the Romans was published in 1734, and his *Spirit of the Laws* was published in 1748.[40]

There is, however, one modern historian whom Smith speaks of in the manner of the ancients. It is Machiavelli. Smith notes that Machiavelli and Guicciardini are the "two most famous modern Italian historians" (*LRBL*, ii.69).[41] But he goes further and singles out Machiavelli in particular for praise:

> [Machiavelli] seems to have had chiefly in his view to prove certain maxims which he had laid down, as the impolitickness of keeping up a standing army, and others of the same sort, generally Contradictory to the politics of the times.... He [Machiavelli] is to be commended above most modern writers on one account, as he does not seem to favor any one party more than another and therefore is generally candid in his relation.... Machiavelli is of all Modern Historians the only one who has contented himself with that which is the chief purpose of History, to relate events and connect them with their causes without becoming a party on either side. (*LRBL*, ii.69–70)

Smith recognizes the mark of the true historian in Machiavelli's writings, even as he also recognizes the rough edges. Smith elsewhere notes that one of Machiavelli's "heroes" was Castruccio Castracani of Lucca and admits that Machiavelli "is not indeed a man of the nicest morality even for his own times" (*WN*, III.iii.19 and *TMS*, VI.i.16,

[39] Compare *CAS*, 31.

[40] Smith does refer to Montesquieu in the *Lectures on Jurisprudence* (*LJA*, ii.150, iii.34, iii.37, iv.2, and *LJB*, 113–44) and *The Wealth of Nations* (*WN*, I.ix.17, II.iv.9, iv.9.47, and V.i.f.40).

[41] Compare *CAS*, 129.

respectively).[42] Nonetheless, Smith admires Machiavelli's style, which he compares to that of Aristotle in that each eschews ornamentation in order to "trust solely to the strength of their arguments and the ingenuity and *newness* of their thoughts and discoveries" (*LRBL*, i.84–85, emphasis added). And Smith says that Machiavelli writes of Cesare Borgia's cunning murders at Senigallia "with that pure, elegant, and simple language which distinguishes all his writings" (*TMS*, VI.i.16).[43] Smith continues:

> He [Machiavelli] gives a very particular account of it.... He talks of it very coolly; is pleased with the address with which Cesare Borgia conducted it; has much contempt for the dupery and weakness of the sufferers; but no compassion for their miserable and untimely death, and no sort of indignation at the cruelty and falsehood of their murderer. (*TMS*, VI.i.16)

In short, Machiavelli offers new and disinterested (perhaps even amoral) causal accounts in an elegant style. It would not be difficult to see him as a model historian on Smith's account.

Smith refers once to Machiavelli's *Florentine Histories* (*WN*, V.ii.a.6). The *Florentine Histories* were commissioned in 1520 by Cardinal Giulio de' Medici and were presented to him in 1525 (by which time he had ascended to the papacy as Clement VII).[44] Although Giulio had made Machiavelli the official historiographer of Florence, it is far from clear that the *Florentine Histories* are a straightforward historiographical account. Machiavelli says in the Dedicatory Letter that he is

[42] Machiavelli most likely wrote *The Life of Castruccio Castracani* in Lucca in 1520 while on a minor diplomatic mission at the behest of Giulio de' Medici. It was published in 1533.

[43] Smith refers to Machiavelli's Il modo che tenne il duca Valentino per ammazar Vitellozo, Oliverotto da Fermo, il signor Pagolo et il duca di Gravina Orsini in Senigaglia, which was published in 1533.

[44] Strictly speaking, the *Florentine Histories* were commissioned by Pope Leo X (Giovanni de' Medici), although Giulio's intervention as an intermediary was key. Machiavelli presented eight books to Giulio in 1525 and did not write any additional ones. All citations of the *Florentine Histories* are from the translation by Laura Banfield and Harvey C. Mansfield (Princeton: Princeton University Press, 1988).

writing of "those times which, through the death of the Magnificent Lorenzo de' Medici, brought a change of form [*forma*] in Italy." He says that he has striven to "satisfy everyone" while "not staining the truth." In the preface to the *Florentine Histories*, Machiavelli says that his intent is to write down "the things done inside and outside by the Florentine people" (*le cose fatte dentro e fuora dal popolo fiorentino*) and that he changed his original intention in order that "this history may be better understood in all times."[45] Though Book I is ostensibly a narrative concerning the time from the decline of the Roman Empire to 1434, in Book II he calls Book I "our universal treatise," thus implying that it is more than a simple narrative, that history is perhaps a dialectic between the twin causes of virtue and fortune.[46]

Smith also refers once to the *Discourses on Livy*, which Machiavelli probably began to write in 1513 in the aftermath of his imprisonment and torture at the hands of the Medici (*WN*, V.i.g.2).[47] In the preface to Book I, Machiavelli says that "no sign" of ancient virtue remains[48] and that neither prince nor republic can be found that imitate the examples

[45] Banfield and Mansfield translate *dentro e fuora* as "home and abroad," though they note the literal translation of "inside and outside" (6 n. 1).

[46] *Florentine Histories* II.2. See the translators' introduction to the Banfield and Mansfield edition, viii.

[47] As far as I can tell, Smith does not ever refer to Machiavelli's *Prince* or *Art of War*. This is particularly surprising because of Smith's admission that "the art of war...is certainly the noblest of all arts" (*WN*, V.i.a.14). Machiavelli in *The Prince* says that the art of war is the only art which is of concern to one who commands (14.58) and that a prince should thus never lift his thoughts from war, even and perhaps especially in peacetime (14.59). Machiavelli thus recommends, among other things, that a prince should "read histories and consider in them the actions of excellent men, should see how they conducted themselves in wars, should examine the causes of their victories and losses, so as to be able to avoid the latter and imitate the former" (14.60). All parenthetical citations of Machiavelli are given by chapter number and page number (e.g., 14.58) and are from Harvey C. Mansfield, trans., *The Prince*, 2nd ed. (Chicago: University of Chicago Press, 1998).

[48] Compare the prologue of Machiavelli's *Mandragola*.

from the ancient histories.[49] He laments the fact that there is no longer a "true knowledge of histories" and judges it necessary to write upon the books of Livy that have not been "intercepted by the malignity of the times." He claims that those who read his writings can "more easily draw from them that utility for which one should seek knowledge of histories." It is a work that is ostensibly a commentary on Livy's history but in which Machiavelli regularly alters or omits Livy's words; in which he disagrees with Livy outright; in which he implies that the Bible can be considered a history; and in which he repeatedly praises Xenophon's "life of Cyrus" as a history.[50]

The one passage of the *Discourses* to which Smith refers explicitly is the first chapter of Book III, which speaks of the necessity to return to beginnings and of the manner in which St. Francis and St. Dominic rescued Christianity from utter elimination. It is almost as if Smith believes that Machiavelli is the only true modern historian because he is the only one who attempts to rescue the past from the malignity of modern times, because he is the only one who dares to make the past breathe again. In the way that Livy is a recapitulation of Herodotus and that Tacitus is a recapitulation of Thucydides, it is tempting to suggest that Machiavelli is somehow the recapitulation of Xenophon, that he somehow embodies in modern garb the ancient historical standard of style and penetration. And insofar as he sees himself not only as recovering but as surpassing the ancients, Machiavelli is perhaps deserving of the honor that Smith bestows upon him. As Harvey Mansfield has noted, the last word of the *Discourses* is *Massimo*—

[49] All citations of the *Discourses on Livy* are from Harvey C. Mansfield and Nathan Tarcov, trans. *Discourses on Livy* (Chicago: University of Chicago Press, 1996).

[50] *Discourses on Livy* I.12 is an example of Machiavelli's alteration of Livy's words, and I.58 is an example of Machiavelli's disagreement with Livy. Machiavelli implies that the Bible is a history at II.5. Machiavelli praises the "life of Cyrus" as a history at II.13, III.20, III.22, and III.39. Compare 14.60 of *The Prince*. Xenophon's work is of course not entitled the "life of Cyrus" but the "education of Cyrus" (*Cyropaedia*).

Maximus, the greatest. *Io* ("I") is the first.[51] Machiavelli may be not only the first modern philosopher but also the first modern historian.

[51] Harvey C. Mansfield, *Machiavelli's New Modes and Orders* (Chicago: University of Chicago Press, 1979) 441.

4 | Visible Hands

Ethics and the Market

Jennifer Baker

The sociologist Juliet Schor tells us that most Americans, when asked, express some measure of deep reservation about market systems, but we fail to put these reservations in a way that "coheres into a persuasive, well-articulated critique." [1] The philosopher Michael Sandel has published a book titled *What Money Can't Buy: The Moral Limits of Markets* that suggests markets "crowd out morals."[2] The philosopher and economist Elizabeth Anderson has begun arguing that our standard approaches in political philosophy, all manner of egalitarian accounts of justice, rest on a "myth" about the market, a myth shared by conservatives: the idea that the market responds to merit.[3] And, of course, we still live among CEOs who insist that a degree of profit-seeking that we find nefarious is indeed "God's work."[4]

There are some justifications that we might or might not have available that make nary a difference to anyone. The justification of the market, I'd suggest, is unlike this. Our concerns about the market, our inarticulateness about the market, our misdescriptions of it: these things, if addressed, could affect our political perspectives and our moral assessments of the market. We have, I mean to argue, so obscure an

[1] Juliet B. Schor, "The New Politics of Consumption," *The Boston Review* (Summer 1999), http://new.bostonreview.net/BR24.3/schor.html (accessed 18 September 2014).

[2] (New York: MacMillan, 2012), 93.

[3] Elizabeth Anderson, *Tom Paine and the Ironies of Social Democracy*, The 2011–2012 Dewey Lecture in Law and Philosophy, recorded 29 February 2012, University of Chicago Law School.

[4] L. Blankfein, "Blankfein Says He's Just Doing God's Work," *New York Times*, 9 November 2009.

understanding of the market that this actually interferes with and hinders our being able to hold aspects of it, including even our own behavior, up for assessment. In this paper I argue for a remedy. I suggest that the justification of the market that we need is of a certain type, with features I will try to list, and that it will need to work at this, rather unusual, level of specificity: the specific moral norm that accounts for acceptable market behavior. The reason for our need for such a norm (and I will suggest one, in conclusion) is because our confusion about the market is so deep. It is not that we have *no* ideas about the purpose and function of the market; we have a host of bad ones.

Business Ethics, Economics, and Philosophy of Economics on the Market

It must seem very unlikely that we lack a justification of the market like the one I am after. With much academic work being done, how is it possible that a matter like justifying the market (at the level of norms) could have fallen by the wayside? I think we can chalk it up to insufficient interdisciplinarity.

For example, we might assume (and an ethical theorist might assume) that the field of business ethics is where to look for justification of the market and its practices, but that field *assumes*—it does not *argue for*—the justification of the market. It does this wholly uncritically, as evidenced by its lack of engagement with philosophy of economics. On the occasion when the issue of its justification comes up, one might find breezy and unexamined statements, such as: "The primary justification for a market system is that it provides an efficient procedure for meeting people's needs and desires for goods and services."[5] But for the most part, business ethicists develop "normative frameworks," a kind of hybrid and shortened account of ethics that can be easily summed up for application. That these frameworks lack the specifics of ethical theory is why they can be so easily applied, but this means they do nothing to address the

[5] David Holley, "A Moral Evaluation of Sales Practices" *Business & Professional Ethics Journal* 5/1 (1986): 3–21.

justification of the person behaving well in business, who wonders about the kind of system she is supporting.

Economists cannot justify the market either, of course, even though they demonstrate its efficiency.[6] This efficiency is what must be justified (some say it is a Utilitarian view that lurks behind economics.[7] But even if so—this must be presented and then examined if it is to work as justification.) Though there has been some debate, even mainstream economists agree that the standard model of economic rationality is designed to treat a phenomenon like moral motivation as if it is not unique.[8]

[6] That markets lead to efficient outcomes is a claim that can be established despite market imperfections such as externalities, imperfect information, geographically distinct markets. The work of Eleanor Ostram showed that there is a range of voluntary, collective associations that over time can evolve efficient and equitable rules for the use of common resources. (*Governing the Commons: The Evolution of Institutions* [NY: Cambridge, University of Cambridge Press, 1990])

[7] S. Meikle, *Aristotle's Economic Thought* (Oxford: Clarendon Press, 1995), 106.

[8] J. Baker, "Virtue and Behavior," *Review of Social Economy: Incorporating Ethical Theory into Models of Economic Choice* 67/1 (2009): 3–24. Note that Michael Sandel's interpretation of economics is not at all what I am referring to. He claims that economists fail to recognize there is such a thing as non-economic value. This is very strange to say, given the research agendas of so many prominent economists who study non-economic value. Some of these economists have responded to Sandel in print: "My colleagues and I found dramatic evidence of this positive relationship between markets and morality in our study of fairness in simple societies—hunter-gatherers, horticulturalists, nomadic herders, and small-scale sedentary farmers—in Africa, Latin America, and Asia. Twelve professional anthropologists and economists visited these societies and played standard ultimatum, public goods, and trust games with the locals. As in advanced industrial societies, members of all of these societies exhibited a considerable degree of moral motivation and a willingness to sacrifice monetary gain to achieve fairness and reciprocity, even in anonymous one-shot situations. More interesting for our purposes, we measured the degree of market exposure and cooperation in production for each society, and we found that the ones that regularly engage in market exchange with larger surrounding groups have more pronounced fairness motivations. The notion that the market economy makes people greedy, selfish, and amoral is simply fallacious" (Herbert Gintis, "Giving Economists Their Due," *Boston Review* [May/June 2012]: online).

Does philosophy of economics supply the justification I am after, the sort that helps us assess why and when the behavior of the people engaged in the market is acceptable? A few philosophers of economics have offered thorough arguments to demonstrate that, among types of value, the market honors some values and not others. The market promotes freedom and efficiency. Philosophers of economics, such as Elizabeth Anderson and Debra Satz, are explicit about not addressing their claims at the level of personal ethics.[9] Anderson explains that "the norms governing market relations are impersonal, suitable for regulating the interactions of strangers."[10] That is not to say that the existence of these values is not quite real. Anderson cautions that there will be consequences when we value market goods inappropriately, treating them as shared or political goods will mean we will not be able to capture the value we are after.[11] Debra Satz explains that our tolerance of

[9] D. Satz, Why Some Things Should Not Be for Sale: The Moral Limits of Markets (New York: Macmillan, 2010) 83.

[10] E. Anderson, *Values in Ethics and Economics* (Cambridge: Harvard University Press, 1995) 145.

[11] Anderson's objections to the over-extension of economic methodology are easily represented in the following real-world example. A debate has gone on in various fraternities in campuses across the country: should they allow some members to pay others to do their formal chores? From an economic perspective, the possibility of this is a win-win situation. Those volunteering to clean bathrooms and kitchens for their "brothers" are indeed eager to supplement their incomes in what they see as a convenient fashion. But the proposal has struck others in the fraternities as damaging to the very "fraternity" that the organization was designed to encourage. Tensions like these are supportive of the case Anderson makes concerning the potential for the norms of different domains to clash with each other. She argues that the very values represented by friendship will be subverted if you make the mistake of thinking a friendship can withstand a paid arrangement. Anderson describes the phenomena involved as representative of the "ethical limitations of the market". In short, the market cannot provide everything we have been led to assume it can. All ethical goods are shared: they cannot be traded or treated as commodities and remain the goods they once were. The market can only provide us with goods for "use". Specific and unalterable norms apply to transactions in the market. (You can experience the feeling of a switch between the norms that apply when a friend suddenly asks for a large loan.) Market norms lead to an

illegitimate or "noxious" markets such as would be due to a failure to recognize the values of democracy, relationships, and child labor or organ sales. These theorists have provided accounts ideal for informing policy but we would borrow their reasoning in application to our own behavior no differently than we borrow legal reasoning. It offers well-justified limits on what is generally appropriate, but it is not going to be nearly specific or motivating enough to function as a guide in our day-to-day decisions. We may recognize from their analyses that it is wrong to sell parts of our body, but this does not help us to recognize the right way to market our other wares, let alone how else to behave in the many ways we do in the market.[12]

The Ethical Puzzle

Here is where I would like to make my contribution. Participation in the market, is, I want to argue, an issue that requires that we personally reflect on the purpose of the market, on what the market is in relation to us. This is not to assume any of us will need a bird's eye, and certainly not an economist's, perspective on what the market is. It does mean we will not be maintaining myths about the market or our behavior in it. When we consider the market from perspectives higher or more

efficient exchange of market goods—but these norms are not the ones that sustain our personal lives and most meaningful interactions. When we confuse market and non-market goods, we can make mistakes in either direction. We can try to convince our employees that they are part of a "family" (when they are anything but), or we can think of our spouses as committed to us by contract. Making either of these mistakes is not something we do willingly, according to Anderson, as it blocks us from realizing the very values we considered ourselves to be after (Anderson 1995, p. 159). The remedy to this conceptual confusion, Anderson argues, is that we keep the domains of economics and ethics distinct, and recognize that the value in our personal relationships cannot be "compared" to economic value (Anderson 1995). As for the example, the debates at Harvard over the student-created Dorm-aid are similar. "Maid for Harvard?" *The Daily Crimson*, the Crimson Staff, March 10, 2005.

[12] Ibid., 198.

abstract than that of how the agent herself is reasoning, we hide the particular puzzle of everyday market participation. When we participate in the market, engaging in what some have called "market norms," we are making determinations that bypass the most immediate response to other humans' needs for something more indirect and longer term, selling rather than giving, it is possible to see us as introducing this condition on a need: it must be paid for. This poses not only a seriously theoretical challenge to current account of ethical theory but also a psychological challenge to persons involved in a switch between market and personal norms. The sad and perhaps apocryphal story of Cornelius Vanderbilt on his deathbed, offering to sell—not give—an artwork to his son memorably illustrates what can happen if we leave this "switch" only on.

The ancient philosophers recognized this problem of competing norms, even with their markets, and the Stoics used to debate the following case. An island has been hit by famine and is in desperate need of grain. You have worked to be the first ship to arrive. You know the other ships are not far behind. Must you tell the islanders about the coming ships, or take the profit that you can? There are two considerations: your humanity and your participation in their market. We understand the value of mercy and aid and the recognition of others, so we can understand the call to simply hand over the grain we've brought. On the other hand, human need is never temporary, and ships will have to arrive with grain again. As Cicero records, when we imagine an honest and virtuous ship owner, we realize even he "might be in doubt whether such silence (not revealing the coming ships) would really be immoral."[13] Consider the media images of women in Haiti beginning to sell vegetables not long after the deadly 2010 earthquake. This market activity was taken as a sign of great hope. Surely the ancient famine at Rhodes case is not too different from this more recent example as vegetable sellers were making decisions like the ship-owner.

[13] Cicero, *De Officiis*, Book III.Xii.

Haiti's situation is more vivid to us because it is more recent, and its poverty easy to compare to our affluence. We cheer on the vegetable sellers because they are acknowledging the "right" norm, a norm of market behavior, and one that encourages the finding the most efficient and careful development of resources. Our participation in such norms is necessary. Contributing to the business norms that maintain an economy is something we can justify. It is not, however, and we kid ourselves for thinking it can be, the same as making a direct contribution to another person's well-being.

What the Invisible Hand Is Doing With Us

Economists generally agree that general affluence comes about through a complex process of many components, including a functioning price system, differences in marginal utility, functioning divisions of labor, specialization, cost-conscious buyers, sellers with an incentive to cut their costs. Buyers and sellers must be participating in markets that are large—large enough for reputations to be established and large enough for small innovations to be worth pursuing—that the result is an economy of scale that reduces the cost of per unit production. Of course there are ingredients necessary to this process that we have not yet begun to identify such as complex social norms, intricate legal arrangements that involve titles, transfers, and so forth. Our understanding of what brings about general affluence, what makes a market work, can be thought of as a number of bright beads tied onto a string so that space is left between each. The beads are the features we are fairly certain about, the spaces between them reminders that we are awaiting further detail. As schematic and minimal as our current explanation might be, we can still note how indirect our own role is, when it comes to the "invisible hand."

Though it is Bernard Mandeville, and not the more cited Adam Smith, who cheekily suggests that without greed nations would dissolve, it is still the case that Smith's account imagines us bartering for the best deal. Now, as mentioned, you may be bartering on behalf of needy children who live on your street, but you will still be seeking out a bargain, a good trade. Your bartering may contribute, though this is unguaranteed, in a general, indirect, and perfectly diluted way to general affluence. But there are two problems with the idea that you deserve moral credit for very real contribution to others' well-being. One, the moral credit would have to be proportionate. And that means it would be as small as the certainty and the amount of your influence on general affluence.[14] Two, these bargains are sought for their rewards. Even in the case of a person not buying or trading or working for herself, the Smithian story suggests we do not do these things unless we think we are getting a bargain.

I do not mean to suggest that prudence cannot be complimented or that prudence and morality never intersect. But the limit seems to be one's motive in the case of a beneficial exchange. As moral as your use of what you've secured might be (let's stick with the idea that you hand it over to those in need), the deal itself is engaged in and assessed by amoral norms. Companies that declare themselves socially responsible still attempt to make a profit, in general and from the sale of particular items. Again, it is not equivalent to behavior that responds in an unmediated way to what others need. "Socially-responsible" companies, after all, still charge for their product, regardless of need.

If we cannot assess our individual market contributions, if our intentions are primarily prudential in the marketplace, must we simply compliment what we can (avant-garde artists who never receive an audience, good-hearted managers) and leave participation in the market itself outside of moral evaluation? This is what commonly happens. Business ethicists, again breezily, recommend conventionally moral

[14] This is the "myth" I referred to initially when mentioning Anderson. She invokes the economist F. A. Hayek, who pointed out that even when we give credit to examples like Henry Ford, as someone who contributed to the expansion of the economy, we've obscured the nature of the market. We cannot track contribution in this way (Hayek, *The Collected Works of F. A. Hayek* [Chicago: University of Chicago Press, 1998] 93). To see the market as a place to redress what people deserve is a type of category. The market is never going to be capable of doling out just rewards. "That whole project," Anderson says, "is hopeless" (*Tom Paine and the Ironies of Social Democracy*).

behavior in business, but those in business are often suspicious of how realistic this advice is. We need only recall the Stoic famine example to think that any socially responsible company might simply hand over what others need if we are going to apply conventional moral thought to what they are doing. To avoid the risk of confusion when it comes to how morality applies to markets, we ought to try to find a place for our participation in the market alongside our other, conventionally understood, moral obligations.

The degree of unfairness, the cover for greed, the unpredictable fate of projects we hold very dear: these features of the market provoke much scorn for capitalism and its ethos. Even if your actual participation in the market has you holding firm to everything you believe about morality—you only deal with good people, you make sure they are fairly rewarded, you participate for others and not just yourself—the market itself still fails to exemplify what we believe to be good.

The Dimension of a Proper Justification

Given these complexities, let me try to briefly sketch some of the features of a justification that I have in mind, even though my aim in this paper is to focus on (and come up with) the personal norms that could be used to justify market-based behavior.

For one, this type of justification will not be a matter of political principles that exist at some remove from people's own "comprehensive conceptions" (religious views and their replacements). We need something that works alongside and in our most personally held moral convictions. We are looking for a way to fit a personal obligation to support the market system alongside our other personal ethical obligations.

Second, a justification of the market will need to be sensitive to the benefits of general welfare. Our current ethical approaches do not recognize these benefits to general welfare. Without the integration of our personal ethics we are neglecting something we tacitly assume: that, all else the same, it is good for people to be better off in terms of material provisions. An ethical justification of the market will need to have the means to clearly acknowledge the harm of poverty. Is there any difficulty in doing this? There are, actually, three difficulties

One is how to balance the normative approval of increases in well-being with normative constraints on the means of producing well-being (including easy ones such as no use of coerced labor to more complex ones, such as the requirement that the affluence produced be "general" and benefit the worst-off.)

Another difficulty is how to give ethical approval to a situation that promotes many cases of harm. With affluence comes all sorts of fuel for behaviors that are harmful, to themselves and others. An ethical theory must be able to assess these affluence-related behaviors as harmful while still recognizing the benefit of affluence (in other words, removing the "all else the same" qualification). We would seem to need a theory that is two-pronged. One prong would be used for measuring bad behavior, the other used to measure the more general good of affluence against alternatives to a market that reduce affluence. Without this dual approach, the balance that would be required between the good of affluence and any harm that results from affluence would lead us to a mushy conclusion that could only partially justify the market.

Third, the free market does not seem to be defensible without defending other human rights. We would be taking the market out of context if we pretended it did not depend on the support of institutions that protect rights. Many ethical approaches also defend rights, of course, but are there particular rights that will be acknowledged only when we bring the market under this umbrella with other things we already consider every human to deserve.

The rewards of market participation must be effectively available to all (even if they are received indirectly, i.e., by a person or child who cannot participate in the market). An ethical justification of the market must involve these formal constraints to be consistent with how argument for the good of general affluence comes about: a respect for general human interests. Therefore, participation must be formally open to all adults; access to the market cannot be blocked by law or custom.

We can combine our concern for our ethical obligations with our role in the market by endorsing an ethics that regards every human as worthy of rights and that acknowledges an ethical obligation to promote the well-being of others. This is not hard for us, and most of us in liberal democracy assume we are already in agreement on the good of human rights. But a trickier element is required next— a means of assessing general welfare without moralizing the evaluation.

This is decidedly against the trend in political theory. Several recent efforts to integrate ethical considerations with economics are efforts to moralize economic results or analysis.[15] The concern is that current economic methodology's refusal to recognize the role ethical value plays in our decision-making results in a misdescription of choices, motives, and welfare. Modifications to overly streamlined accounts of preference in economics, such as those undertaken by Amartya Sen, have brought about better analyses and even better predictions in that field.[16] These approaches, as useful as they may be in other contexts, are not designed to address the issue of how we, as agents, are to think of our participation in the market alongside our other behavior, which is the key to a functional justification of the market.

The promise of the type of approach I am proposing is that we can see the choice before the ship owner bringing grain to a famine-torn island.[17] We can recognize his options, the two behaviors he could be justified in choosing. We can call out the CEOs on their lack of humanity or we can recognize their likely contribution to our gradual accumulation of greater general affluence. Or we can do both at the same time. But we will want to assess the content of the controlling norm for any behavior under question. Purely self-interested justifications of

[15] D. Hausman and M. McPherson, *Economic Analysis and Moral Philosophy* (Cambridge: Cambridge University Press, 1996), 1.

[16] Sen, *Development as Freedom* (Oxford: Oxford University Press, 1999).

[17] J. Baker, "Don't Let the Best Be the Enemy of the Good: A Stoic Defense of the Market," in *Accepting the Invisible Hand: Market-Based Approaches to Social-Economic Problems* (New York: Palgrave Macmillan, 2011) 72.

market behavior will no longer work. Attempts to talk about benefitting the economy in general ways, without an attempt to link this justification to empirical results should seem suspicious.

For an example of a practical application, let us look to what the CEO of Goldman Sachs had to say about his company's recent participation in the banking crisis and subsequent bailout: "We're very important; we help companies to grow by helping them to raise capital. Companies that grow create wealth. This, in turn, allows people to have jobs that create more growth and more wealth. It's a virtuous cycle. We have a social purpose."[18] With the assistance of an ethical theory that invokes meaningful categories, we recognize immediately that this is a blanket justification of anything Goldman Sachs might do. No limiting factor to the good of "growing" the economy is acknowledged. We can also acknowledge a social role for banks without conflating this with the practice of virtue. "God's work" lines will no longer do when the invisible hand is placed in its proper context.

The Missing Norm

A focus on how the agent must acknowledge the rationale for her behavior herself puts a certain pressure on theorists to generate an articulable, commonsense explanation of the good of the market. We require a norm that can be used in our own deliberation, as answer to "why am I doing this?" or in consideration of the question, "Am I doing this for the right reason?"

As we have suggested, market-based behavior does not fit the description of other-concern that ethical theorists give us. Ethical theorists are left describing behavior in an incredibly limited fashion, as if we only act when at leisure and at home. I would like to propose that the norm that underlies market behavior, from the simplest transaction to the typically complex, has not been well identified; therefore, no appropriate norm has been explicitly endorsed by an ethical theory nor

[18] L. Blankfein, "Blankfein Says He's Just Doing God's Work," *New York Times*, 9 November 2009.

integrated into an account of virtue. This means we do not yet know how to integrate the good of promoting general affluence into our general understanding of what is good. The result is a type of schizophrenic thinking about our personal behavior and our behavior in the market. This phenomenon has not only been noted in the business ethics literature but is obvious from our everyday efforts to talk about the role of the market (what does "it's just business" mean?). We do not know how to categorize the good of selling vegetables alongside our more rehearsed commitment to the charity and compassion of humanitarianism.

A recent NPR interview with a Haitian reveals this.

> Interviewer: Is anybody working? Is the economy up in any sense at all?
>
> Ms. JOSEPH: Well, you know, where there are people, there's an economy. So there is somewhat of an economy. People are getting things together. They're trying to sell things, and I mean, people need to live. But in some ways, it's extortionate. I mean, the price of gasoline is outrageous. The price of all different kinds of things, of fruits and vegetables, in some places are four and five times what they have been.

So you have got that side of the spectrum, where people are looking to make an extraordinary deal on this situation. And you have the other side of the spectrum, where people are coming together to share whatever resources they have, which is the side that is really going to help the country rebuild.

Here we have what had been regarded as a sign of hope, the buying and selling of vegetables as the sign of market revitalization, categorized as people trying to make a deal for themselves. And, worse still, these deals are regarded as ones taken at the cost of others. We, of course, cannot vouch for the behavior of the venders the interviewee is speaking of. These may be clear-cut cases of some abuse of power. But to pit exploitation against "coming together" is to leave no conceptual route to general affluence. That Haiti has made so little discernable progress since photos of the first food venders were taken only helps to underscore what we are dealing with, when it comes to assessing the market. The market is wily, it is not created in a direct fashion, and it defies conceptual accounting. Even with the resources of contemporary economics and political science, we cannot yet count all of the ingredients necessary to a functioning market.

The "invisible hand" metaphor could be thought to highlight that we don't know what makes a functioning market. Yet we have seen that the idea that we are (in some "invisible hand"-directed way) "promoting general affluence" fails to work as a norm that justifies our own behavior. We'll consider other candidate norms. Our market-based behavior will not make ethical sense until we account (as the invisible hand metaphor does) for the dynamism of market results, the process required to bring about general affluence. Surely one reason the norm that underlies typical market-based behavior has been obscured is because it is difficult to pin down.

A recent feature on CNN is the collected "regrets" of former debt collectors. One interviewee explains,

> If someone told me they only had $150 to their name this month and needed to feed their entire family of five, I would say, "I don't care, this is your fault and you owe the money. Pay it." I would even use blind threats like, "I know where you work" to intimidate them. It was survival of the fittest, and I thought being aggressive was the only way to succeed. And then it became an addiction—being authoritative and abrasive was like a high.[19]

This fits the description of unjustified behavior offered by traditional virtue ethics. Virtue ethicists would focus on these elements of this man's description: the norm of "survival of the fittest" being associated with market success; market success becoming something more than a means to an end (the addictive feeling); the tension (now revealed by the interviewee) between the man's normal concern for others and his on-the-job disregard for their dire situations. The rationale of

[19] "Confessions of Former Debt Collectors," Mel Harsh. http://money.cnn.com/galleries/2010/news/1007/gallery.debt_collectors/

"you owe the money" was not working for him, he "can't wait to get out of this line of work."

What would an ethical approach to market norms recommend? It would suggest that the man rid himself of his current norms or reform the norms that have come into conflict. For what reason is he pursuing market success? Business ethics is capable of providing every norm we might need about the particular practices a businessperson might engage in, but this example demonstrates why we must be able to explain why we should follow ethical norms.

No sustained account of business can maintain that the norm controlling the market is "survival of the fittest." The market does not reward ethical merit, and market results are not regular enough to justify its favoring any particular set of qualities at all. This is an unsatisfying stop-gap measure for people struggling to figure out if there is a justification for being aggressive in business when these same people (e.g., the person quoted in the CNN interview) might never be aggressive in other contexts.

What about a norm such as "contribute to general affluence"? Could this norm explain and justify our behavior in the market, or is it overly general, underdetermine ethical behavior? Business norms are good because they lead to general affluence. Markets are good when they lead to general affluence, yet humanitarian good can result from market behaviors that are not moral at all. We can benefit from accidents and from greed.

There are two other reasons why there is no simple way to derive the good of our market behavior from the good of the market itself. Smith himself advertises that when we trade in the market, we will not have "contributing to general affluence" in mind. We will be focusing on the items at hand. It is to the market's benefit that we examine the construction of sweaters and the heartiness of bread. Self-interest will not be adequate to justify business behavior. Everyone in business uses that as their excuse, and it is in no way guiding nor useful for making distinctions between behaviors. We would eliminate the very issue of business ethics.

The next reason a "contributing to general affluence" explanation of the good of typical business behaviors fails is because of the nature of the "invisible" hand itself. As we have reviewed, we can never know the terms of the test the market is holding or whether we are bringing down the average or setting the bar.

What we are looking for is a norm that can guide us, that can be used by us as we make choices about how to behave in the market. My proposal is that we look to the explanation offered by sophisticated economists, such as Vernon Smith and F.A. Hayek. These economists have been aware that we needed better metaphors for how the market worked. Neither has taken self-interest to be some kind of motor for the market (so ripe for counter-examples from every day behavior). Instead, they focus on the information that is conveyed by choices we make in the market. They do not see the market as some bizarre "survival of the fittest," nor do they see it as a prisoner's dilemma (Smith's experimental economics is a refutation of the very assumptions of game theory). The market is, instead, a form of "coming together" into a cooperative enterprise. This is one where "the mutual adjustment through exchange of the respective (marginal) rates of substitution (or equivalence) which different goods or services have for various individuals" is what determines how we value resources brought for sale. Thanks to the "wonder" of the price system, choices we make in the market is one that can be informed by the ability "to take account, in…decisions about the use of such things, of the better opportunities others might have for their use."[20]

In other words, we could not meaningfully assess the viability of our own personal options—our career options, our housing options, our productive options—because they are inherently social, and a market plays the role of advertising to us what these options will cost us. This explanation keeps places such as Haiti from seeming to suffer from any lack of individual self-interest. Imagine people remain very kind, and a

[20] Hayek, The Collected Works of F. A. Hayek, 95.

dysfunctional economy presents not just a lack of incentives but a lack of information about any incentives. If we do not know what others are expected to be willing to pay for the opportunity we are considering purchasing, we are no better off than a person learning to make metal bowls in craft school before realizing she would need to sell each bowl for $20,000 to make a living at it. (This is a true story.) Even our personal decisions of career require information about price.

Yet, it is not the price people pay for fruit and vegetables in Haiti that signals how much fruits and vegetables are needed. It is clear that in Haiti there may be tremendous need among people who can afford no price. Selling vegetables is cooperative in that the prices for which they are bought informs vegetable producers whether their bringing food to market is worth the effort. In affluent places, we surely ignore this role of prices in the market, and focus on the features more obvious to us such as, yet there is no other explanation for why we cheered when we saw imagines of individual food venders in Haiti. Food was being distributed through aid agencies, after all. The venders were not distributing very much food, but they signaled that Haitians may begin to make a living for themselves. The high prices of the food indicate how dysfunctional Haitian life is for the time being. But partaking in these high prices, if you are a local, is going to be a matter of engaging in the norm the ancient virtue ethicists recognized as that which perpetuates the market. Paying for vegetables, giving sellers a price, is, like our norms of charity and compassion, necessary for human well-being.

Let us focus on what we do not usually focus on. When we sell vegetables and fruit at a stand, we may or may not be pursuing our own self-interest (who even has a clear conception of what that is?). What we can be confident of is that when we sell food we have brought to market, we will treat these items as valuable, and as worth as much as we can get for them. We will be counting pennies out in change, we will be attempting to determine if our price is too low or high to be optimal. We might return home that day realizing the outlay is simply not worth it. The norm we operate is one of "conserving resources." We are not going to give away our wares because to do this would be to squander them. We negotiate because in the context of a market, our aims are pecuniary.

This norm is not a guide to family life or life with friends, that is for sure. But it is a guide to why we behave in the market as we do. Self-interest does not explain a thing that is unique to market transactions. Because resources are limited; because their relative worth to others is of dire importance for their own choices; because, over time, commitment to such a norm allows for the indirect growth of general affluence the regard for commodities as limited seems justified and explanatory. General affluence is the good you are promoting when you make a deal in the market, and you do this directly by committing to the norm of conserving the resources under your current or future control.

One benefit of recognizing this norm is that it is then capable of being weighed against others. There is nothing immediately crucial about acting in a typical business fashion when faced with a choice to act on other humanitarian norms. Neither the store nor the economy will shut down if you offer a family without resources an item free of charge. If we promote the use of this norm, we might lose the propensity for overstating the significance of our behavior in the market in the way we have heard business people do. There is no reason not to think the CEO of Goldman Sachs does not believe what he has said when he explains his company has done "God's work." He can only believe his company's methods are beyond reproach because the significance of the company is not put in context.

Let us review some criteria for this norm we are suggesting:

- a norm that people can articulate without reference to concepts that stand-in for unclear philosophical accounts;
- a norm that is descriptive of what has actually happened in a market transaction;
- a norm capable of being guiding when it comes to the actual choices in the market in a way that a commitment to values such as freedom or efficiency are not;
- a norm we can follow with consistency given our other commitments to what is good.

Provisionally, how about this: *We are behaving justifiably in the market when we are aware that it is the right time and place to treat resources as scarce for the sake of contributing to a market system that generates information that can be used by others immediately, and long term as a means to general affluence.*

How can we assess this norm? It honors the choice we have in the market that the Stoics recognized: to at times refrain from acting as if every situation calls for "business as normal." It matches our behavior. We do not sell bread because others need it. This is not the self-described motivation of bread sellers, though they do often suggest they sell bread for reasons other than to make money. We do not do everything we do in business out of self-interest. We do, however, treat commodities as limited resources. We bid and barter. We do not give commodities away as needed. This norm also helps us recognize our role in the market as one that is dispensable, in an affluent-enough place. This has the potential to change attitudes, too. Finally, this norm can guide us when it comes to our own analysis of our market behavior. The loan collector feels guilty for what he has done. His methods are clearly not in line with his beliefs about what people deserve. Yet he also seems to think his efforts are wholly unjustified. I say this as a person who has received calls from debt collectors: it is not an occupation without a role in promoting general affluence. A norm that explains the connection between our focus on conserving resources can help to justify occupations that have been too casually treated as beyond the pale ethically. Confusion about what is good does not behoove us, whether it generates moralistic views or not. Finally, the norm I have suggested is not catchy. So there is that. Economists tell me I could just propose "maximize surplus," even after they hear my explanations for how inappropriate the direction to "maximize" is. So, there may still be that, too. And by "that" I mean: a notable need for more interdisciplinary discussion on how we ought to regard the market.

5 | On Vernon's Smith

Ryan Patrick Hanley

Students of Adam Smith have reason to be grateful to Vernon Smith; indeed, they have two reasons. First, in developing the fundamental distinction between personal and market exchange that undergirds some of the experimental work for which he won a Nobel Prize, Vernon Smith credits Adam Smith as a predecessor and inspiration, an honor which would no doubt make the modest Scot blush, but which specialists on his thought will quite willingly accept on his behalf. Second, in reflecting on his debts to Adam Smith, Vernon Smith sets forth a distinction that is in its own right of great benefit to Adam Smith specialists and which deserves greater attention than it has received: namely the distinction between reciprocated and non-reciprocated exchange behaviors that Vernon Smith suggests are the key to solving the notorious "Adam Smith Problem."

Clearly then there is cause for mutual admiration and appreciation, yet still one might wonder: are Adam Smith and Vernon Smith in fact playing on the same team? In less colloquial language: are Vernon Smith's conclusions—and indeed his very questions—the same as Adam Smith's? In a very real sense, the answer is yes. But there is also reason to think there might be more divergence than convergence on three specific fronts. First, Adam Smith is keen to defend the existence of non-reciprocated ethical behavior and indeed to celebrate such behavior as the peak of virtue. Second, Adam Smith defends intended beneficent activity as a necessary political good. Third, Adam Smith emphasizes the distinction between "social" and "unsocial" passions, regarding this as a better means of distinguishing the passions than the familiar typology of selfish and altruistic or self-regarding and other-regarding.

Vernon Smith seems to depart from Adam Smith on each of these fronts: his account of reciprocity in small group exchange relegates non-reciprocated behavior to the realm of self-interested actors in large-group exchange; his emphasis on the limits of rational intentionality leads him to be skeptical of political expressions of intended beneficence; and his approach to moral psychology—even as it leads fruitfully beyond debates over egoism and altruism—points in a quite different direction from Adam Smith's distinction between the social and the unsocial.

What then to make of these divergences? Here there may be room for a potentially productive engagement. This engagement would eschew the blood sport question ("who's right?") and instead ask a more fruitful question, namely: are there other ideas set forth by Adam Smith beyond those already considered by Vernon Smith that would benefit from the scrutiny of the experimentalist? Working under the hopeful suspicion that the answer to this latter question is yes, the present essay focuses on three such ideas, wonderfully elaborated by Adam Smith and of potential interest to both experimental economists and historians of economic thought: non-reciprocated beneficence, intended beneficence, and social vs. unsocial behavior.[1]

Vernon's Smith

To begin: one of the most striking elements of Vernon's work is its generous acknowledgment of the work of his predecessors. And while this corpus identifies several such predecessors by name—from Scots such as Hume to Austrians such as Hayek—it seems fair to say that the influence of Adam is especially prominent and celebrated by Vernon, as others have also recently emphasized.[2] In this vein, we might begin by briefly sketching how Vernon characterizes his debts to Adam in helping

[1] For simplicity's sake, I refer to "Adam" and "Vernon" in what follows in order to minimize the distracting repetition inescapable if full names are used.

[2] See Maria Pia Paganelli, "Smithian Answers to Some Puzzling Results in the Experimental Literature," in *Elgar Companion to Adam Smith*, ed. Jeffrey T. Young (Cheltenham: Edward Elgar, 2009); Paganelli, "The Same Face of the Two Smiths: Adam Smith and Vernon Smith," *Journal of Economic Behavior and Organization* 78 (2011): 246–55; and Jonathan Wight, "Sentiments and Motivations in Adam Smith and Vernon Smith," *Forum for Social Economics* 42 (2013): 298–301.

him to formulate his central ideas. Vernon describes these debts in four specific essays: his 1997 distinguished guest lecture to the Southern Economic Association,[3] the introductory chapter to his more recent monograph *Rationality in Economics*,[4] a brief reply to his critics, published under the title "What Would Adam Smith Think?,"[5] and most recently his essay "Adam Smith: From Propriety and Sentiments to Property and Wealth."[6]

The first of these four essays takes as its point of departure the famed "Adam Smith Problem": that is, the ostensible tension between the other-directed and benevolent moral psychology on which the social system of *The Theory of Moral Sentiments* (*TMS*) is said to be founded and the self-interested moral psychology on which the system described in the *Wealth of Nations* (*WN*) is said to be predicated. Smith scholars have long debated whether there really is such a problem insofar as Adam is concerned; a great deal of ink has been spilled on the subject since *Das Problem* was set forth by August Oncken in 1898.[7] That said, however relevant or irrelevant *Das Problem* is to our understanding of Adam, what drives it—the apparent tension between seemingly self-interested and seemingly altruistic tendencies in human behavior—has been and continues to be an important heuristic in the history and practice of the social sciences. Yet it was Vernon's achievement to suggest—with reference to Adam's insights and his own experimental results—that the conventional formulations of the "tension" are the result

[3] Vernon Smith, "The Two Faces of Adam Smith," *Southern Economic Journal* 65 (1998): 1–19.

[4] Vernon Smith, *Rationality in Economics: Constructivist and Ecological Forms* (Cambridge: Cambridge University Press, 2008).

[5] Vernon Smith, "What Would Adam Smith Think?" *Journal of Economic Behavior and Organization* 73 (2010): 83–86.

[6] Vernon Smith, "Adam Smith: From Propreity and Sentiments to Property and Wealth," *Forum for Social Economics* 42 (2013): 283–97.

[7] See Leonidas Montes, "Das Adam Smith Problem: Its Origins, the Stages of the Current Debate, and One Implication for Our Understanding of Sympathy," *Journal of the History of Economic Thought* 25 (2003): 63–90.

of a misunderstanding. That is, against the idea that there are somehow two Adams, or even two sides of human nature, Vernon, following Adam, argues that there is only a single human nature that simply expresses itself in different ways under different conditions and in different contexts. In his words, to see that "what would appear to be directly contradictory views of human nature held by Adam Smith" (e.g., "noncooperative self-interest and other regarding sympathy") are "not contradictory," we must "distinguish impersonal market exchange and personal exchange."[8] By reorienting our focus to the question of the relevant context, we come to see that the ostensible "tension" in our psychology is more apparent than real. Further, "if we recognize that a universal propensity for social exchange is a fundamental distinguishing feature of the hominid line, and that it finds expression in both personal exchange in small-group social transactions and in impersonal trade through large-group markets," we reach two useful conclusions.[9] First, the conventional dichotomy between egoism and altruism will come to be seen as resting on a category mistake; mired in the debate over how to understand human nature, the conventional dichotomy obscures our capacity to appreciate that the apparent differences are attributable simply to the different expressions of our natures in different contexts. This has payoffs on multiple fronts, not least of which is that it illuminates the deficiencies of all systems that see to reduce the mind to "a general purpose logic machine" in which "all decision tasks, regardless of context, constitute maximization problems subject to external constraints."[10] However crucial this may be, there is also a payoff for students of Adam as this reorientation of focus away from "human nature" to contexts of expression helps us see that Adam "was talking about the juxtaposition of positive reciprocity and self-loving, or noncooperative behavior." Put slightly differently, "the puzzle" implicit in

[8] Vernon, "Two Faces," 2.

[9] Ibid., 3.

[10] Ibid., 7.

Das Problem is how a single being can be both cooperating and non-cooperating, and the "key" to its solution is a distinction between impersonal large group exchange and social small group exchange.[11] This will need to be addressed more fully below, but for now the important point is Vernon's claim that Adam was working with two main categories: positive reciprocity (understood as the reciprocal benevolence exhibited by individuals in small groups) and non-cooperative behavior (or self-interested utility maximization in large groups).

In *Rationality in Economics* these same themes are further developed, and indeed in a way that further illuminates Vernon's debts to Adam. These debts are in fact acknowledged from the start, with Vernon paying homage in his preface to the "incredible Scottish Enlightenment" and "Scottish geniuses," naming Hume and Smith in particular. [12] In becoming bolder in his praises of the Scots, Vernon also becomes somewhat bolder in his treatment of the Adam Smith Problem; indeed here we are forthrightly told that the ostensible Problem is in fact "an artificial problem" founded on the failure to appreciate the distinction between "personal exchange" and "impersonal exchange in markets."[13] Now, all this is essentially familiar from the earlier piece. But what is new here is the theoretical framework in which the distinction is cast, for now the key problem is taken to be chiefly epistemological. In particular, the heart of the problem lies in the distinction between the two forms of rationality invoked in the book's subtitle: the "constructivist" rationality by which an agent purposefully establishes a normative solution to a specific practical problem, and the "ecological" rationality embodied in the complex system of social norms and moral rules that is part of our cultural and evolutionary inheritance and which reflects the aggregated and distilled collective wisdom that emerges from human interaction in the absence of conscious human design.[14] And here too Vernon insists

[11] Ibid., 8; cf. 16–17.

[12] Vernon, Rationality in Economics, xvi.

[13] Ibid., 7.

[14] Ibid., 2.

that the Scots were the true pioneers of this distinction, insisting that the "coexistence" of these two forms of rationality was in fact "well understood" by Smith and Hayek alike.[15] Here again Vernon is well positioned to remind Smith specialists of something all-too-often overlooked: that Adam was himself well aware of the complex range of types of social interaction, and the consequent need for us to employ different mental mechanisms in different contexts, an idea that has recently been given new life in the specialist debate over the extent of Adam's ostensible "cosmopolitanism." [16] For our purposes, the significance of the distinction between the constructivist and ecological lies in its implications for understanding other-regarding behavior. First, ecological rationality to some degree serves as a substitute for conscious intended beneficence; that is, one of the benefits of a focus on ecological rationality is that the wisdom embodied in the adaptively evolved brain and the norms and codes of successful groups can supplant traditional focus on the moral psychology of other-directed agent motivation—a notoriously messy business. Second and similarly, the ecological rationality that has reciprocity at its core provides a more compelling explanation for other-directed behavior than the explanations neoclassical economic models have been able to provide. One of the chief benefits of the experimental approach, Vernon suggests, is that it enables us to "observe other-regarding behavior that supports more cooperation than the standard [neoclassical] model predicts."[17] But not only does it establish the reality of a greater degree of other regarding behavior than allowed to *homo economicus*, but it also provides a more compelling explanation for such. Vernon is skeptical of efforts to "model these other-regarding behaviors as due to other-regarding preferences (utility) in the tradition of static equilibrium theory." Such bending-over-backwards to

[15] Ibid., 7.

[16] Fonna Forman-Barzilai, *Adam Smith and the Circles of Sympathy* (Cambridge: Cambridge University Press, 2010).

[17] Vernon, *Rationality in Economics*, 9; Paganelli, "Smithian Answers"; Paganelli, "Same Face," 247–48; and Wight, "Sentiments and Motivations," 299.

explain other-directedness is doomed, as "this model confounds reputation-based reciprocal motives to cooperate through exchange with the notion that cooperation requires preferences to be altruistic."[18] Herein lies the upshot: Vernon's method of accounting for other-directed motives via reiterated reciprocity liberates us from having to subscribe to either the morality of pure altruism or the neoclassical claim that other-directed action is explicable only as "other-directed utility"; in Vernon's words, "there is no inherent contradiction between self-regarding and other-regarding behavior, and as we shall see, the latter well serves each individual under the common cultural norms of reciprocity sharing as it derives from repeat interaction."[19]

These themes, so central to Vernon's long-standing engagement with Adam, have recently been restated and even further developed. In a response to his critics Vernon again returns to what he calls the "remarkable insights" of Adam concerning "the mainsprings of other regarding behavior in human sociality." Several of these are now familiar, including the distinction between *TMS* and *WN* on the grounds that the former's focus is "personal social exchange" while the latter's is "impersonal market exchange."[20] Also familiar is the claim that "contemporary notions of reciprocity in economics, and reciprocal altruism in biology, are inadequate as oversimplified mechanical reductions, in comparison with the concept as Smith applies it to human interaction."[21] But what receives greater emphasis in this piece than in the previous discussions is Adam's interest in moral psychology proper. Indeed here it is clear that so far from merely limiting his accounts of human behavior to what can be observed in social interaction, a principal aim of *TMS* is said to be to probe "what might be going on inside of people's heads."[22] What seems to be going on inside these heads is

[18] Vernon, Rationality in Economics, 9.

[19] Ibid., 21.

[20] Vernon, "What Would Adam Smith Think?," 83.

[21] Ibid., 84. Also quoted in Paganelli, "Same Face," 248.

[22] Vernon, "What Would Adam Smith Think?," 83.

sympathy, "the dynamic core of human sociality" but what is truly striking about this is the extent of this claim: "in the absence of human sympathy, we are bereft of having any sense of self," as the individual "*cannot even be defined* independently" of mutual sympathies.[23]

This claim receives even further emphasis in his most recent essay on Smith. Here Vernon brings together his long-standing skepticism concerning the adequacy of the model of the rational utility maximizer with his explicit reconsideration of the nature of the individual. In so doing he reiterates the significance of appreciating differences in context,[24] and emphasizes the specifically "predictive" significance of Smith's theory of beneficence and resentment.[25] Here I want to focus principally on his claim here that "far from championing the individual's pursuit of self-love, *Smith saw the individual as not even defined except in a social context*."[26] With this last remark Vernon speaks to one of the most interesting and important debates for Smith specialists today, one to which we will need to return later. Put simply: do we owe our sense of ourselves solely to our sympathetic interactions with others? Put slightly differently: are we merely social constructions constituted by our intersubjective interactions with other human beings, or is there an element of our natures that resists or transcends such intersubjectivity?

Non-Reciprocated Ethical Behavior

This is of course a large question, and has been extensively treated by recent commentators elsewhere.[27] The present essay restricts itself to

[23] Ibid., 84 (italics original).

[24] Vernon, "Smith: From Propriety to Wealth," 285–87, 294.

[25] Ibid., 288–91; see also Vernon, "Adam Smith and Experimental Economics: Sentiments to Wealth," forthcoming in *Adam Smith: A Princeton Guide*, ed. R. Hanley (Princeton: Princeton University Press).

[26] Vernon, "Smith: From Propriety to Wealth," 288 (italics original).

[27] See, e.g., Hanley, *Adam Smith and the Character of Virtue* (Cambridge: Cambridge University Press, 2009), 135–50; and Forman-Barzilai, *Smith and the Circles of Sympathy*, 75–105.

those aspects of *TMS* that bear on the specific problems at hand: non-reciprocated beneficence, intended beneficence, and social vs. unsocial. Our departure point for discussion of the first point is Vernon's distinction between reciprocated and non-reciprocated behavior. As noted above, Vernon's conception of reciprocity serves as an alternative to the account of altruism to be found in the traditional account of *homo economicus*. Thus where the traditional model is prone to interpret altruism in terms of a maximized utility of pleasure, in the system that Vernon defends, expressions of altruism need to be understood within the context of personal exchange in small groups; where the neoclassical model reduces all behavior to utility maximization, Vernon's differentiates between reciprocated and non-reciprocated behavior, associating beneficent behavior in small groups with the former and self-interested behavior in large groups with the latter. But with this we come to the central question: how does Vernon's response to *homo economicus* compare to Adam's?

In this section I want to argue that Vernon's and Adam's responses in fact diverge on a key point: namely that where Vernon distinguishes between two types of behavior—reciprocated beneficence and non-reciprocated self-interest—Adam consciously adds to these a third: non-reciprocated beneficence. More specifically: central to Adam's theory of normative ethics is a type of behavior that is performed without hope or expectation of any sort of reciprocity or cooperation whatsoever (and in this sense operates like self-interest), but which is motivated by genuine concern for the well-being of others (and in this sense operates like beneficence). This category is not a central focus of Vernon's analysis but is central to *TMS*, as its well-known first line attests: "How selfish soever man may be supposed, there are evidently some principles in his nature, which interest him in the fortune of others, and render their happiness necessary to him, though he derives nothing from it except the pleasure of seeing it" (*TMS*, 1.1.1.1).[28] Vernon of course knows this line well, and

[28] Citations to *TMS* and WN take the standard section and paragraph references of the Glasgow edition.

quotes it directly. And his reasons for being interested in it are clear; as Smith scholars know, Adam's target in this opening line and opening section is the egocentrism defended by Hobbes and Mandeville, and the parallels between Adam's attempt to refute egocentrism by calling attention to the existence of the "pleasure" that virtuous spectators take in apprehending the well-being of others deserves comparison to Vernon's response to the attempts of theories of utility maximization to account for the existence of altruism. For our purposes, a different side of Vernon's response that demands attention. Specifically, Vernon regards this element of Adam's response as something of a disappointment as it suggests that Adam's conception of beneficence "is not clearly connected in [his] thinking with the informal social exchange of favors and goods." As a result, Vernon suggests, Adam regarded beneficence "as unexplained input," chalking it up "to design by the great Director of nature, Providence, the Judge of hearts, and so on." In this light Adam's conception of beneficence is "the ultimate conversation stopper," as for him "it was just too much to see in gifts, the hidden benefits of gifts in return." And it is this that Vernon aims to remedy by demonstrating that this "pleasure" is in fact best accounted for "from the expectation of reciprocal benefits."[29]

Herein lies a key difference between Vernon and Adam. Vernon's claim is that "Smith never asked why, outside of Divine design, otherwise selfish humans derived *nothing* from beneficence to others 'except the pleasure of seeing it.'"[30] This falls short of doing complete justice to the complex accounts of the provenance and functions of conscience and praiseworthiness in *TMS*. For our purposes, the most important question concerns what relationship there might be between the accounts of non-reciprocated beneficent behavior in Adam's treatments of praiseworthiness and conscience and Vernon's distinction between reciprocal benevolent behavior and noncooperative self-

[29] Vernon, "Two Faces," 17.
[30] Ibid., 17.

interested behavior. This question is all the more significant given the fact that Adam's own most pointed defenses of non-reciprocated beneficent behavior are presented as responses to Mandeville's reduction of all moral motivation to mere egocentrism, just as Vernon's own most pointed defenses of reciprocated beneficent behavior are presented as responses to contemporary reductions of all human activity to utility maximization.

Adam's response to Mandeville is principally given in two places in *TMS*: 7.2.4 ("Of licentious systems") and 3.2 ("Of the love of Praise, and that of Praise-Worthiness..."). These again are complex passages that raise questions that go beyond what we can treat here,[31] which we have to limit to the question of reciprocity. On this front, what is striking here is the degree to which Adam emphasizes the reality of the human capacity to act beneficently without any hope of reward or further reciprocity and specifically without any hope of augmented reputation. This is particularly evident in Adam's account of the "love of virtue." Adam introduces the love of virtue by distinguishing it from two other dispositions: the love of praise and the "love of true glory." Lovers of praise, he explains, care only about getting praise from others, merited or not. Lovers of true glory, on the other hand, are concerned to *deserve* the praises of others, but share with the lovers of praise a deep solicitude for praise itself. This latter disposition finds a contemporary analogue in Jon Elster's account of the phenomenon of "approbativeness" as exhibited by those driven by "the desire to be thought of well by others," and which Elster identifies as "a false coin that may have to substitute for the true coin of altruism and morality."[32] Where Adam departs from both Mandeville and Elster is in his insistence that there exists a third and higher disposition, that of the lovers of virtue. Lovers of praise and lovers of true glory are regarded from this perspective as decidedly second-rate, for virtue in its fullest sense emerges only when we are indifferent to any

[31] Hanley, *Smith and the Character of Virtue*, 92–99.

[32] Jon Elster, *Explaining Social Behavior: More Nuts and Bolts for the Social Sciences* (Cambridge: Cambridge University Press, 2007) 98.

external reward for our behavior: "The man who acts solely from a regard to what is right and fit to be done, from a regard to what is the proper object of esteem and approbation, *though these sentiments should never be bestowed upon him*, acts from the most sublime and godlike motive which human nature is even capable of conceiving" (*TMS,* 7.2.4.10; italics added). This is Adam's trump card, and indeed it is one that he would play not only in this passage, which dates from the first (1759) edition of *TMS*, but also in some of the key revisions that he would make three decades later to the sixth (1790) edition. Here again he insists that "though a wise man feels little pleasure from praise where he knows there is no praise-worthiness, he often feels the highest in doing what he knows to be praise-worthy, *though he knows equally well that no praise is ever to be bestowed upon it*" (*TMS,* 3.2.7; italics added). Indeed what truly defines the peak of excellence is *indifference* to reciprocity and reputation effects; thus the good man who "has the most perfect assurance of the perfect propriety of every part of his own conduct" not only "neglects" and "despises" all recognition, but "[h]is self-approbation, in this case, stands in need of no confirmation from the approbation of other men," as "[i]t is alone sufficient, and he is contented with it"—this self-approbation indeed "if not the only, is at least the principal object, about which he can or ought to be anxious" (*TMS,* 3.2.8). On these grounds, it seems fair to say that at the heart of Adam's response to Mandeville is an effort to carve out a place for the reality and primacy of beneficent behavior performed without any hope of reciprocation, and specifically without any hopes of augmented reputation—an approach quite different from that in which the limits of non-cooperative self-interest are established by reciprocal behaviors.

So what implications does this have for Vernon? A few suggestions might be ventured. First, attending to Adam's conception of praiseworthiness and the love of virtue may lead to some slight adjustment of Vernon's account of praiseworthiness. Vernon's most direct account of praiseworthiness (so far as I know) is to be found in the most recent of the three pieces examined above. Here he suggests that Adam's account of praiseworthiness "perhaps explains why, when you do me a favor, I may thank you but also add, 'I owe you one.' My acknowledgment of a debt to you adds praiseworthiness to my thankful praise of your actions."[33] This seems absolutely right in one crucial sense; the "I owe you one" declaration conveys the judgment of "merit" or "desert" that is clearly central to Adam's account of praiseworthiness. Yet this is only half of the function of praiseworthiness in Adam's system. For beyond its role in our efforts to judge desert or merit, praiseworthiness also plays a crucial role in Adam's account of action-motivation. Here what matters to the lover of virtue is not merely others' expressions of our praiseworthiness (as Vernon's example nicely captures) but also the precise way in which we are moved to act as a result of our self-consciousness of our own praiseworthiness—an aspect of the story that receives its fullest treatment in the accounts in the "desire" or "love of praiseworthiness" as distinct from the mere "love of praise" (e.g. *TMS*, 3.2.25–32). In short, this love of praiseworthiness, understood as an internalized conception of honor, is important because it leads us to act in a certain way and particularly in those instances in which we cannot expect to be either praised or blamed for so doing, and indeed "to do the right thing even if there is nobody there to praise or blame us."[34]

This leads to another question: what response might Vernon have to Adam's quite insistent claims about the excellence of non-reciprocated beneficent behavior? There are several options available. One would be simply to dismiss such claims altogether, either on the grounds that these are behaviors exhibited by very few people (a point to which we return below) or that such "perfectionist" concerns are not in fact central to *TMS*.[35] Another equally simple option might be to say that this is the sort of stuff that goes beyond what experimental economics can or should be concerned with and forms a part of that side of *TMS* to which Vernon generously calls attention in noting that personal exchange "is central to

[33] Vernon, "What Would Smith Think?," 84.

[34] Paganelli, "Smithian Answers," 187–88; cf. Wight, "Sentiments and Motivations," 300–301.

[35] Forman-Barzilai, Smith and the Circles of Sympathy, 106–34.

but certainly not all of the content of Smith's first book, which dealt broadly with human sociality."[36] And it also might be possible simply to regard all of this concern for praiseworthiness as merely the after-the-fact synthesis of our individual experiences into a moral code—the process by which reciprocity can become "internalized as conscience."[37] I suspect that in the end the concern is not so easily dismissed insofar as it speaks so directly to the central claims here at stake concerning the association of beneficence with reciprocity. When Adam insists so pointedly that for a genuinely good person, the self-approbation that he or she experiences while doing well—even and especially if he or she is not recognized for such by others—"is alone sufficient," he suggests that the end of morality lies not in reciprocation or cooperation but in a very one-sided sort of giving that challenges our concepts of exchange. Put in more familiar terms, we might borrow a phrase from Gordon Tullock, who closed his essay on "Adam Smith and the Prisoners' Dilemma" with the suggestion that in large groups in which individuals can choose with whom they wish to exchange, known self-interested non-cooperators are in time likely to find that they have "no one to noncooperate with."[38] For Adam's genuinely virtuous person, animated by a desire to give without hope of receiving in return, the optimal activity is precisely that non-reciprocated beneficence in which the objects of our beneficence are assumed to be non-cooperators from the start.

Intended Beneficence

A second point where Vernon and Adam seem to diverge concerns intended beneficence. Here the point at issue concerns the question introduced above with reference to ecological and constructive

[36] Vernon, Rationality in Economics, 7.

[37] David M. Levy and Sandra J. Peart, "Sympathy and Approbation in Hume and Smith: A Solution to the Other Rational Species Problem," *Economics and Philosophy* 20 (2004): 337; and esp. Paganelli, "Same Face," **[page?]**

[38] Gordon Tullock, "Adam Smith and the Prisoners' Dilemma," *Quarterly Journal of Economics* 100 (1985): 1081; also quoted in Paganelli, "Same Face," 248.

rationality. As we saw, in Vernon's work there is a consistent claim that many of the outcomes we find praiseworthy or otherwise desirable are often attributable to actions in which such ends formed no part of the design or intention. On Vernon's account, this in fact forms "the key proposition articulated by the Scottish philosophers": that "to do good for others does *not require* deliberate action to further the perceived interest of others."[39] What exactly does this mean? Does this in fact capture Adam's own position?

To begin with the first question: to some degree Vernon's claim here is one that is today quite familiar (at least to readers of Hayek). That even our seemingly amoral actions often have beneficial unintended consequences is today at least a well-known if hardly universally accepted claim. This seems to be essentially what Vernon has in mind when he suggests "that unintended good for others could flow from doing well for yourself."[40] What makes Vernon's claim especially interesting is first his identification of its provenance; in his text, Vernon identifies Mandeville as its originator and Adam as "influenced" by it. So too at the 2002 Nobel ceremony, where in praising the "discoveries of the Scottish philosophers," Vernon singles out Hume for his insight "that the rules of morality are not the conclusions of reason" and that honorary Scot Mandeville for his observation that "'the worst of all the multitude did something for the common good.'"[41] Adam, as it happens, was not mentioned on this occasion. This is itself significant because it leads us to wonder whether in fact an emphasis on the limits of rationality and the beneficial consequences of self-interested behavior in fact captures either the whole or the heart of Adam's own system, however well it might describe Hume or Mandeville.

[39] Vernon, *Rationality in Economics*, 18 (italics original).

[40] Ibid., 18.

[41] "The Grumbling Hive," in *Fable of the Bees*, ed. F. B. Kaye (Indianapolis: Liberty Fund, 1988) 9; Vernon, "Toast," *Nobel Prize Lecture*, Stockholm, Sweden, 8 December 2002.

In what follows, I argue that this emphasis not only fails to capture Adam's intention but also may well distort it. My evidence for this is three key passages from *TMS*. In these three passages, Adam sets forth a series of strikingly direct claims concerning the intentional beneficence that is to be expected of a wise and virtuous man in both his private and his public capacity. In light of our present concerns, what is striking in each of these passages is the pronounced emphasis on intended beneficence. For example, in his account of the peak figure of his ethics, the wise and virtuous man, Adam insists that

> [h]e is never so elated as to look down with insolence even upon those who are really below him. He feels so well his own imperfection, he knows so well the difficulty with which he attained his own distant approximation to rectitude, that he cannot regard with contempt the still greater imperfection of other people. Far from insulting over their inferiority, he views it with the most indulgent commiseration, and, by his advice as well as example, is at all times willing to promote their further advancement. (*TMS*, 6.3.25)

The excellence of the most excellent man seems to consist in both his generous attitude to others as well as his active exertion for their benefit. So too the excellent public servant:

> The civil magistrate is entrusted with the power not only of preserving the public peace by restraining injustice, but of promoting the prosperity of the commonwealth, by establishing good discipline, and by discouraging every sort of vice and impropriety; he may prescribe rules, therefore, which not only prohibit mutual injuries among fellow-citizens, but command mutual good offices to a certain degree. (*TMS*, 2.2.1.8)

One fears that this striking account of the magistrate's positive duties is often overlooked owing to either a misreading of the debate with Kames that is its immediate context in the text, or a hurry to get to Adam's powerful critique of the dangers of the man of system. In any case, neither the account of the wise and virtuous man nor the account of the virtuous public magistrate is an anomaly. Each embodies what Adam takes to be the defining principle of human nature, which is itself something quite different than the propensity for reciprocal exchange:

> Man was made for action, and to promote by the exertion of his faculties such changes in the external circumstances both of himself and others, as may seem most favourable to the happiness of all. He must not be satisfied with indolent benevolence, nor fancy himself the friend of mankind, because in his heart he wishes well to the prosperity of the world. That he may call forth the whole vigour of his soul, and strain every nerve, in order to produce those ends which it is the purpose of his being to advance, Nature has taught him, that neither himself nor mankind can be fully satisfied with his conduct, nor bestow upon it the full measure of applause, unless he has actually produced them. (*TMS*, 2.3.3.3).

This is a striking conception of human nature, one not often associated with Adam but yet central to his thought.

The key question of course is what we ought to do with these observations, and indeed what bearing they have on the claims that Vernon is centrally concerned to develop. One strategy might simply be dismissal; perhaps the concerns about intentional beneficence reflected in the passages above are not really central to Adam's project and that his fundamental concerns lie more in containing "men of system" than encouraging men of virtue. Or one might concede that Adam did think these central, but that his project is something of a hodge-podge and thus better regarded as a stock of ideas from which to pick and choose rather than as a system that needs to be unpacked and reconstructed and understood as a whole. Or one might say that this is simply part of that side of *TMS* that cannot be captured by exchange. To my mind the interesting question is how we ought to understand Adam's commitment to spontaneous order and unintended consequences in light of his emphasis on intended beneficence.

More particularly, this emphasis challenges us to be clear about what we mean when we say "that unintended good for others could flow from doing well for yourself." It seems to me that sometimes this is shorthand for the view that "the unintended good that is done for others and which flows from doing well for yourself is sufficient for the purposes of preserving human order, and efforts at intended beneficence are supererogatory and need not necessarily be encouraged." And sometimes it is shorthand for the view that "the unintended good that is done for others and which flows from doing well for yourself is sufficient for the purposes of preserving order, and since beneficent efforts often lead to pernicious albeit unintended consequences they should be actively discouraged." But either way, there is some reason to think that this position differs from Adam's own view, which the passages above seem to suggest is better described in the terms of the present discussion as "the intended good that is done for others and which comes from putting the interests of others ahead of your own is at once a moral and a political good."

Several important recent works have argued on the basis of a similar interpretation that Smith's politics were in fact more progressive than his popular reputation would seem to suggest.[42] This is not however a question that we can pursue here. Instead, we limit ourselves to asking to what degree does Vernon want to side with the position outlined just above, namely that "the intended good that is done for others and which comes from putting the interests of others ahead of your own is at once a moral and a political good?" In some obvious sense there are clear parallels; what else is the beneficent activity of some first movers in dictator games if not a recognition that in at least some contexts it is good to put the well-being of others before one's own? But the much more difficult and more interesting question is how we are to draw the line of demarcation that will allow us properly to distinguish those contexts in which intended beneficence is desirable and those in which it is pernicious.

[42] See esp. Samuel Fleischacker, *On Adam Smith's Wealth of Nations: A Philosophical Companion* (Princeton: Princeton University Press, 2004); Amartya Sen, "Introduction," in *The Theory of Moral Sentiments*, ed. Hanley (London: Penguin, 2010).

Egoism and Altruism

This penultimate section turns to one of Vernon's central achievements: namely the resources he provides for transcendence of the debate over egoism and altruism. Comparing Vernon to Adam is particularly apt on this front because the transcendence of this debate was every bit as much Adam's intention in his day as it is Vernon's in ours. At the same time there seems to be a subtle but significant difference in Vernon's and Adam's routes to this end—a difference, moreover, that might be usefully exploited by Vernon to further advance his position.

To introduce this, it might be useful to begin with a bit of historical context, just enough to see the similarities between the battles that Adam and Vernon are fighting. To tar with a broad brush: a chief debate of eighteenth-century British moral philosophy concerned the definition of human nature, and specifically the question of whether accounts of human nature and human action ought to give primary emphasis to selfish motives or to other-directed motives. The principals in this debate (here again speaking broadly) were on the one hand, the philosophers that Hume associated with what he called the selfish system of morals (Hobbes, Locke, and Mandeville) and those who opposed their egocentric reductionism (most notably Shaftesbury, Hutcheson, and Butler). This debate dominated much of the ethics of the first half of the eighteenth century, but in large part it was not until mid-century that real progress began to be made. For it was then—and specifically through the contributions of Hume and Rousseau—that the dichotomy of selfishness and selflessness or egoism and altruism began to be productively transcended. In particular, and for all their other many disagreements,[43] both Hume and Rousseau agreed that the essential question for students of human motivation was not whether human nature was somehow fundamentally either egoistic or altruistic but rather how the self-directed and the other-directed passions that are both

[43] See John T. Scott and Robert Zaretsky, *The Philosopher's Quarrel: Rousseau, Hume, and the Limits of Human Understanding* (New Haven: Yale University Press, 2009).

undeniably present in human nature and human action work together. In Hume's terms, this inquiry takes the form of understanding how that "particle of the dove, kneaded into our frame, along with the elements of the wolf and serpent" can be most productively directed,[44] and in Rousseau's terms, it takes the form of understanding how two passions natural to man (self-love and compassion) interact to define both natural and cultivated morality.[45] It was in this precise context, and indeed with Hume and Rousseau as two of his chief influences, that Adam composed and published *The Theory of Moral Sentiments*, which centered around the question of the relationship of the self-directed to the other-directed.

How exactly did Adam understand this relationship, and how does his view compare to Vernon's? For Vernon, the key to this relationship, as we have seen, lies in an appreciation of the necessary relegation of the self-directed and the other-directed to separate spheres. But Adam's solution seems to involve some additional elements. To some degree these include his redefinition of self-love itself; in Adam's hands, self-love, so far from being reducible to any simple sort of egocentrism or selfishness, is a dynamic passion capable of both evolution and education in a manner that renders it compatible with promotion of the interests of others. But it also concerns the way in which Adam divides the passions. Against the reductive binary of selfish and selfless, Adam suggests a classification founded on a tripartite distinction: "social" and "unsocial" and "selfish." These are the three principal categories of *TMS*, 1.2, and it is a distinction that deserves more attention than it has generally received.[46] It also deserves attention from those interested in Vernon's project insofar as it would seem to provide further evidence for—and

[44] Hume, *An Enquiry Concering the Principles of Morals*, ed. Tom Beauchamp (Oxford: Oxford University Press, 1998) 74.

[45] Rousseau, Discourse on Inequality, Part I.

[46] Though on this front see Lisa Herzog, "Higher and Lower Virtues in Comnmercial Society: Adam Smith and Motivation Crowding Out," *Politics, Philosophy, and Economics* 10 (2011): 5–6.

perhaps even clarify—Adam's distinction between social and selfish contexts.

Adam presents this distinction chiefly at *TMS*, 1.2.3-5. Here I want to focus on one specific element of it: namely the effect of this tripartite distinction on our understanding of the "selfish" passions. For in a very real sense, the substitution of the tripartite distinction for the old binary distinction between selfless and selfish reorients the selfish from its original position on one extreme pole and places it in the middle, thereby neutralizing it. A brief turn to the text can help make this clear. Adam's discussion begins with what he again calls the "unsocial" passions. As Adam makes clear, he has a very specific idea in mind in calling these "unsocial," an idea that emerges largely from his identification of "hatred and resentment, with all their different modifications" as the chief "unsocial" passions (*TMS*, 1.2.3.1). Hatred and resentment are unsocial, he explains, because they are unpleasant in both their experience and their apprehension. They are "disagreeable to the spectator" insofar as witnessing them often "disgusts us" and "disturbs our sympathy" and they are "not less so to the person who feels them" as they "are the greatest poison to the happiness of a good mind" for in their experience we feel "something harsh, jarring, and convulsive, something that tears and distracts the breast" (*TMS*, 1.2.3.5 and 7). Their "unsocial" (or perhaps even better, "unsociable") aspect is evident. But for all this, Smith insists that these passions are nevertheless "regarded as necessary parts of the character of human nature" (*TMS*, 1.2.3.3). By this he means that they are the foundation of justice, an evolution developed in detail in *TMS*, 2.[47] Even here Adam insists that the only way to understand how the obviously unsocial passions in fact promote social ends is to shift perspective, for even though what he calls their "immediate effects" are mischievous, their "remote effects" ought to be welcomed (*TMS*, 1.2.3.4). Thus Adam's conscious effort to shift our perspective, and

[47] See esp. Spencer J. Pack and Eric Schliesser, "Smith's Humean Criticism of Hume's Account of the Origin of Justice," *Journal of the History of Philosophy* 44 (2006): 47–63.

indeed in two ways: first to have us shift time horizons to differentiate between short-term and long-term effects,[48] and second to shift our analytical focus from the subjective feelings of an individual to the benefits of the group. It is this second shift that provides further justification for Vernon's own efforts to shift our focus away from the subjective and atomistic experience of *homo economicus* and to increase our appreciation of the influence of group context in explaining specific behaviors. Adam's emphasis on this shift continues in his discussion of the other two classifications. The discussion of the "social" passions that follows is the shortest of the three, perhaps since it is the least controversial and most intuitive. That "[g]enerosity, humanity, kindness, compassion, mutual friendship and esteem, all the social and benevolent affections" are immediately pleasing to both actors and spectators Adam seems to think sufficiently obvious and non-controversial and thus not in need of much elaboration or defense (*TMS*, 1.2.4.1). What does deserve pause is his account of the "third set of passions," here labeled "the selfish passions." In contrast to what one might have expected on turning to this section, one finds here no treatment of greed or pride or envy or any of the other selfish passions familiar from Hobbes and Mandeville. The selfish passions, as defined here, are rather the feelings we experience on reflecting on "our own private good or bad fortune." And what is remarkable in Adam's treatment is that far from regarding our concern with our private fortune as either a motivating force to be celebrated or a corrupting influence to be repressed, this concern is treated as a decidedly neutral phenomenon, which in fact "holds a sort of middle place" between "those two opposite sets of passions, the social and unsocial" (*TMS*, 1.2.5.1). Adam evidently thinks this an important enough observation to repeat it later, claiming that the selfish passions hold "a sort of middle place, between the social and unsocial affections" (*TMS*, 3.6.6). The upshot of this is to remove concerns for our own welfare

[48] See esp. Gordon Davis, "Philosophical Psychology and Economic Psychology in David Hume and Adam Smith," *History of Political Economy* 35 (2003): 269–304.

from the morally charged realm of self-interest or self-regard and to encourage readers to see such concerns merely as natural and necessary phenomena that are universally exhibited.

A further advantage of attending to this tripartite distinction, it seems to me, is that it provides further evidence for Vernon's claim that Adam's perspective is that of the group rather than the isolated autonomous individual. It may also serve to clarify exactly what we mean when we say this. One suspects that Adam does not himself want to defend what many of his latter-day readers want to defend when they make this claim: namely that human individuality is merely a social construct. Adam's own claim is more nuanced: namely that from the specific perspective of the student of group dynamics, *homo economicus* is not a helpful concept insofar as the well-being of a group in its totality demands attention as well as the well-being of the individual. It is this frame-shift, more evident here than any other single place in *TMS*, which establishes a context that enables us to employ a normative language to describe certain actions as virtuous or vicious, praiseworthy or blameworthy.

Experimenting with Adam

The aim of this essay has been to make a modest call for a renewed engagement between students of the past and students of the present on the grounds that each stands to benefit from the wisdom of the other, and particularly with regard to what we might learn both about and from Adam Smith. Vernon's analysis has much to teach Smith specialists especially concerning Adam's understanding of the importance of exchange contexts and the function of reciprocity; the textual evidence from *TMS*, 2.1.1.5 and 6.2.1.19 that he adduces demonstrates this masterfully.[49] I also hasten to add that there is much else in Vernon that deserves the attention of students of Adam beyond what this paper has been able to treat (e.g., the suggestive remark that Adam "may have had

[49] Vernon, "What Would Smith Think?," 84.

some of the earmarks of high-functioning autism or Asperger's Syndrome"[50]). Leaving this for another occasion, we close by echoing and extending two recent reminders that there remains much in Adam that deserves further exploration by behavioral and experimental economists. As such studies have shown, Adam's analyses of such phenomena as the desire to be regarded by others and the propensity to admire the rich are fertile sources of "unexploited ideas,"[51] just as his analyses of the psychological phenomena of resentment and praiseworthiness can help to explain several results in the experimentalist literature that deviate from the expected conclusions of rational choice.[52] In this vein, I close by suggesting a few additional ways in which experimental methods might complement the theoretical insights of Adam to illuminate particularly key but obscure elements of human behavior.

First, what accounts for the sort of non-reciprocated beneficence described above? Here is one instance in which a combination of the experimental methods of Vernon and the theoretical analysis of Adam can be especially fruitful. Two experimental results are particularly salient on this front. First, experimenters frequently report increases in rates and frequency of giving in dictator games when perceived social distance is minimized and solidarity of giver and receiver is increased by providing givers personal information about receivers.[53] Second, experimenters also report that even in anonymous one-shot dictator games, a small

[50] Vernon, *Rationality in Economics,* 19n2.

[51] Nava Ashraf, Colin F. Camerer, and George Loewenstein, "Adam Smith, Behavioral Economist," *Journal of Economic Perspectives* 19 (2005): 140–42.

[52] Paganelli, "Smithian Answers."

[53] See, e.g., Elizabeth Hoffman, Kevin McCabe, and Vernon L. Smith, "Social Distance and Other-Regarding Behavior," *American Economic Review* 86 (1996): 653–60; Iris Bohnet and Bruno S. Frey, "Social Distance and Other-Regarding Behavior in Dictator Games: Comment," *American Economic Review* 89 (1999): 335–39; Fernando Aguiar, Pablo Brañas-Garza, and Luis M. Miller, "Moral Distance in Dictator Games," *Judgement and Decision Making* 3 (2008): 344–54; and Gary Charness and Uri Gneezy, "What's in a Name? Anonymity and Social Distance in Dictator and Ultimatum Games," *Journal of Economic Behavior and Organization* 68 (2008): 29–35.

percentage of givers (typically about 10 percent) exhibit altruistic behaviors that significantly deviate from the expected rate of giving in a subgame perfect Nash equilibrium.[54] What accounts for this latter behavior? Conventional explanations invoke cooperation and reciprocity or altruism and "warm glow" (the desire to maximize the internal pleasure from self-consciousness of having acted virtuously, a concept that itself deserves analysis against the Smithian notion of praiseworthiness). The real answer may lie in what can be inferred from the first piece of experimental data; herein lies the significance of Adam's theoretical analysis. That beneficence varies proportionately to social distance was well known to Adam, as his notorious story of the Chinese earthquake attests (*TMS*, 3.3.4) and several recent scholars have emphasized.[55] But what Adam also understood equally well is that the hallmark of the benefactor who transcends the seeming limits of spatial propinquity is not simply a predisposition to altruism or to reciprocity, but rather *precisely the capacity to internalize mechanisms that overcome social distance and increase a perceived feeling of solidarity with others*. In this sense, the key fact about the wise and virtuous man is not that he is more caring or more compassionate than others, but rather that he is at all times animated by a deep sense of equality and solidarity with others; in Adam's words, he is animated by a sense of "real modesty" concerning his own merits as well as a "full sense of the merit of other people," including "those who are really below him" (*TMS*, 6.3.25). This is itself merely a development of one of Adam's most fundamental claims: that the most important disposition of the truly virtuous individual is his or her capacity to regard him or herself as "but one of the multitude in no respect better than any other in it" (*TMS*, 2.2.2.1, 3.3.4, 6.2.2.2). It is this sensitivity to solidarity, and not acute affective concern for others,

[54] Catherine C. Eckel and Philip J. Grossman, "Altruism in Anonymous Dictator Games," *Games and Economic Behavior* 16 (1996): 187; Alexander K. Koch and Hans-Theo Normann, "Giving in Dictator Games: Regard for Others or Regard by Others?" *Southern Economic Journal* 75 (2008): 227–28.

[55] See, e.g., Forman-Barzilai, *Smith and the Circles of Sympathy*, 50–52, 141–60.

that mitigates the genuinely virtuous person's egocentrism and maximizes his beneficence.

Taken together with the experimental data, Adam's analysis suggests that what may distinguish that small number of "altruists" or "wise and virtuous" who consistently act beneficently even in conditions in which "no praise is ever to be bestowed" (*TMS*, 3.2.7), is not a mere predilection to altruism or warm glow, but rather their internalization of mechanisms that overcome social distance and promote their identification with others on the basis of shared humanity. In this sense, Smith might be seen as providing a more developed account of how some agents come to achieve that sense of solidarity that his contemporary and friend Hume called "humanity" and which Hume judged in fact to be the necessary foundation of any legitimate ethical system even as he professed himself unable to account for its origin beyond merely positing it to be a natural sentiment.[56] Equally significant is that the alternative this possibility offers to models of cooperation or reciprocity. Paganelli has recently and helpfully demonstrated how Smithean conceptions of imagination, sympathy, and the desire to be praiseworthy help to explain how we internalize norms of cooperation.[57] In addition to helping us better to understand how typical agents often come to internalize norms of cooperation and reciprocity, Adam may well also help us to appreciate the alternative route taken by a particular type of virtuous agent whose non-cooperative beneficence is founded ultimately on a belief in and commitment to human solidarity rather than other-directed affect or concern for mutually beneficial outcomes.

Second, how ought we to understand the relationship between "self-directed" and "other-directed" behaviors? These terms are today largely thought preferable to the older and unwieldy dichotomy of egotism vs. altruism; thus Herbert Gintis's recent declaration that the concept of

[56] See Hanley, "David Hume and the 'Politics of Humanity'," *Political Theory* 39 (2011): 205–33.

[57] Paganelli, "Same Face," *passim*.

self-regard is to be preferred to the concept of self-interest as it gets us beyond "much pseudophilosophical discussion."[58] Without questioning that the categories of self-regard and other-regard are genuine improvements on egotism and altruism, one might still wonder whether this improvement is sufficient unto itself. Here again Adam stands poised to contribute to our efforts at conceptual clarity. A central lesson of *TMS* is that a strikingly wide sphere of human behavior is at once both self-regarding and other-regarding; thus the indignation that drives us to gratify our private desire for revenge is the foundation of the juridical systems that preserve the public peace and order, just as the sympathy that leads us to commiserate the suffering of others also renders us solicitous for their recognition and esteem. If so, then the attempt to establish whether a given action or even a given motive is ultimately self-regarding or other-regarding seems no less reductionist than the attempt to define our motives and our outcomes as either egotistic or altruistic; self-regarding motives often have other-directed effects (as indignant men know) just as other-regarding motives often have self-directed effects (as lovers of true glory know). If the ambitions of experimental economics are limited strictly to presenting data concerning outcomes, this may not be problematic. If experimental economics ultimately aspires to providing insight into motivation as well, then Adam's analysis—and in particular its sensitivity to identifying and disaggregating those components of our actions and our sentiments that are self-regarding from those that are other-regarding—will continue to be indispensible.

Author's note: Earlier versions of this paper were presented to the George Mason University Workshop in Philosophy, Politics and Economics; the NYU Colloquium on Market Institutions and Economic Processes; the Seminaire Philo-Éco of the Pôle d'histoire de l'analyse et des représentations économiques (PHARE) of Université Paris 1

[58] Gintis, *The Bounds of Reason: Game Theory and the Unification of the Behavioral Sciences* (Princeton: Princeton University Press, 2009) 46.

Panthéon-Sorbonne; and the 2011 Annual Meeting of the Southern Economic Association in Washington, DC. For these invitations I am very grateful to Peter Boettke, Mario Rizzo, Benoit Walraevens, and Maria Pia Paganelli. I am also grateful to Maria Pia Paganelli for generously sharing her own essay on the two Smiths, and to Doug Den Uyl, Eric Schliesser, Jason Aimone, Justus Meyers, and Daniel Klein for many helpful comments. A special note of thanks is in order to Vernon Smith, who generously read and responded to an early draft of the manuscript.

6 | Serenity and System in Smith and Hayek

Art Carden

Introduction

In Part VI of *The Theory of Moral Sentiments*, Adam Smith asks us to consider "The Character of Virtue."[1] In Part VI, section II he compares and contrasts worldviews with different implications for human flourishing and different prescriptions for how people "whose public spirit is prompted altogether by humanity and benevolence" can most effectively discharge that humanity and benevolence. Friedrich Hayek, one of his intellectual heirs, explained in the twentieth century how a "Great Society" protects liberty through abstract principles governing conduct rather than attempts to impose specific outcomes through the articulated rationality of the one Adam Smith called "the man of system."[2]

Sowell explained the constrained and unconstrained visions of humanity as follows: "The constrained vision is a tragic vision of the human condition. The unconstrained vision is a moral vision of human intentions, which are viewed as ultimately decisive."[3] In the constrained vision, human nature is immutable and resources are scarce. It is, as

[1] This essay is based on remarks I made at the Elliott Conference on "The Moral and Political Philosophy of Adam Smith" at Mercer University (3-4 April 2013) and was supported in part by a summer research grant from Samford University. I also benefited greatly from the discussions we held at a Liberty Fund seminar on Friedrich Hayek in August 2013. Thanks to Francis Hector for transcribing parts of the talk that form the basis of this essay. *TMS* refers to the Liberty Fund's online edition of *The Theory of Moral Sentiments*; *WN* refers to the Liberty Fund's online edition of *The Wealth of Nations*.

[2] Thomas Sowell (*A Conflict of Visions* [New York: Basic Books, 2007] 47ff) refers to the "articulated rationality" of those of the unconstrained vision who see the social project as precisely that: a *project* whereby wise stewards armed with the power of reason deliberately fashion institutions in such a way as to produce specific, desirable outcomes.

[3] Ibid.

Sowell points out, a tragic vision of humanity. In the unconstrained vision, however, human nature is malleable. People are perfectible. Human institutions can be uprooted and the wet clay of humanity can be formed and shaped according to the intentions, visions, and articulated rationality of those in charge of running society. These visions are contrasted against one another in *TMS*. Smith contrasts man's moral limitations against man's moral ambitions and argues that our ability to intervene advantageously in others' affairs is more limited than we might think.

In VI.II of *TMS*, Smith contrasts two visions of humanity. The first is one espoused by one we will call "the man of serenity"; while this is not Smith's term, it captures the attitude Smith describes. The man of serenity's good intentions are tempered by social and technological constraints. The second is Smith's "man of system." The "man of humanitarian system," to use Coyne's phrase, has attempted to use force to create economic development in poor countries, often with either nothing to show for it or with actually negative results.[4] Attempts to create liberal democracy in poor countries have been unsuccessful, as have attempts to create economic development.

Smith's broad project considered the origins and implications of sympathy (in *TMS*) and the origins and implications of "self-love" (in *WN*).[5] Overall, he developed an analytical system that helps us understand how order and harmony emerge from seemingly chaotic and incomprehensibly complex processes. Smith in the eighteenth century and Hayek in the twentieth century offered compelling defenses of the "obvious and simple system of natural liberty," showing that it is difficult to intervene advantageously in others' affairs. The results of intervention—even humanitarian intervention—suggest that

[4] Christopher Coyne, *Doing Bad by Doing Good: Why Humanitarian Action Fails* (Stanford: Stanford Economics and Finance, 2007), 27.

[5] James Otteson, "Adam Smith and Social Justice," Lecture at the Institute for Humane Studies, Humane Studies Fellowship Research Colloquium Fairfox VA, 15 November 2013.

humanitarians should be more humble and less confident in their ability to improve others' lives. The contrast between these visions is evident in *TMS*.

Serenity and System: Two Visions in The Theory of Moral Sentiments

The twentieth century was a century-long debate over whether society can be organized or whether society self-organizes. In the first case, production is directed centrally by moral and intellectual surrogates who assume from the general populace the right and responsibility to make decisions about what is to be produced, how, and how it is to be distributed. This is done in accordance with a central plan that replaces the "anarchy of production" endemic to a decentralized, free market system with rational planning guided by the higher wisdom of the central planners.

The problem is that knowledge about individuals' opportunity costs, tastes, preferences, and available technologies is never presented to central planners as *data* (things given) but only emerges through the marketplace as people confront "the particular circumstances of time and place."[6] Mises argued that rational economic calculation is impossible under socialism because reliable prices cannot emerge unless the means of production are privately owned and, therefore, traded in markets.[7] The economic critique of central planning is not that market prices are a more efficient way of transmitting knowledge than a central plan; rather, it is that market prices are meaningful whereas "prices" determined by central planners or identified through complex formal models are not. One of Hayek's contributions was to note that even if efficient central planning could be done with a large enough computer, the economic problem is fundamentally of a different kind: a society's knowledge does not and

[6] Friedrich A. Hayek, *Individualism and Economic Order* (Chicago: University of Chicago Press, 1948) 81.

[7] Ludwig von Mises, *Socialism: An Economic and Sociological Analysis* (1922; repr. Indianapolis: Liberty Fund, 1981).

cannot exist in a central repository. It is dispersed among some seven billion (and counting) minds, and it is embodied in and transmitted by the prices arising from voluntary trade.

These insights have their roots in Smith, but not only in *WN*. They go back to *TMS* as well, and are perhaps best embodied in two passages about the motivations and abilities of the one Adam Smith called "the man of system" and his counterpart with a more constrained vision of his own abilities, a prudent humanitarian we will call "the man of serenity."

A famous prayer is attributed to Reinhold Niebuhr: "God, grant me the serenity to accept the things I cannot change, / The courage to change the things I can, / And the wisdom to know the difference."[8] This sentiment is foreshadowed in a passage in *TMS*:

> The man whose public spirit is prompted altogether by humanity and benevolence, will respect the established powers and privileges even of individuals, and still more those of the great orders and societies, into which the state is divided. Though he should consider some of them as in some measure abusive, he will content himself with moderating, what he often cannot annihilate without great violence. When he cannot conquer the rooted prejudices of the people by reason and persuasion, he will not attempt to subdue them by force; but will religiously observe what, by Cicero, is justly called the divine maxim of Plato, never to use violence to his country no more than to his parents. He will accommodate, as well as he can, his public arrangements to the confirmed habits and prejudices of the people; and will remedy as well as he can, the inconveniencies which may flow from the want of those regulations which the people are averse to submit to. When he cannot establish the right, he will not disdain to ameliorate the wrong; but like Solon, when he cannot establish the best system of laws, he will endeavour to establish the best that the people can bear. (*TMS*, VI.II.41).

The man of serenity, or "the man whose public spirit is prompted altogether by humanity and benevolence," has all these characteristics.

[8] The text is available at Wikipedia among many other online sources: https://en.wikipedia.org/wiki/Serenity_Prayer (accessed 2 December 2013).

First, he recognizes that he might not have the ability to topple "the established powers and privileges" of the society in which he finds himself, and he recognizes that the unintended consequences of doing so may be worse than allowing them to continue.

This isn't to say that he is completely inactive or that he does not take the opportunity to alter "the established powers and privileges" when it would be advantageous. Rather, he possesses the courage to change the things he can and the wisdom to know the difference as, "like Solon, when he cannot establish the best system of laws, he will endeavor to establish the best that the people can bear"(*TMS* VI. II.41). To use a bit of modern wisdom, he might think locally or globally, but he acts locally. This isn't to say that his work is geographically constrained to his immediate community. Rather, the man of serenity sticks to what he knows, whom he knows, and where he knows without acting based on views that are largely speculative. The man of serenity earnestly wishes for a better world but recognizes that he faces constraints that may be non-negotiable. He works to change what he can change (his immediate surroundings) and prays that God would change what he cannot (the hearts of men).

The farther we go from our immediate intellectual, cultural, and social surroundings, the less likely it is that we will be able to act in a way that is advantageous to those further removed. In Colossians 4:5 (KJV), Paul exhorts us to "walk in wisdom toward those who are without, redeeming the time." Wisdom differs from mere good intentions in much the same way that beneficence differs from benevolence. Meaning to help someone and wanting to help someone (benevolence) is all well and good. Beneficence—actually helping people—is much more difficult.

The "man of serenity" is likely to be a more effective champion of the social good than the "man of system" Smith discusses shortly after. In a famous passage, Smith writes,

> The man of system, on the contrary, is apt to be very wise in his own conceit; and is often so enamoured with the supposed beauty of his own ideal plan of government, that he cannot suffer the smallest deviation from any part of it. He goes on to establish it completely and in all its

> parts, without any regard either to the great interests, or to the strong prejudices which may oppose it. He seems to imagine that he can arrange the different members of a great society with as much ease as the hand arranges the different pieces upon a chess-board. He does not consider that the pieces upon the chess-board have no other principle of motion besides that which the hand impresses upon them; but that, in the great chess-board of human society, every single piece has a principle of motion of its own, altogether different from that which the legislature might choose to impress upon it. If those two principles coincide and act in the same direction, the game of human society will go on easily and harmoniously, and is very likely to be happy and successful. If they are opposite or different, the game will go on miserably, and the society must be at all times in the highest degree of disorder. (*TMS*, VI.II.42)

The man of system treats social problems like engineering problems. Solving them, in this view, is a matter of assembling willpower and computational resources. He discounts the preferences and assumes to know the abilities of all members of his Great Society, and he presumes that he can direct their actions with the same ease with which he arranges pieces on a chessboard, or Lego bricks, without acknowledging that people have their own "principle(s) of motion" (*TMS* VI.11.42) that cannot be known by a single mind. They are endowed with knowledge about the particular circumstances of time and place that the man of system cannot know; they know more about their tastes, available resources, opportunity costs, and intimate acquaintances than anyone else, and this knowledge cannot be deployed through the actions of a central planner.

Smith took this insight further in *WN*, when he wrote of "the statesman":

> The statesman who should attempt to direct private people in what manner they ought to employ their capitals would not only load himself with a most unnecessary attention, but assume an authority which could safely be trusted, not only to no single person, but to no council or senate whatever, and which would nowhere be so dangerous as in the hands of a man who has folly and presumption enough to fancy himself fit to exercise it. (*WN*, IV.2.10)

The statesman is something of a "madman in authority," to adopt John Maynard Keynes's phrase. He is trying to solve a problem that is not just difficult: he is trying to solve a problem that is impossible for someone in his or her position to solve. Smith counseled that central planning is less than counterproductive. It is also dangerous in that it appeals to the conceit of the interventionist statesman. The danger comes from the statesman's folly, which is to presume that he can make good use of power in the pursuit of specific ends chosen by moral and intellectual surrogates endowed with superior reason.

Friedrich Hayek was one of the most prominent intellectual heirs of Smith's vision. Liberal institutions, those that direct what Hayek called "the Great Society," do not have any overarching purpose or consciously directed goal. [9] Indeed, they are rarely consciously designed and implemented. One twentieth-century institutional manifestation of the unconstrained vision was the rise of collectivism, first as an idea propounded by the intellectuals and second as an arrangement of institutions in collectivist countries. Hayek described collectivism as follows:

> The common features of all collectivist systems may be described, in a phrase ever dear to the socialists of all schools, as the deliberate organization of the labors of society for a definite social goal. That our present society lacks such "conscious" direction toward a single aim, that its activities are guided by the whims and fancies of irresponsible individuals, has always been one of the main complaints of its socialist critics.[10]

The man of system and the statesman are necessarily partial. They must pick winners and losers in accordance with their conception of the good society, and Hayek makes this point in contrasting the liberal state with the illiberal state:

[9] Friedrich A. Hayek, *Law, Legislation and Liberty, vol. 2: The Mirage of Social Justice* (Chicago: University of Chicago Press, 1976), 36–68.

[10] Friedrich A. Hayek, *The Road to Serfdom* (1944; repr. Chicago: University of Chicago Press, 2007) 100.

> Where the precise effects of government policy on particular people are known, where the government aims directly at such particular effects, it cannot help knowing these effects, and therefore it cannot be impartial. It must, of necessity, take sides, impose its valuations upon people and, instead of assisting them in the advancement of their own ends, choose the ends for them. As soon as the particular effects are foreseen at the time a law is made, it ceases to be a mere instrument to be used by the people and becomes instead an instrument used by the lawgiver upon the people and for his ends. The state ceases to be a piece of utilitarian machinery intended to help individuals in the fullest development of their individual personality and becomes a "moral" institution—where "moral" is not used in contrast to immoral but describes an institution which imposes on its members its views on all moral questions, whether these views be moral or highly immoral. In this sense, the Nazi or any other collectivist state is "moral," while the liberal state is not.[11]

Illiberal and collectivist states are "moral" according to Hayek not in that what they do is morally good (as it most certainly isn't) but in that they restrict the citizens' range of permissible views as to what is and is not right. In a liberal state, by contrast, people are free to have different values and different preferences. A "moral" state, according to Hayek, is one in which people's values are in effect chosen for them.

Hayek continues by highlighting some of the decisions that must be made by the man of system:

> When we have to choose between higher wages for nurses or doctors and more extensive services for the sick, more milk for children and better wages for agricultural workers, or between employment for the unemployed or better wages for those already employed, nothing short of a complete system of values in which every want of every person or group has a definite place is necessary to provide an answer.[12]

Hayek goes on to point out a predictable irony in the consequences of central planning. Central planning substitutes the articulated

[11] Ibid., 115.
[12] Ibid., 116.

rationality of moral and intellectual surrogates for the systemic rationality of a liberal economic and political system.[13] Planners do not create a "more rational" substitute for the "anarchy of production." Here is Hayek again:

> In fact, as planning becomes more and more extensive, it becomes regularly necessary to qualify legal provisions increasingly by reference to what is "fair" or "reasonable"; this means that it becomes necessary to leave the decision of the concrete case more and more to the discretion of the judge or authority in question.[14]

People have diverse tastes and talents, and planning eliminates the contexts in which these tastes and talents can be deployed to the satisfaction of individual wants and ends. Central planning destroys information. Otteson noted that for Smith, voluntary trade was the way we learn how to best use our own time, talent, and treasure to do the things that we think valuable.[15] As Sowell describes it, "what is called 'planning' is the forcible *suppression* of millions of people's plans by a government-imposed plan."[16] The planners suppress the mechanisms that generate knowledge about people's tastes and opportunity costs and impose upon people a central (and artificial) scale of values. The effects can be particularly pernicious when we consider the effect of a taste for status on the wealth of a nation under more coercive (as opposed to more voluntary) institutions.

Status, Serenity, and System in the Catallaxy

People are not always motivated by material consumption. Sometimes, we want to move up in the social hierarchy. Status-seeking differs from trade in that status-seeking is to a much larger degree a zero-sum game. If we are going to acquire status, then someone else has to lose it. If the desire for status is deeply ingrained and if the demand

[13] Sowell, *A Conflict of Visions*.

[14] Hayek, *Road to Serfdom*, 116.

[15] Otteson made this point in "Adam Smith."

[16] Thomas Sowell, *Intellectuals and Society* (New York: Basic Books, 2009) 53.

for status is relatively inelastic, people will shift their status-seeking to margins other than income and consumption. Furthermore, the people doing the taxing and redistributing are presumably subject to the same status-seeking pressures and proclivities.

Smith relates the tale of "the poor man's son" in *TMS*:

> The poor man's son, whom heaven in its anger has visited with ambition, when he begins to look around him, admires the condition of the rich.... He studies to distinguish himself in some laborious profession. With the most unrelenting industry he labours night and day to acquire talents superior to all his competitors. He endeavours next to bring those talents into public view, and with equal assiduity solicits every opportunity of employment. (*TMS*, IV.I.8)

Smith goes on to describe the trials and travails (and ultimate regrets) of the poor man's son after he has wasted his life chasing a proverbial whirlwind. Under Smith's "obvious and simple system of natural liberty," or in what North et al. call an "open-access order," people earn economic rents by innovating, or at least by producing more at lower prices.[17] Innovation and production create wealth for the innovators and the producers (therefore raising their status), but it also creates wealth for everyone else. When the means to status run through government, people earn places in the social hierarchy not by creating wealth for others, but by establishing positions of dominance and authority. In what they call an "open access order," status goes to those with the ability to convince others to act. In what they call a "limited access order," status goes to those with the most discretion to compel others to act.

Hayek writes in defense, therefore, of the "Rule of Law":

> Indeed, the Rule of Law, more than the rule of contract, should probably be regarded as the true opposite of the rule of status. It is the Rule of Law, in the sense of the rule of formal law, the absence of legal privileges

[17] Douglass C. North, John Joseph Wallis, and Barry R. Weingast, *Violence and Social Orders* (Cambridge: Cambridge University Press, 2009).

of particular people designated by authority, which safeguards that equality before the law which is the opposite of arbitrary government.[18]

In this passage, Hayek highlights the importance of an abstract order based on the Rule of Law. In this setting, people are legal (if not material) equals. If people have a taste for status, then the material inequality generated by a society governed by the Rule of Law is arguably the most benign form of inequality. The Rule of Status, which is the alternative to the Rule of Law, creates uncertainty for entrepreneurs and investors because it makes the law itself subject to those who are in the positions of "lawmakers." Furthermore, as people compete for position in a society governed by the Rule of Status, they consume real resources in zero-sum status-seeking.

McCloskey argues that a change in rhetoric explains the wealth of the western world.[19] Specifically, beginning in Holland and then later moving to England, public opinion about the bourgeoisie changed. Status was earned by the innovators and entrepreneurs. Being a merchant came to be considered not merely tolerable, but virtuous. Commerce tempers the darker angels of our nature—our vanity, for example—by channeling it toward activities that make others better off.

One of the most important things students learn in an introductory economics class is that trade creates wealth. People who can move up the social hierarchy by being adept and astute traders may be seeking wealth only as a means to the ultimate goal of high status, but their status-seeking activities produce benefits for others in the form of more and better goods and services. There will always be those among us who are motivated by vanity and a desire for status. The institutional question is not "what can we do to reform or remake human nature?" because it is not within our power to do so. Rather, the institutional question is

[18] Hayek, *Road*, 116–117.

[19] Deirdre N. McCloskey, *Bourgeois Virtues: Ethics for an Age of Commerce* (Chicago: University of Chicago Press, 2006); *Bourgeois Dignity: Why Economics Can't Explain the Modern World* (Chicago: University of Chicago Press, 2010); *Treasured Bourgeoisie* (forthcoming).

"under what conditions will vanity and desire for status manifest in social benefit?" If the poor man's son is going to waste himself upon the altar of his own vanity, it is far better that he should do so by producing and trading rather than by seeking power.

By participating in the market economy, or what Hayek called "the catallaxy," people are participating in a social process that no single mind can articulate and that no single mind can understand. Smith and others working in the same tradition have pointed out that the way to achieve your own goals it is to help other people achieve *their* goals.[20]

Expanding the extent of the catallaxy gives us the greatest hope for long-run institutional change. Hayek summarizes this in a discussion of what he calls "the Great Society," which is simply an outworking of what Smith called "the obvious and simple system of natural liberty":

> It is often made a reproach to the Great Society and its market that it lacks an agreed ranking of ends. This, however, is in fact its great merit which makes individual freedom and all its values possible. The Great Society arose through the discovery that men can live together in peace and mutually benefiting each other without agreeing on the particular aims which they severally pursue. The discovery that by substituting abstract rules of conduct for obligatory concrete ends made it possible to extend the order of peace beyond the small groups pursuing the same ends, because it enabled each individual to gain from the skill and knowledge of others whom he need not even know and whose aims could be wholly different from his own....
>
> The important point about the catallaxy is that it reconciles different knowledge and different purposes which, whether the individuals be selfish or not, will greatly differ from one person to another. It is because in the catallaxy men, while following their own interests, whether wholly egotistical or highly altruistic, will further the aims of many others, most of whom they will never know, that it is as an overall order so superior to

[20] See Mises (*Socialism*) and Hayek (*Individualism*) for discussions of the impossibility of rational economic calculation without private ownership of the means of production.

> any deliberate organization; in the Great Society the different members benefit from each other's efforts not only in spite of but often even because of their several aims being different.[21]

The catallaxy is, in short, an institutional environment in diversity is most meaningful. It is an order that is "means-connected and not ends-connected," to use Hayek's words again. Hayek notes that some view this as an undesirable characteristic, but again, it allows us to preserve the fundamental diversity of humanity because we are linked by common humanity and a relatively small set of abstract principles rather than a common (and unavoidably homogeneous) humanity bound by an imposed hierarchy of ends.

Serenity and System Applied: Making the World a Better Place at Gunpoint

Smith, and later Hayek, Sowell, and others, have cautioned us against the presumption that we can intervene advantageously in others' affairs. This might leave a bad taste in the mouths of those who have identified and chronicled horrors upon horrors throughout history and around the world. Identifying horror and fixing horror are two separate things: that bad people are doing bad things does not mean that good people can fix it. That the poor man's son will waste his life seeking status in a commercial society does not mean that he will not waste his life seeking status in more socially destructive ways in a non-commercial society. Furthermore, as Christopher J. Coyne has argued, intervening in complex systems creates unanticipated (and often negative) unintended consequences.[22]

In his 2007 *After War: The Political Economy of Exporting Democracy*, Coyne details American failures to "export liberal democracy at gunpoint" and notes that even if we set a relatively low bar for "success" (leaving the object of our intervention with institutions as good as

[21] Hayek, *Law*, 109–110.

[22] Coyne, *After War: The Political Economy of Exporting Democracy* (Stanford: Stanford Economics and Finance, 2007); Coyne, Doing Bad by Doing Good.

modern-day Iran's), American intervention does not have a particularly encouraging track record. In *Doing Bad by Doing Good: Why Humanitarian Action Fails*, he introduces us to "The Man of the Humanitarian System" and explains how and why government humanitarian action is sometimes doomed to failure.[23]

Coyne explains how attempts to create stable and desirable institutions in Somalia failed, noting that "the establishment of a central government of the Republic of Somalia did not yield benefits to members of Somali society at large. Instead, the central government was seen as a tool to be used by a few to expropriate the many."[24] Indeed, the existence of international aid infrastructure had the unintended consequence of encouraging violence as competing groups sought control over Mogadishu on the (perhaps reasonable) belief that this would mean control over a renewed flow of aid dollars.[25] It is unlikely that liberal democracy can be grafted into a dysfunctional society from outside; as Boettke et al. note, institutional changes are "sticky" when they are consistent with the underlying pattern of preferences and opportunities.[26] Coyne documents numerous instances in which people coordinate on liberal democratic institutions or on pathological institutions during and after reconstruction.[27] In Germany and Japan after World War II, for example, the institutional conditions for prosperity were already in place. In societies like Somalia, they are not.

How, then, do we get sustained economic growth? Occupiers are "constrained by a country's existing cultural endowment."[28] What can we do about it? Coyne suggests extending the reach of the catallaxy wherever

[23] Coyne *After War*, 27.

[24] Coyne, *After War*, 147.

[25] Ibid., 145.

[26] Peter J. Boettke, Christopher J. Coyne, and Peter T. Leeson, "Institutional Stickiness and the New Development Economics," *American Journal of Economics and Sociology* 76 (2008): 331–58.

[27] Coyne, *After War*, 47–48.

[28] Coyne, *After War*, 57.

possible.[29] Borrowing from Tyler Cowen, Coyne notes that trade is a way to create the appropriate cultural soil in which liberty can grow (which is perhaps a better metaphor):

> Consider for instance that many of the autocracies with which the United States has engaged in large-scale trade (such as Mexico, South Korea, and Taiwan) have moved toward liberal democracy, relative to their starting point, as a result of a larger trade-produced commercial middle class and its demands for political participation. While trade may not lead to countries assuming a mirror image of the West, trade can plant the seeds of tolerance and a willingness to agree to disagree, traits that [philosopher Kwame Anthony] Appiah notes are central to any notion of global peace.[30]

Attempts to do this through humanitarian channels have largely failed, as well. Coyne summarizes the research on foreign aid and explains how and why "the man of the humanitarian system" is unable to create long term growth.[31] The causes of growth are largely systemic and unintentional. We are obviously capable of creating intentional benefits for others, but in a complex society most of the social benefits we create are purely unintentional.[32]

Conclusion

Adam Smith offers a constrained vision of the human condition. We cannot fundamentally change human nature, nor can we be certain (or even confident) that our schemes to influence their incentives will lead to a game that goes advantageously. Following Smith, Friedrich Hayek explains how "the Great Society" emerges as the result of a commitment to abstract principles of order rather than commitment to

[29] Ibid.

[30] This was a remark Coyne made at a panel discussion of his book at Mississippi State University on 6 March 2013. I paraphrase: we don't know how to create liberal democracy. We don't know how to create long-run economic growth.

[31] Coyne, *Doing Bad*.

[32] Sowell, *Conflict of Visions*, 15.

specific desirable outcomes. Given that people pursue status, granting them the ability to use force to generate desirable outcomes can backfire because it then encourages status-seeking in the political arena rather than the marketplace.

Coyne shows that even when we mean well, pretending that people have principles of motion other than those we choose to impress upon them can be dangerous at worst and minimally effective at best.[33] He shows how we cannot export liberal democracy or economic development at gunpoint and suggests instead that the best way to proceed is not to surgically repair a society's institutions but to extend the catalaxy—the realm of trade and voluntary cooperation. This can be done through freer trade in labor and freer trade in goods that helps till and fertilize the institutional and cultural soil in which economic growth takes place.

[33] Coyne, *After War; Doing Bad.*

7 | Adam Smith's Juggler and Its Practical Relevance Today

Scott Beaulier

I. Introduction

According to the United States Treasury, the US deficit for 2013 was $680 billion.[1] The federal government's inability to balance its budget in 2013 and persistent run of large deficits, which have been a consistent feature of America's federal budget since 2000, have resulted in a US debt in excess of $17 trillion today.[2] The dismal budgetary picture we see in the United States and through most nation-states around the world is not unique; the persistence of deficits and debt here and elsewhere is something Adam Smith predicted and raised concerns about in an important and somewhat underappreciated section of *The Wealth of Nations*:

> When national debts have once been accumulated to a certain degree, there is scarce, I believe, a single instance of their having been fairly and completely paid...publick bankruptcy has been disguised under the appearance of a pretend payment.... When it becomes necessary for a state to declare itself bankrupt, in the same manner as when it becomes necessary for an individual to do so, a fair, open, and avowed bankruptcy is always the measure which is both least dishonorable to the debtor, and least hurtful to the creditor. The honour of a state is surely very poorly provided for, when in order to cover the disgrace of real bankruptcy, it has recourse to a juggling trick of this kind.... Almost all states, however, ancient as well as modern, when reduced to this necessity, have upon some occasions, played this very juggling trick. (*WN*, 929–30)

[1] Jean Sahadi, "U.S. Deficit Falls to $680 Billion," CNNMoney, http://money.cnn.com/2013/10/30/news/economy/deficit-2013-treasury/ (accessed 22 January 2014).

[2] Stephen Dinan, "U.S. Debt Jumps a Record $328 Billion—Tops $17 Trillion for First Time," *Washington Times*, 18 October 2013.

In Smith's day, the sovereign and his "juggling tricks" were of chief concern. The lack of transparency in accounting, which remains a problem in modern economies, made it difficult for people to know the true costs of government finances. The juggler's tendency, moreover, to distract the people through gimmicks like one-off expenditures and war propaganda led to further confusion about the state's true finances. But, according to Smith, the juggling cannot go on forever. A day of reckoning comes when the sovereign either inflates away the currency through seignorage and debasement or admits the game is over. Honesty from sovereigns, of course, is not the predicted outcome, and we instead observe a historical pattern of deficits, debt, and debasement.[3]

Here in the US, the "juggler" is alive and well, as he tries to keep the large balls of Social Security, Medicare, and Medicaid in the air on the one hand, while new balls of bailouts and the Affordable Care Act are added to the mix. America's lackluster economic performance since the "Great Recession of 2008" has made delivering generous benefits to Americans difficult for lawmakers. Since tax increases are unpopular, and since they would stifle America's already slow recovery, the tactic of borrowing against future growth and future Americans—what the economist Laurence Kotlikoff describes as "intergenerational theft"[4] has become the modern-day US juggler's preferred tactic. The juggler in the US is not one party or one person, but, rather, the system in general, which concentrates benefits on current voting Americans and disperses costs on others. The collective result of our juggling tricks is not a $17 trillion, but, in fact, amounts to a true unfunded liability of more than

[3] Further discussions about Smith's work on juggling tricks can be found in Scott Beaulier and Peter Boettke, "Deficits, Debt, and Debasement," *Cato Policy Report* 33/4 (July/August 2011) and Peter Boettke and Christopher Coyne, "The Debt Inflation Cycle and the Global Financial Crisis," *Global Policy* 2/2 (2011): 184–89.

[4] Laurence Kotlikoff and Robert Rosenthal, "Some Inefficiency Implications of Generational Politics and Exchange," *Economics and Politics* 5/1 (1993): 27–42.

$200 trillion.[5] The true liability of $200 trillion reflects all of the promises our government has made to all Americans living today, and the true liability calculation assumes current revenues will continue to be taken in. Such numbers, which are never given much attention in Washington, DC, are the stuff Smith was talking about in the passage above and are cause for a more honest conversation about government finances.

II. Pretend Payments and Juggling Tricks

For Smith, the practice of pretend payments and juggling tricks "gradually enfeebled every state which has adopted it" (*WN*, 928). The Italian republics, Spain, England, and France were all, according to Smith, enfeebled by the juggler back in the 1760s when Smith was writing *Wealth of Nations*. And, the same schemes of pretend payments and juggling tricks present throughout Europe in Smith's day are omnipresent today, as evidenced by crises in Greece, bailouts of the European periphery, and signs of crisis here in the United States.

Crisis and a turn by politicians toward "improper" forms of funding are the inevitable first steps once a state is enfeebled enough by juggling. In the United States, the massive increases in transfer spending (i.e., redistributing money from one person to another), coupled with steady increases in discretionary and defense spending, means large deficits will burden us for the foreseeable future. The momentary slow-down in spending we observed after the 2012/2013 sequester has come to an end, and even the sequester was a minor shift in the trajectory of spending, rather than a fundamental change.

Deficits occur when government expenditures exceed tax revenues. They lead to higher interest rates and a crowding out of private sector investments. They generate unpredictability in policy because they herald rising taxes. Since they cannot be left unpaid, governments finance deficits by issuing bonds, which are IOUs promising to repay the

[5] Laurence Kotlikoff, "U.S. Is Bankrupt and We Don't Even Know It," *Bloomberg News*, 10 August 2010.

principal (with interest) over time. Over the past fifty-five years, the United States government has spent 20.2 percent of all US income at the federal level. Over the same period of time, however, the government has collected 18.1 percent of income. The two-percentage point difference has been financed in the bond market, and our $17 trillion in debt is the result of our constant reliance on bond issuance to cover our excessive spending.

Publicly held debt in the United States currently stands near 70 percent of gross domestic product and, according to the Congressional Budget Office, it will rise to near 100 percent by 2025. As debt rises, interest rates rise, taxes rise, and politicians become more and more tempted to inflate the currency to hide their excessive spending. Inflating away our problems by using a country's central bank to print money, purchase bonds, artificially hold down interest rates, and prolong the juggling trick is something economists call "debasement." It is what Smith called a "pretend payment" of debt because money being used to pay on an obligation is worth less, thanks to monetary mischief, than it appears.

In Smith's day, governments debased their currencies by trimming small amounts of metal off of their coins. They would gather the shavings, melt them down, create new coins, and circulate them. Such actions allowed them to maintain higher levels of spending, but they stand out today as blatant examples of debasement. When the Federal Reserve or other central banks flood the Treasury market with new fiat currency, they are eroding the value of currency in real terms, while allowing authorities to spend beyond their means for a bit longer. They are using a slight variation—a modern-day version—of the same "juggling tricks" to achieve their ends: kicking the deficit and debt problems plaguing nation-states off into the future and, in so doing, hiding the full cost of repayment to the public.

While trimming physical coins in Smith's day made debasement of currency a somewhat easier problem to track, there are troubling signs indicating central banks are busy juggling away in modern economies too. The Federal Reserve's balance sheet, for example, has expanded from a stable, quite constant level of about $800 billion in 2007 to more than $4 trillion today.[6] The quintupling of assets on the Fed's balance sheet has helped to fuel one of the longest bond market rallies in US history, and Treasury yields, which reflect the cost of government borrowing, have been kept artificially low thanks to the Fed's meddling. The Fed's "quantitative easing" programs and reluctance to taper its most recent program, which Fed watchers call "QE3," have helped keep mortgage rates near record low levels as well. Like interest rates in the bond market, artificially low mortgage rates create distortions for both borrowers and lenders, and they encourage an overinvestment in housing and a steady bidding up of housing prices. While the Fed's binge of asset purchases has not shown up in traditional inflationary indicators like the Consumer Price Index, it has spilled over into Treasury and housing inflation. Since QE3 was introduced in September 2012, for example, housing prices have increased by more than 11 percent.[7]

By entering the market and purchasing toxic assets and government securities—assets private buyers were not interested in purchasing at the prevailing price—the Fed expanded the money supply. Prices have risen in both markets, and each dollar earned by other citizens in the economy is worth less than it was before the Federal Reserve's actions. Milton Friedman famously stated, "Inflation is always and everywhere a monetary phenomenon in that it is and can be produced only by a more rapid increase in the quantity of money than in output."[8] The pernicious effects of money increases outstripping increases in economic output are just beginning to be felt in the US and elsewhere.

While the juggler metaphor set up by Smith hints at people being distracted and confused about the true state of government affairs, there is some evidence they have, in the past, been keenly aware of the

[6] http://www.federalreserve.gov/monetarypolicy/bst_recenttrends.htm

[7] http://us.spindices.com/indices/real-estate/sp-case-shiller-us-national-home-price-index

[8] Milton Friedman, "The Counter-Revolution in Monetary Theory," *Institute of Economic Affairs Occasional Paper* 33 (1970): 11.

government's actions. During major wars and economic crises, for example, Americans are willing to live with larger deficits and more debt. Our country's public debt as a fraction of GDP rose to 109 percent of GDP during World War II, for example. After the war, debt as a fraction of GDP steadily fell to just 24 percent of income by 1974. Even as recently as 1980, total national debt for the United States was just $1 trillion (in present-day dollars). Over the past thirty-five years, though, and with no major wars or depressions on the scale of America's Great Depression, the United States has managed to add $16 trillion to its national debt, and all projections indicate there is no end in sight when it comes to growth in our country's public debt.

III. Taking Balls Away from the Juggler

Smith's recognition of the juggling tricks in public finances, although chiefly concerned with the historical examples in the aforementioned section of *The Wealth of Nations*, is an accurate statement about the nature of public finances more generally. Monarchies, dictatorships, and democracies all face the same challenge of keeping their people happy on the one hand while advancing their own interests on the other. The public choice revolution in economics[9] of the_1960s shed light on the fact that even democratic governments from the same inherent problems Smith described 240 years ago.

As public choice economics has taught us, elected officials face similar incentives to kings and queen. They want to maintain power; they want legacies; and they want to raise funds for their own agendas at the lowest possible cost. To raise revenue, they either can tax people now, tax people later (and issue IOUs in the form of debt now), or inflate. Tax hikes on current citizens are widely unpopular, so governments throughout history have sought to "kick the can down the road" by deferring taxes through borrowing and using inflation to pay for wars,

[9] James Buchanan and Gordon Tullock, *The Calculus of Consent* (Ann Arbor: University of Michigan Press, 1962).

major public works projects, etc. The bias in nation-states, according to Smith and public choice economists, is towards "juggling tricks" and "free lunch" policies, which deliver some perceived benefit to people now at the expense of everyone in the long run.

The strong incentive for jugglers to exist in the domain of public finance, coupled with the large body of historical evidence indicating nation states almost always succumb to ruinous financing, has led many economists to focus on institutions, rules, and mechanisms capable of limiting the power of governments. Many economists have called for an independent central bank; others, such as Milton Friedman and John Taylor, have suggested central banks should at least be following broad monetary rules instead of making decisions based on discretion. Similar calls for rules, such as a balanced budget amendment at the federal level or spending rules tied to economic growth, have been suggested.

Rules and alternative institutions are appealing because they limit the tricks the juggler can play, and they take certain juggling opportunities off the table. These measures may be appealing in theory, but they are difficult to imagine in practice because they involve leaders falling on their swords and sacrificing short-term political benefits for the greater long-term good. Thus, taking balls away from the juggler probably requires a more radical set of concomitant fiscal reforms.

Reverse revenue sharing, for example, would get the federal government out of the business of taxing and would delegate the revenue correction problem to the states. Unlike the Articles of Confederation, which encouraged free-riding by states, each state could be required to contribute to the federal government. Rather than being trapped in a system that hampers citizens and creates massive deadweight losses through a one-size-fits all federal system, people could "vote with their feet" and choose different tax systems in different states.

Solutions such as reverse revenue sharing as a way to limit the juggler, of course, are a reach when the current realities of economic and political reform are considered. Radical reforms with the broad goal of limiting the juggling tricks, however, become more and more crucial with each trillion dollar increase in our country's debts. And, the longer any country waits to deal with its fiscal problems, the more radical the reforms must be, which, in the limit for Smith often means an open and avowed bankruptcy.

IV. Putting an End to the Cycle of Juggling Tricks

The alternative to reforming now, according to Smith, is inevitable bankruptcy later. Experiences in the private sector and municipal bankruptcy shed some light on what a larger federal write-down might look like. The millions of Americans entitled to benefits through Social Security and Medicare, for example, might experience a "haircut" on the benefits they actually receive. State-owned assets, such as the 20 percent of US land controlled by the federal government, could be auctioned off. Taxes across the board would rise.

By failing to pay on our $17 trillion of promises made and nearly $200 trillion of true liabilities, Americans would see the emperor (or juggler, in Smith's case) has no clothes. People's expectations about government promises would be dashed. The moment when the jugglers are discovered is a moment when people realize many government promises were nothing more than empty rhetoric; they were, as Dani Rodrik, describes them nothing more than, "Promises, Promises."[10] Smith remains silent on whether the discovery moment is a good thing, but he insists on an open and transparent process of bankruptcy to correct the tricks. As the tricks are fully revealed, the government's credibility and its ability to borrow in the future would be compromised. As we have indeed observed at the municipal level and across many countries susceptible to default, interest rates on future debt issuance soar, and the long-term consequences of reneging persist.

Short of bankruptcy, our best hopes for limiting the juggler in modern-day economies may very well be to call on people to "think big" and consider radical alternatives to the current system. Breaking free

[10] Dani Rodrik, "Promises, Promises: Credible Policy Reform Via Signaling," *Economic Journal* 99 (September 1989): 756–72.

from the cycle of deficits, debt, and debasement requires thinking about the necessary and proper functions of a nation state. For Smith, it meant calling on the British Empire, for example, to give up on amusing "the people with the imagination that they possessed a great empire on the west side of the Atlantic" and instead "realize this golden dream, in which they have been indulging themselves, perhaps, as well as the people; or, that they should awake from it themselves, and endeavor to awaken the people" (*WN*, 947).

Basic financial realities, in other words, prompt a day of reckoning. The day of reckoning comes, as it did for Great Britain during colonialism and as it appears to be coming for the United States, thanks to our bloated welfare state. For the US in 1776, the juggler's tricks meant an end to British rule and the beginning experiment called the American experience. For us today in 2015, when the juggler and his pretend payments are made obvious to all, perhaps freedom and demands for liberty emerge as a byproduct of an otherwise insane financial moment, just as they did for America during the time of Smith's writing on the topic in 1776.

8 | Liberal Learning in the Marketplace

Thinking About Liberal Education With Adam Smith

Joseph M. Knippenberg

I make no claims to a high level of expertise in the philosophy of Adam Smith. This is the first time I have spoken about Smith outside of a classroom setting. I assign selections from *The Theory of Moral Sentiments* and *The Wealth of Nations* in a sophomore-level core course, so the students and I discuss his work without any of us proposing to specialize in it. The irony of approaching Smith in this way is certainly not lost on me.

Nonetheless, I think that it makes sense to think about liberal education with Smith because we live, work, educate, and are educated in a "market society." It is impossible not to think about the "job market," the "higher education marketplace," and so on. The notion of liberal education certainly antedates the ascendancy of the capitalist market, and the question of how the two fit together, if at all, ought to be taken seriously by all those who profess to be devoted to liberal learning in the contemporary world.

Let me take as my point of departure Smith's discussion of the division of labor in Book I of *WN*. There he argues that this very division of labor is the principal cause of the wealth of nations, perhaps the most important consideration in an account of the human good. The great collective wealth, from which we all benefit to one degree or another, follows from the division of any complex work into a multitude of smaller tasks. In the course of explaining why this arrangement is so productive, Smith makes a number of arguments, the last of which has to do with the role of inventions and machinery in enabling us to accomplish these smaller and simpler tasks more efficiently and hence more productively. Many labor-saving machines are themselves, he avers, products of the division of labor: “Men are much more likely to discover easier and readier methods of attaining any object, when the whole attention of their minds is directed towards that simple object, than when it is dissipated among a great variety of things.”[1]

There are a few of things about this statement that are noteworthy. In the first place, Smith is stating what is arguably a general truth about the human mind: at least when it is seeking means toward an end, it gains power through a narrowed focus. In any human endeavor, it would seem, specialization seems to produce greater results than synopsis and synthesis, than taking a sort of grand overview. The latter seems, as Smith says, to be kind of “dissipation,” hardly a compliment in any circumstance. Second, this observation has no necessary bearing on theory for its own sake. Means-end rationality, or (if you will) instrumental reason, profits from this narrow focus. It is hard to believe that (grand) theorizing as an end in itself would similarly benefit. It would not then be “grand,” would it?

I shall return to this last point soon and then again later, when I consider what Smith has to say about “unproductive labor.” At the moment it is sufficient to note that when one is—as Smith is—concerned with the wealth of nations, narrow specialization seems to be the order of the day. Of course, this may be as much a reflection on the natural limitations of the human mind as anything else: the proud multi-tasker probably does most of his or her tasks rather badly. And Smith appears in general not to be too impressed by human genius, referring as he does (for example) to the “vanity” of the philosopher who thinks himself so much naturally better than the common street porter.[2]

Immediately after making this argument about specialization and the improvement of productive processes, Smith revises it slightly, averring that *some* (not “many”) of the improvements come from a different source:

[1] Robert L. Heilbroner, ed., *The Essential Adam Smith* (New York: W. W. Norton, 1986) 165. *WN* I.1.

[2] Ibid., 170.

> Many improvements have been made by the ingenuity of the makers of the machines, when to make them became the business of a peculiar trade; and some by that of those who are called philosophers or men of speculation, whose trade it is, not to do anything, but to observe every thing; and who, upon that account, are often capable of combining together the powers of the most distant and dissimilar objects.[3]

Here we have theory, not necessarily as an end in itself or for its own sake, but as a "trade" that specializes in synthesis. Indeed, Smith is quite explicit about the "trade-like" quality of philosophy thus understood: "In the progress of society, philosophy or speculation becomes, like every other employment, the principal or sole trade and occupation of a particular class of citizens."[4]

The one who engages in theoretical synthesis or synopsis is a specialist just like everyone else, even if his or her specialty involves a broader sweep of vision and less focus on a simple object. But Smith is not yet done with his account of specialization in philosophy:

> Like every other employment too, it is subdivided into a great number of different branches, each of which affords occupation to a peculiar tribe or class of philosophers; and this subdivision of employment in philosophy, as well as in every other business, improves dexterity, and saves time. Each individual becomes more expert in his own peculiar branch, more work is done upon the whole, and the quantity of science is considerably increased by it.[5]

In a sense, this might seem to defeat the purpose of synopsis and synthesis, if the philosophers are specialists just like everyone else. Smith may be right about the "quantity" of science being "considerably increased by it," but what about the quality? If philosophy is specialized, how can the objects compared be "most distant and dissimilar"? What we have here is something that seems most closely to resemble the division

[3] *WN* I.2.
[4] *WN* I.1.
[5] Ibid.

of the academy into disciplines, with synthesis occurring perhaps in an interdisciplinary or multidisciplinary setting. It seems to be more of an antithesis to than an apotheosis of liberal learning.

Thus far, we might argue that—so far as he is concerned with the wealth of nations—Adam Smith seems to be no great friend of liberal learning in the traditional sense. He does not adopt the Aristotelian gentleman's disdain for professionalization or specialization, and he certainly does not seem to care for what we might call Socratic philosophizing for its own sake. If theory is for the sake of practice—for the sake, that is, of increasing the wealth of nations—we would seem to gain everything by specialization and apparently lose nothing by abandoning the traditional liberal view.

There are two caveats worth noting here. The first follows from Smith's reference to "the quantity of science" that is increased by specialization. Strictly speaking, this is a "theoretical," not a practical, concern. Regardless of any payoffs in productivity or wealth, specialization would increase the quantity of science. We should favor it, even if we were not necessarily concerned with increasing the wealth of nations. If we care about knowledge for its own sake, in other words, we might favor specialization just as much as if we cared solely about increasing wealth. If there are two facets of the concern with liberal learning—one opposing "professionalization" in the name of breadth, the other favoring theory as an end in itself—Smith's claim would seem to suggest the two are at odds: those who wish to promote knowledge for its own sake would also have to favor specialization. We cannot have it both ways.

A second caveat seems to tend in a different direction. As I noted a few moments ago, if the "philosophers or men of speculation" are indeed increasingly specialized, it would be difficult for them genuinely to combine together "the powers of the most distant and dissimilar objects." If this combination is indeed desirable—either for innovation or for its own sake—it cannot be promoted by mere specialization.

Let me put these two points together in the following, somewhat paradoxical, way. Specialization increases the quantity of science but undermines the possibility of a certain sort of innovation—not that which depends upon it, but rather that which depends upon synopsis and synthesis. Scientists who diligently till their own disciplinary gardens contribute to the quantity of science and to the wealth of nations (whether they intend the latter or not). But their disciplinary discipline (if I may be permitted such an awkward expression) militates against a certain kind of innovation, one that requires ignoring or breaking disciplinary boundaries. The latter undertaking cannot be justified by any sort of attention to the wealth of nations, until it can, that is, until it produces the unexpected result that adds to the sum of our knowledge and/or to our wealth. In other words, for the sake of innovation, productivity, and wealth, we may have to indulge mere, apparently pointless, curiosity, because it from time to time will produce something genuinely new and important. Such mere curiosity will increasingly go against the grain of a society devoted to specialization and wealth creation, but it is difficult to see how such a society can, in the end, do without it.

There is some good news and some bad news here. The good news is that, left to their own devices, different people will pursue different paths, with the result that some may be attracted to a "trade" that involves comparing different and dissimilar objects. We could be the beneficiaries of the unintended consequences of ordinary (or extraordinary) human curiosity. The bad news is that, especially in the short term, the market is likeliest to reward the narrow specialization that shows the most promise of producing immediate results.

Toward the end of *WN*, Smith returns to this issue. The context here is his account of the responsibility of government to provide certain public goods, in particular, education. He presents education in the first instance as a remedy for the stultifying and narrowing effects of the division of labor, which leads many to become "as stupid and ignorant as it is possible for a human creature to become."[6] The remedy for this is

[6] *WN* V.1.3.2.

not for everyone to become liberally educated—heaven forbid!—but for the state to provide for, in essence, universal primary (and secondary?) education. In the course of making this argument, Smith contrasts "barbarous" and "civilized" societies. In the former, human beings are called upon to provide almost all their needs on their own, with the result that "[i]nvention is kept alive, and the mind is not suffered to fall into that drowsy stupidity, which, in a civilized society, seems to benumb the understanding of almost all the inferior ranks of people."[7] In the latter, the only people, it seems, who are afforded similar challenges to keep their minds flexible are the theorists:

> In a civilized state...though there is little variety in the occupations of the greater part of individuals, there is an almost infinite variety in those of the whole society. These varied occupations present an almost infinite variety of objects to the contemplation of those few, who, being attached to no particular occupation themselves, have leisure and inclination to examine the occupations of other people. The contemplation of so great a variety of objects necessarily exercises their minds in endless comparisons and combinations, and renders their understandings, in an extraordinary degree, both acute and comprehensive.[8]

While most people in a "civilized society" run the risk of a certain sort of dehumanization, paying dearly for the great opulence to which they contribute through the division of labor, a few stand to gain extraordinarily by taking advantage of that opulence to gain leisure and contemplating the very complexity that a fully developed division of labor produces. Here Smith's concern is not with productivity, but rather with what we might call intellectual acuity, the development of which requires both "leisure and inclination."

He does not neglect the social and political consequences that might follow from this development. If we do not find positions for these people so we can take advantage of their learning, "their great abilities, though honorable to themselves, may contribute very little to the good

[7] Ibid.

[8] *WN* V.1.3.2.

government or happiness of their society."[9] In other words, if such people are not afforded the opportunity to apply in practice what they have gained through theory (in the original sense of observation or contemplation), government and society stand to gain little or nothing from their "great abilities." It is not clear what Smith has in mind here, as he speaks of these observers "happen[ing] to be placed in some very particular situations,"[10] as if their influence would not be by anyone's design, but rather by accident (thanks, perhaps, to the "invisible hand").

It is worth noting in this connection that Smith speaks here of the possible benefits to either government or society. He is not obviously calling for those with political power to elevate these people into positions of political leadership or responsibility. After all, those who "happen to be" in positions of political power may not themselves be capable of recognizing great intellectual talent when they see it. It is just as likely that they will elevate crackpots as geniuses. And in any event it is very likely that they will elevate those who are saying, or are willing to tell them, what they want to hear. As Smith says in a different context, "I have never known much good to be done by those who affected to trade for the public good."[11]

Furthermore, as Smith makes abundantly clear on more than one occasion, it is not just the manner in which our intellects serve our interests, but also the limited character of our intellects, that justifies modesty in this connection:

> The statesman, who should attempt to direct private people in what manner they ought to employ their capitals, would not only load himself with a most unnecessary attention, but assume an authority which could not safely be trusted, not only to no single person, but to no council or senate whatever, and which would nowhere be so dangerous as in the

[9] Ibid.

[10] Ibid.

[11] *WN* IV.2.

hands of a man who had folly and presumption enough to fancy himself fit to exercise it.[12]

Smith does not deny that there is a public good; he simply denies that we, generally speaking, have the capacity to discern it or the interest to pursue it as something apart from our own interests. He implies that landowners might have the leisure necessary to discern that good, but all too often their leisure leads to "indolence."[13] Even in this case, Smith suggests that it is not so much their intellect (even rightly applied) as it is the "strict and inseparable"[14] connection of their interest with the public interest that would enable them to promote the latter, were they able to discern it.

Where do all these considerations leave us? Let me offer a couple of preliminary conclusions. First, the market rewards the narrowness of specialization, rather than breadth of vision, however much it relies upon the latter for certain sorts of innovation. Second, when a person who happens to specialize—so to speak—in synthesis and synopsis offers something for the benefit of society, there is no guarantee that society will pay attention, and no reliable program for assuring that it will. Indeed, programs meant to bring innovation to the marketplace from "on high" run the risk simply of putting in place, and indeed reinforcing, the selfish or mistaken judgment of a political leader. Under these circumstances, people like Smith himself, whose intellect ranged widely over a number of subjects, would seem to be orphans, not favored by the marketplace and favored by the government only at their peril.

If there is a saving grace, it comes from the very market that discourages what my institution has long called the "humane generalist." Here I would advance two considerations, one from Smith's discussion of productive and unproductive labor and the other from his treatment of education. What unites them is that the great abundance produced by a "civilized" society with a fully developed division of labor leaves room for

[12] Ibid.

[13] *WN* I.II conclusion

[14] Ibid., 225.

all sorts of "waste." Not every one of Smith's capitalists will be one of Max Weber's Calvinists who abhors leisure and invests every last penny of his or her profit back into the business. Rather, some will consume (so to speak) "luxury goods" like liberal education and the arts.

Let me begin with Smith's account of productive and unproductive labor. The former, he says, produces something of value that is "vendible"[15]; in other words, there is a product external to the labor that can be sold, yielding a revenue that leaves a profit beyond the human and material costs of production. By contrast, unproductive labor leaves no such profit. The services of an unproductive laborer "generally perish in the very instant of their performance, and seldom leave any trace or value behind them, for which an equal quantity of service could afterward be procured."[16] Thus people "waste" money on servants or entertainment, when they could invest it productively and turn a profit. Smith's list of unproductive laborers is quite telling:

> The sovereign, for example, with all the officers both of justice and war who serve under him, the whole army and navy, are unproductive laborers.... In the same class must be ranked, some both of the gravest and most important, and some of the most frivolous professions: churchmen, lawyers, physicians, men of letters of all kinds; players, buffoons, musicians, opera singers, opera dancers, etc.[17]

Many on the list arguably receive (at least in our day and age) what might be called a liberal education. And since, as Smith next observes, the "annual produce of the land and labor of the country"[18] pays the wages of both productive and unproductive laborers, the more that is devoted to the latter, the less that can be devoted to the former. When our productive laborers are very productive, we can afford more unproductive laborers as well. When a nation is wealthy, it has room for

[15] *WN* II.3.
[16] Ibid.
[17] *WN* II.3.
[18] Ibid., 235.

more people who do not obviously contribute to its wealth. Of course, there is a perfectly reasonable "bias" in favor of productivity, but it is hard to imagine a nation without both grave and frivolous unproductive laborers.

If there is anything that those of us on the unproductive side of things ought to take away from Smith's account, it is that we should probably not bite the hand that so profligately feeds us. The more wealth that is generated by productive labor, the more that can be "wasted" on us. We can decry the bias in the marketplace against our sort of undertaking, but, as I said, this is a perfectly reasonable bias, one that contributes to the very wealth that ultimately supports us.

The second consideration takes as its point of departure Smith's remarks about "the employments…in which people of some rank and fortune spend the greater part of their lives."[19] Unlike the jobs that are stultifying and narrowing, "[t]hey are almost all of them extremely complicated, and as such exercise the head more than the hands."[20] Furthermore, they "are seldom such as harass them from morning to night," leaving them "a good deal of leisure, during which they may perfect themselves in every branch either of useful or ornamental knowledge of which they may have laid the foundation, or for which they have acquired some taste in the earlier part of life."[21] Leaving aside for the moment whether our people of some rank and fortune have (or allow themselves) as much leisure as did Smith's contemporaries, we can see here both that a developed economy affords opportunities for what we now call lifelong learning and how we in the liberal arts can prepare the way for it. Our task is to lay the intellectual foundations and to cultivate our students' taste.

In the end, we are compelled, I think, to take the good with the bad. A Smithian market economy does not favor either leisure or liberal learning; it does not smile upon either theory for its own sake or upon

[19] *WN* V.1.3.2.

[20] Ibid.

[21] Ibid.

taking a broad view of the world. But it does produce wealth and hence leisure, and (thankfully) leaves it up to individuals how they will use that leisure. Some may give themselves over to frivolity (think *Duck Dynasty*, poker night with the guys, or a neighborhood Bunko party), but others will not use it productively, but nonetheless well. How they use it depends in some part at least upon us, the teachers.

What we should not do, as teachers, is complain about the marketplace and invite someone with authority to "fix" it. To see why, we need only consult the ways in which our political leaders generally approach higher education. They focus on efficiency of delivery, "college completion" (without any real regard for whether those who complete their education actually learn anything), and (when they do pay attention to content) workforce development. Education doubtless is an economic development tool, but it is or can be much more than that. That "more" can only flourish in the spaces left by the market economy. It is a luxury good, available to those who are fortunate enough to acquire a taste for it. It has always in a sense been that; we can only hope that it will continue to be available for those who seek it.

9 | Is Adam Smith a Buddhist?

Contemplative Inquiry and Political Philosophy

Eduardo Velásquez

> "Unless," I said, "the philosophers rule as kings or those now called kings and chiefs genuinely philosophize, and political power and philosophy coincide in the same place, while the many natures now making their way to either apart from the other are by necessity excluded, there is no rest from ills for the cities, my dear Glaucon, nor I think for human kind, nor will the regime we have now described in speech ever come forth from nature, in so far as possible and see the light of the sun. That was what for so long was causing my hesitation to speak: seeing how paradoxically it would be to say. For it is hard to see that in no other city would there be private and public happiness."[1]

> "Science in its core, in its active, living core it is pure contemplation. It has little or nothing to do with manipulation."[2]

I

Of all the possible areas of study universities offer, why do students major in political science? Of those who major in political science, how many enter politics after earning a Bachelor of Arts degree? Say students believe that no career in politics is viable without a law degree. Who among the hundreds of B.A.- J.Ds. win a seat in local, state, or national

[1] *The Republic of Plato: Translation with Notes by an Interpretive Essay by Allan Bloom*, 2nd ed. (New York: Basic Books, 1991) 153–54.

[2] *Monte Grande* (July 30, 2007). Icarus Films. Directed by Franz Reichle. Online. https://vimeo.com/30813744, accessed July 2, 2013. Quotation begins at 22 minutes, 18 seconds.

government? Did a *science* of politics get them in office? Once there, did a science of politics provide the method of good government?

Prudence is arguably the principal virtue of politics, not *science*. Judgments are contextual. The right choice in one context isn't in another. Policy is compromise. In emergencies the opposite is true. Political action in the service of life and death is often swift and decisive. Devotion to principle necessary in one context is folly and political suicide in another. Discerning the right means to right ends doesn't unfold in an uninterrupted deduction of causes to effects.

Were a science of politics the way to political virtues, those would not be, as some claim of science, "value free." Our global political landscape depicts a variety of regimes, from despotism to democracy. Say we agree that discerning the relative merits of despotic and democratic arises from a detached, indifferent, and morally neutral perspective. Is the judgment in favor of one over another morally neutral?

Scientists may rightly wonder about any and all claims to a scientific study of politics. Walk over to the science lab and ask a chemist, biologist, or physicist whether she thinks politics is a science. Can't you see them raise both hands to the side of each ear flexing index and middle fingers then saying really do you think there is a "science" of politics? Political scientists harbor the same doubts. For example, search for "science" at the American Political Science Association (APSA), the premier academic and professional association governing all manner of things political science. At the APSA the study of politics is parsed into forty-something sub-disciplines, the proliferation of which isn't likely to abate: "State Politics and Policy," "Sexuality and Politics," "Women and Politics Research," "Politics, Literature, and Film," "New Political Science," "Experimental Research," "Law and Courts," and "Canadian Politics." The APSA recognizes Canada but not Germany, Barbados, or South Korea. Why? Is the answer *science* or *expediency*? The APSA legitimizes "African Politics Conference Group" and "European Politics and Society" but not Asia, Middle East, Latin America, or the Caribbean. Again, why? Three sub-fields are deemed worthy of the name "science." None among them all is "philosophy." Political philosophers in the discipline of political science labor under the auspices of "Politics, Literature, and Film" and "Foundations of Political Thought." For political philosophers in political science the choice is between politics as fiction or as foundation. We can only wonder whether thus subsumed, philosophy is not science; in fact, it isn't really "thought."

Most introductions to political science do not include Adam Smith. *The Theory of Moral Sentiments* (*TMS*) looks like a constellation of stories, each one of them brilliant, but not by any stretch of the imagination.

There are a few paths from political science into contemplative studies, whose authority rests on the neurosciences. Within academic political philosophy, contemplation is barely mentioned. It won't be long, however, before we hear scholars debate contemplation in Hannah Arendt, Josef Pieper, Pierre Hadot, Eric Voegelin, Leo Strauss, Alexander Nehamas, and Michel Foucault. "Projects" on political emotions will find fodder in Merleau-Ponty's *Phenomenology of Perception*. Francisco Varela's co-authored *The Embodied Mind: Cognitive Science and Human Experience* is likely to become a "seminal text" in an emerging contemplative political science and/or philosophy. All of a sudden we'll remember the phenomenological sources of Voegelin and Strauss's critique of behavioral political science. That is a start, and there is much to recommend.

I am not here to extol the virtues of Adam Smith's *TMS* as a science. That said, I am persuaded that *TMS* is contemplative because it is phenomenological. To say that Smith's *TMS* is phenomenological is not quite the same as saying that Smith wrote about phenomenology. I am suggesting that Smith's *TMS* is a phenomenological exercise. The *TMS* brings readers to contemplative experiences. It also represents empirical evidence of those experiences. Smith's *TMS* is scientific. It is *theoretical*. To understand Smith we must come to terms with what the book does. Smith *shows* considerably more than he *tells*.

II.

Contemplative studies is a young discipline. It remains amorphous and ill-defined. The Association for Contemplative Mind in Higher Education was founded in 2008. To date, it has little or no traction in political science. "Contemplation" may sound just as esoteric as "philosophy." Substitute "mindfulness" for "contemplation," and we move farther from a science of politics as conceived by the likes of Thomas Hobbes. Naming Smith's *TMS* "mindful" isn't likely to inspire much confidence among the professoriate in the science of politics. Mindfulness may be about yoga or navel-gazing, nothing to do with the hardcore stuff of *Realpolitik.*

Not without, after all, due cause. Consider the short history of mindfulness in American culture. Google "mindfulness" and see for yourself. Even among Buddhist traditions of comprehensive mind training you will find no single, abstract entity called *mindfulness*. Within those traditions mindfulness has a place, it is usually *right* mindfulness, among the practices of life-long mind training. In American culture, mindfulness is considered to be a fad, so much so that contemplative neuroscientists studying brain and behavior refer the various distortions of mind-body disciplines in American pop culture as "McMindfulness." This disparagement is not without good reason. Mindfulness is therapy, business, and burlesque. On Amazon.com, a search for mindfulness returns 10,000 results. A sure sign that mindfulness is here may be the publication of *Mindfulness Workbook for Dummies*. While perhaps not a first-tier peer-reviewed journal, *Psychology Today* published "Mindfulness to Enhance Sexual Pleasure" and "How Mindfulness Makes for Yummy Sex."

Mindfulness also went corporate in a hurry. It is at the core of human and non-human "resource" management at Google, Target, and General Mills, and not only for the corporate executive toiling at the top of the ladder. There is vitality and vigor in contemporary pop culture mindfulness. The Seattle Seahawks organization is one among numerous professional sports teams with mindfulness programs for athletes and staff.[3] From sports to politics, mindfulness is rapidly becoming *the* oldest game in town. Ohio Congressman Tim Ryan, author of *The Mindful Nation*, touts the virtues of mindfulness as personal practice and public policy.[4] Cultural historians of our generation may very well look back at the turn of the twenty-first century and agree that mindfulness was America's third or fourth "Great Awakening."

In colleges and universities in the United States, the word isn't *mindfulness*. It is *contemplation*. The differences are and aren't semantic. Mindfulness is a word with an etymology rooted in the East; contemplation is of the West. From the Sanskrit *smṛti*, mindfulness is loosely translated into "awareness," from the Pali *sati* "memory." Contemplation resonates with mindfulness. Two of the leading lights of the contemplative movement in higher education refer to contemplation as follows:

> There are many kinds of contemplative practices, and they are used to achieve many different outcomes. The word contemplation derives from *contemplari*, to "gaze attentively," but the word was originally linked to the act of cutting out or creating a space, as in "to mark out a space for observation." The word temple comes from this definition: a place reserved or cut out for observance. In many ways, the practices we are discussing provide this space for students to allow them to observe and gain insight. Introspection is inward (*intro*) looking (*specere*)— the mental act of attending carefully to what is occurring within, often in response to an activity, theory, or text.[5]

[3] Alyssa Roenigk, "Lotus Pose on Two," *ESPN Magazine*, 21 August 2013, http://espn.go.com/nfl/story/_/id/9581925/seattle-seahawks-use-unusual-techniques-practice-espn-magazine, (accessed 28 November 2013).

[4] Tim Ryan, *A Mindful Nation: How a Simple Practice Can Help Us Reduce Stress, Improve Performance, and Recapture the American Spirit* (Carlsbad, CA: Hay House, 2012).

[5] Daniel Barbezat and Mirabai Bush, *Contemplative Practices in Higher Education: Powerful Methods to Transform Teaching and Learning* (Wiley). Kindle Edition. P. 21, Location 790.

Riding on a wave of dazzling discoveries in the neural net, "contemplative inquiry" and "contemplative studies" are permeating all academic disciplines. The consequences are staggering. Via contemplative mind in higher education there is a movement underfoot reinvigorating, revolutionizing, and radically reinterpreting the intellectual structures of the "Western university" (this gross abstraction will have to do for now). Nothing akin to contemplation has been seen in the Western university since its conception in the academies of ancient Greece and the schools of medieval Europe. The two principal academic and professional associations that authorize and support contemplative inquiry are the Center for Contemplative Mind in Society (CMS) and The Association for Contemplative Mind in Higher Education (ACMHE). Appropriately, both call themselves contemplative, not mindful or mindfulness. Mindfulness is derived from various Eastern practices, contemplation from Western. Contemplation affirms what is already in the traditions of higher education in the West. Indeed, as those who understand the West's grounding in the contemplative traditions of classical Greece and medieval Christianity will attest contemplation is arguably the Western university's reason for being.

Contemporary contemplative inquiry wasn't reborn in the womb of Plato, Aristotle, St. Augustine, and St. Thomas Aquinas. Contemporary contemplative inquiry returned to the "West" via the "East." Howsoever commonplace the alliance between Western science and Tibetan Buddhism may become in the years ahead, we shouldn't cease to be amazed by the alliance. Cognitive scientists at the frontier of brain and behavior research went in search of the postulates of Western science in the meditating brain of Tibetan Buddhist monks. Ancient practices developed with no Western science whatsoever and in no need of assistance from Western science are not thought to illumine the qualities of mind essential a proper understanding of mind and a good life.[6] From

[6] Hundreds of studies argue the benefits of non-discursive mindfulness practices. A brief introduction could start with Makiko Kitamura, "Harvard Yoga Scientists Find

that initial encounter of Western brain-mind-body science and Buddhist practices begins the recovery of Western contemplative modes that were Western schools' *raison d'etre*.

III.

Contemplation has been written about, its virtues of mind-disciplines extolled, and practices promulgated from the beginnings of the Western academy. We've been reminded by near contemporaries of the vitality of contemplation in Western modes by writers so varied they are not easily coalesced into a "school of thought." Josef Pieper, Pierre Hadot, Hannah Arendt each narrates the history of contemplative inquiry in the West. Before them, phenomenologists such as Franz Brentano, Edmund Husserl, German and French existentialists then offered alternatives to scientific rationalism. Out of philosophical phenomenology several eclectic and unconventional thinkers, among them Leo Strauss, Eric Voegelin, and Maurice Merleau-Ponty began to open up a contemplative space. The first two are well known among political scientists for their scathing critiques of the prevailing "science" of politics. They also wrote in ways that confounded readers who expected a Rational socio-scientific discourse. Recall, Smith writes an enactment, not merely an explanation.

We notice a lull as political science continued its quest to transform itself into a science, and for the last few decades political philosophy continues as a second rate subdiscipline of political science. This is true in liberal arts colleges as well where the Western tradition as a whole is upheld and passed on to the next generation. Whether academic contemplation will go the way of pop culture mindfulness is an open question.

Adam Smith may very well be helpful. For through him we may see that there is a rich contemplative tradition within the frame of Western

Proof of Meditation Benefit," *Bloomberg*, 21 November 2013, http://www.bloomberg.com/news/2013-11-22/harvard-yoga-scientists-find-proof-of-meditation-benefit.html, (accessed 29 November 2013).

Rationalism that expanded our understanding of Reason. Smith wrote out of the excess of Enlightenment rationalism from within that tradition. He offered a theory of embodied and emotive rationality. Smith wasn't alone, of course. Jean-Jacques Rousseau also called into question the rational, self-serving egoist. We see the same temperament in the novels of Jane Austen. Politics and society are not fabrications from the rational calculus of consent among beasts in a lawless state of nature. Smith's teacher, David Hume, also harbored doubts about the qualities and characteristics of rational "natural laws." Hume's story of "identity" is foreboding and prescient, compare Hume to Daniel Dennett's fictive self.[7]

Smith offers a perspective that may assist anyone who finds pleasure in reading old books of philosophy and wondering what all the fuss about "contemplation" means. The case for Smith's "Eastern" sensibilities, if you wish to call them that, are present in Hume. Alison Gopnik makes a plausible case for a flesh and blood encounter between David Hume and Buddhism. If Hume knew of Buddhism, he most likely learned it from Charles Francois Dolu, a Jesuit scholar in residence at the Royal College of La Flèche between 1723 and 1740. Those dates are not insubstantial, for in those years Hume wrote his monumental *The Treatise of Human Nature* (1735–1737), in residence at the Royal College of La Flèche.[8]

Howsoever important historical connections are, my purpose is not to suggest that Smith's teacher and friend David Hume was a devotee of Buddhism and hence Smith would be also. After a decade of reading and rereading Smith, I first shared thoughts of Smith's affinities with Eastern thought. I suggested to an audience at the McDonald Center for

[7] Daniel Dennett, "The Self as a Center of Narrative Gravity," in F. Kessel, P. Cole and D. Johnson, eds., *Self and Consciousness: Multiple Perspectives* (Hillsdale, NJ: Erlbaum, 1992).

[8] Alison Gopnik, "Could David Hume Have Known about Buddhism? Charles Francois Dolu, the Royal College of La Flèche, and the Global Jesuit Intellectual Network," *Hume Studies* 35/1 and 2 (2009): 5–28.

America's Founding Principles at Mercer University during the 6th Annual A. V. Elliot Conference, April 2013, how we might imagine Smith as an "embodied" political philosopher.

I did not offer a contemplative Smith that was "historically based," however. My awareness of Smith's Eastern affinities did not come from reading academic journals. They came from within my own contemplative practices. Through practices that called me to see my own mind in action and not to mistake that action for my reading of a theory, I began to see how Smith moves toward contemplative and mindful states of mind. Conceptually, Smith's "sympathy" reworks "pity" and "compassion." Smith's ephemeral "self" that is constituted through the gaze of another "self," his sober analysis of "systems" of utility all resonate with what emerges from the burgeoning new field of contemplative studies.

For the occasion of this essay and book, I offer the reader preparatory work. I am not here to rain down conclusions that establish a new "contemplative Smith." In due course we shall see an industry of Smith's contemplative "spectator," "bystander," "impartial spectator," demigod in the breast," and "conscience."

Arriving at the prospects of Smith "contemplative philosopher" requires that we acknowledge a simple distinction: namely, between contemplation in Smith's philosophy or theory and Smith a philosopher contemplating. The distinction might be seen as between (1) a scientist scanning, measuring, and representing the mind of a monk in the midst of contemplative practice and (2) contemplation from within the practice of a contemplating monk.

IV.

In the aftermath of the Second World War a relatively unknown teacher and scholar delivered a pair of lectures in Bonn, Germany. Imagine an academic standing before an audience calling into question the imperative of "work" in the thicket of postwar reconstruction? Yet this is precisely what Josef Pieper did. Undergraduates reading *Leisure: The*

Basis of Culture in political philosophy courses often react with the same incredulity and indignation.[9] Pieper's *Leisure* is an unflattering mirror of the state of education, and we teachers of undergraduates are framed by the same image. By propagating the idolatry of "total work," Pieper said, the victorious allied forces unwittingly succumbed to their totalitarian foe. Having "won" the war on the ground and in the air, they lost hearts and minds, dare I say their own souls to inhumane and totalitarian ideologies. "For assuming all too rashly, for the moment, that our new house is going to be built in the Western tradition," Pieper said well aware of his audience's reaction "—a thing so arguable that it might almost be said to be the decision which is hanging in the balance—it is essential to begin by reckoning with the fact that one of the foundations of Western culture is leisure."[10]

Leisure is not spare time, holiday, a weekend or vacation. It is not a restorative pause before and after activities. Most emphatically Pieper separated leisure from idleness. Leisure "is a mental and spiritual attitude."[11] It is a form of "that silence which is the prerequisite of the apprehension of reality." [12] Contemplation, insofar as it points etymologically to "look" (the Latin *contemplatio* and the Greek *theoria*), "means to open one's eyes receptively to whatever offers itself to one's vision." [13] Contemplative leisure opens space for those inaudible ministrations of insight and intuition (*simplex intuitus*). We have not solved the riddle of inside and outside, me and you, I and other. We do know that mind is complex and interdependent. Greek philosophers and

[9] Among the few undergraduate theses I supervised at Washington and Lee University, I call attention to Rachel Alexander, "Contemplation in Political Philosophy," Washington and Lee University, Honor's Thesis, Department of Politics, 2013, http://academia.edu/3261891/Contemplation_In_Political_ Philosophy (accessed 15 July 2013).

[10] Ibid., 46.

[11] Ibid., 49.

[12] Ibid., 26.

[13] Ibid., 28.

Medieval Christians were not simpletons. They knew what we are now rediscovering: that mind is *Ratio*, "the power of discursive, logical thought, of searching and examination, of abstraction, of definition and drawing conclusions";[14] and that mind is *Intellectus* or "non-discursive vision."[15] Mind is "both these things in one...simultaneously *ratio* and *intellectus*." Knowing and the "process of knowing is the action of the two together."[16]

According to Pieper, leisurely contemplation is "the source of the distinction between *artes liberales* and *artes serviles*, the liberal arts and servile work."[17] In Greek leisure is *skole*, in Latin *scola*. "The word used to designate the place where we educate and teach is derived from a word which means 'leisure'. 'School' does not, properly speaking, mean school, but leisure." [18] We should not mistake leisurely contemplation for quietude or resignation. In *Happiness and Contemplation*, Pieper wrote, "acting does not consist only in building, establishing, producing, struggling, killing. Cognition, for example, is true activity. That is to say, it is a realization of the potentialities inherent in the living cell."[19]

If Pieper is correct and contemplation is the *raison d'être* of Western culture, and of universities whose purpose is to cultivate and transmit culture, how then do we find ourselves yet again turning the wheel of samsara? How did science displease contemplation? Paradoxically, the answer is the Western intellectual tradition itself. By various twists and turns we arrive at Immanuel Kant (1724–1804), who in Pieper's story hammers a wedge in between knowledge and contemplation. For Kant knowledge proper is discursive and rational. *Ratio* and *ratio* alone is knowledge. Contemplation is not. Kant's philosophy provides, sustains,

[14] Ibid.

[15] Ibid., 29.

[16] Ibid., 28.

[17] Ibid., 21.

[18] Ibid., 19–20.

[19] Josef Pieper, *Happiness and Contemplation*, trans. Richard and Clara Winston (South Bend: St. Augustine's Press, 1998) 55–56.

and amplifies intellectual justifications for the procedures of modern science including its dependence on forms of mathematical representtation.

I say "paradoxically" because university students and faculty did not until recently identify contemplation within the traditions of Western education. Leaving aside those with an interest in the theories and histories of contemplation, university men and women learned of contemplation via "mindfulness" or "contemplative initiatives" sprouting rapidly throughout the United States and Europe. The boldest is at the University of Virginia, where the "Contemplative Sciences Center" (CSC) is looking very much like the intellectual hub of Thomas Jefferson's university.[20] A $12 million dollar gift by a wealthy alum helps.[21] So does publicity. On 15 October 2013, several hundred students, faculty, and staff sat on the front lawn of Mr. Jefferson's "Academical Village" for guided meditation. Leading them from the front steps of the famous rotunda were none other than Deepak Chopra and Arianna Huffington.[22] That said, it would be rash to conclude that CSC is a sideshow in the game of rankings. Glance at the guest speakers, courses, the integration of the various schools via contemplation, compare the deployment at UVA with other contemplative initiatives, we may rightly wonder if UVA is the shape of what is to come in higher education.

The contemporary contemplative movement in higher education is young. The first professional academic society, the Association for

[20] See the CSC website: http://www.uvacontemplation.org/ (accessed 25 November 2013).

[21] Jayson Whitehead, "Yoga U: Is the Contemplative Sciences Center the answer to UVA's 'reputation gap,' or an expensive New Age Sideshow?" *Cville Weekly* (online), 5 September 2012.

[22] Jane Kelly, "Hundreds gather for Deepak Chopra-led meditation on UVA's lawn," *UVA Today* (online), 15 October 2013, http://news.virginia.edu/content/hundreds-gather-deepak-chopra-led-meditation-uva-s-lawn, accessed November 25, 2013.

Contemplative Mind in Higher Education (ACMHE), was established in 2008; its parent organization, the Center for Contemplative Mind in Society (CMS) in 1997. CMS launched the first call for papers in 2013. Reach back a bit further and the connections between Western science and Buddhism start to appear. Few doubt that contemplation would be in the academy today had it not been for the Mind and Life Institute (MLI). Mind and Life began as an intellectual experiment between His Holiness the 14th Dalai Lama, entrepreneur R. Adam Engle, and neuroscientist Francisco J. Varela. The first Mind and Life Dialogue was held in the Dalai Lama's small audience room in Dharamsala in October 1987. It was structured as a weeklong conversation between Buddhism and the cognitive sciences, and included the Dalai Lama, six scientists, two translators, and a few observers. From the very beginning, Varela had a vision of the opportunity for interdisciplinary collaboration. He recognized that science had become the dominant paradigm for investigating the nature of reality, and in developing a knowledge that could help improve the lives of humans, other animals, and the planet. The scientific method is in current parlance empirical, it depends on technology, all in the service of third-person "objective" observation. Be that as it may, Varela was adamant that well-refined contemplative practices and introspective methods could likewise be used as instruments of investigation. He was convinced that modern science was unconvincingly an exclusively third-person investigation, would to the benefit of science incorporate into its analytical paradigm first- and second-person observation, analysis, and methodologies.[23]

Mind and Life invites forgotten and disparaged "humanities" back to the seat of knowledge. Scientists at Mind and Life ignited a conversation about the relationship between disciplines said to be "personal," "cultural," "subjective," and "value laden," on the one hand, and put them into conversation with rigorous, empirical, experimental

[23] Mind and Life Institute website, http://www.mindandlife.org/about/history/ (accessed 25 November 2013).

sciences of brain and behavior, on the other In a nutshell, this is what the fledgling "Contemplative Studies" is trying to do.

Contemplative neuroscience was not the making of renegade scientists on a spiritual quest to the East. By the logic and structures of Western rationalism, scientists steeped in the ways of Western science went in search of new modes of inquiry impelled by the weight of their own history. In the late nineteenth and early twentieth century, theories of relativity and quantum mechanics called into question a mechanistic universe operating in absolute space and time. Observations of quantum "phenomena" are within the frame of classical mechanics, obviously. Scientists cannot do science and dispense with the perspective of the observer, however. There is no view from nowhere. Isaac Newton's universe of natural laws, causes and effects is still our "world," of course. When we turn our technologies inside the basic constituents of "matter," we discover probabilities—not certainties. It is as if we have been prompted to rediscover the awful and wonderful disjunctions and continuities in a moral universe just as we recently discovered them in a physical universe. Not by coincidence alone does it seem that one of the founders of the contemplative movement, former director of CMS, ACMHE, and now president of Mind and Life, is Amherst College professor of physics Arthur Zajonc.

V.

Adam Smith's is probably the most cited and least read author in the Western canon. He is not favored as political theorist. Economists claim him but not as a social scientist. Philosophers don't include him among philosophers. The book he labored over the course of his life, published in various editions, revised until his death in 1790, is the little known *The Theory of Moral Sentiments* is not the first to land on college syllabi. One reason may be that the *TMS* is a riddle. And the riddle is in the title. The book announces a "theory" of moral "sentiments." Emotions, feelings, and passions can be *theorized* but aren't themselves theory. Reading the *TMS* hides a disjunction between body and mind. Take for example that few "theorists" appear in the *TMS*, not until the end. Throughout Smith provides vivid examples students relate to immediately as if he were speaking here and now. Smith's examples are literary. His metaphors of "concord," "pitch," "tone," "harmony" are musical. His prose is florid, vivid, and ever so close to events as we "experience" them. Smith is emerging as a phenomenologist.[24]

Maybe not genuinely a scientist, Smith has begun to emerge as a philosopher of science.[25] He is a scientist sufficiently skeptical of science to know what science is and isn't, what it does and doesn't, and how. Smith's judicious deployment of mechanisms explaining sentimental and sympathetic causes and effects corresponds well with his rhetorically deft employment of Newtonian metaphors describing human psychology and behavior. Reading Smith's political economy in the light of "survival of the fittest" and "social Darwinism" seems to make sense for commercial peoples. [26] Smith's "revival" as phenomenologist includes Smith as methodological Newtonian and "quasi-social- psychologist." [27] These paths are likely to founder when the new proto-phenomenological, proto-neuroscientific Smith "scholarship" tries to navigate in between the straights of Scylla and Charybdis. Unable to reconcile the "is" and the "ought" scholars will ask: Is there is a third way? Gazing in the direction of that marvelous hybrid of philosophical phenomenology and cognitive science that became contemplative inquiry and is becoming academically viable and compelling contemplative studies they will find neither succor nor solace. Why? To repeat, contemplative neuroscience is not contemplative practice. I may not live to see the hypothesis tested. They

[24] Christel Fricke and Dagfinn Føllesdal, eds., *Intersubjectivity and Objectivity in Adam Smith and Edmund Husserl: A Collection of Essays* (Frankfurt: Ontos, 2012).

[25] Leonidas Montes and Eric Schliesser, eds., *New Voices on Adam Smith* (New York: Routledge, 2006).

[26] Robert H. Frank, "The Invisible Hand, Trumped by Darwin?," New York *Times*, 7 July 2009, http://www.nytimes.com/2009/07/12/business/economy/12view. html?_r=0 (accessed 1 December 2014).

[27] Gustav Jahoda, *A History of Social Psychology: From the Eighteenth Century to the Second World War* (New York: Cambridge University Press, 2007).

may come in closer vicinity to one another, but never shall the two meet. Allow me to address this distinction by looking back at the origins of contemplative neuroscience out of which contemplative studies is born.

VI.

Francisco Varela is arguably the leading intellectual light of academic contemplation. His life in the service of knowing mind inspired the dialogues that became the MLI. *The Embodied Mind: Cognitive Science and Human Experience* establishes the need for and the possibility of contemplative neuroscience. "Neuro" was already bandied about by the time Varela co-authored *The Embodied Mind*. Scientists aren't likely to say the book is "science." Neither are philosophers likely to say it is "philosophy." We agree for the time being that it is neuro-phenomenology.

Few read *The Embodied Mind* as a history of Western thought. That is not surprising. Francisco Varela, Evan Thompson, and Eleanor Rosch did not write intellectual history. Yet in their admittedly cursory overview of Western philosophy, Varela and colleagues turn the history of Western philosophy into "proto-quasi-cognitive science." Published in 1991, *The Embodied Mind* comes to the marketplace just as the sciences of brain, behavior, and cognition were disturbing traditional modes of philosophy. Philosophy, revered by ancient philosophers as queen of the sciences, was interred in an graveyard called the "humanities." We know why. Liberal "arts" (in contradistinction to the not-so-liberal "sciences") are supposedly anachronistic, avatars, relics of historical curiosity, of no immediate import, and certainly not science. Varela, Thompson, and Rosch were not so crude. Their compassion for defunct disciplines was not borne of nostalgia, deference to tradition, or misplaced filial piety. In their view, science was at an impasse. Science needed a step outside of science to see science. Friedrich Nietzsche's poignant although posthumously published insight that the nineteenth century is distinguished not for the triumph of science, but of the scientific method over science is apropos.[28]

At first glance the step Varela and his colleagues take when inquiry about the nature of science seems to be toward philosophy. Look for philosophy, and it quickly fades. "If philosophy in the West no longer occupies a privileged, foundational position with respect to other cultural activities such as science or art," Varela and colleagues write, "then a full appreciation of philosophy and its importance for human experience requires that we examine the role of philosophy in cultures other than our own."[29] The statement is conditional. Cognitive science brought "great excitement among philosophers (and the public at large)" for it then permitted philosophers to "see their tradition in a new light."[30]

So, out of the cave came the philosophers. Just as soon as the sojourners step out into the light of day, the sun sets. Science resurrects philosophy but not as philosophy:

> Were we to entertain the idea that there is no hard-and-fast distinction between science and philosophy, then philosophers such as Descartes, Locke, Leibniz, Hume, Kant, and Husserl would take on a new significance: they could be seen, among other things, as protocognitive scientists (Or as Jerry Fodor puts it, "In intellectual history, everything happens twice, first as philosophy and then as cognitive science.") Might this not also be the case for philosophical traditions with which we are less familiar?[31]

This conditional sentence I quoted in the context of the historical narrative is marvelous. It is merely a suggestion or hypothesis. Ending the passage with a question is also oh so Socratic. Philosophy *qua*

[28] Friedrich Nietzsche, *The Will to Power*, 466.

[29] Francisco Varela, Evan Thompson, and Eleanor Rosch, *The Embodied Mind: Cognitive Science and Human Experience* (Cambridge: Massachusetts Institute of Technology Press, 1993) 21.

[30] Ibid.

[31] Ibid.

philosophy is not dead. Western philosophy is dead. We may therefore entertain the prospect of an enlightening "Eastern" philosophy.[32]

Were Varela and colleagues indicting the entire Western philosophical tradition, that would amount to throwing the proverbial baby out with the proverbial bathwater. After all, isn't science arguably the highest achievement of Western rationalism? And isn't rationalism what philosophy in the West was before it was science? In the early 1990s Western intellectuals had indicted the Western tradition as hyper-rationalist "logocentrism" and "Socratism." Some of you may remember the vitriol among scholars soon after the publication of Allan Bloom's best-seller *The Closing of the American Mind: How Higher Education has Failed Democracy and Impoverished the Soul of Today's Students* (1987).

Varela and his colleagues acknowledge a debt to a philosophical tradition in the West: "We like to consider our journey in this book as a modern continuation of a program of research founded a generation ago by the French philosopher Maurice Merleau-Ponty."[33] The co-authors of The Embodied Mind said on behalf of Merleau-Ponty that "Western scientific culture requires that we see our bodies both as physical structures and as lived, experiential structures, in short, as both 'outer' and 'inner,' biological and phenomenological." "Western scientific culture" (perhaps not to be confused with science) did not then have a phenomenology proper to it. Science required a discipline of inner experience amenable to scientific experimentation, measurement, and verification. *The Embodied Mind* offered the "possibility of circulation between the sciences of mind (cognitive science) and human experience."[34]

In *The Embodied Mind*, philosophy diagnoses philosophy's ills; yet philosophy cannot save philosophy from itself. Despite the "progress" that accrues from philosopher to philosopher in the Western tradition,

[32] Ibid.

[33] Ibid., xv.

[34] Ibid.

each and every rebirth is riddled by a genetic defect. That is, the defect of strictly rationalist modes of introspective inquiry and discourse. The last gasps of life in the Western tradition are into intellectual oblivion of postmodernism and deconstruction. According to Varela and colleagues, Merleau-Ponty is unwittingly a child of Edmund Husserl. And Husserl is a child of Franz Brentano.

The defects of that inheritance show up in Varela's characterization of Husserl through the inheritance of Brentano's "notion of intentionality."[35] Husserl modified it to include "a specific procedure for examining the structure of intentionality."[36] Intentionality should be based on the structure of experience itself, Husserl argued, "without reference to the factual, empirical world."[37] Husserl called this "bracketing" (*epoché*), "for it required that one put out of action as if in brackets, one's ordinary judgments about the relation between experience and the world."[38] Phenomenologists speculated about the first movements of mind. They answered with "intentions." What are intentions? Husserl called them "intuitions" prior to experience. Only as prior may we speculate that intentions, not as reactions to outside stimuli. This may sound a lot like non-judgmental awareness. One could read Jon Kabat-Zinn placeholder for mindfulness into phenomenology: paying attention in a particular way: on purpose, in the present moment, and non-judgmentally.[39]

[35] Ibid., 15

[36] Ibid., 16.

[37] Ibid.

[38] Ibid.

[39] J. Mark G. Williams and Jon Kabat-Zinn, "Mindfulness: Diverse Perspectives on its Meanings, Origin, and Multiple Intersections of Science and Dharma," *Contemporary Buddhism* 12/1 (May 20011). Kabat-Zinn said that "mindfulness" is a stand in for the "Dharma," which I must say is delightfully wicked. For it now sends all those who discovered there is no "mindfulness" in the traditions of the East, and indeed no such abstract "mindfulness" exists, Kabat-Zinn offers of the Dharma as an apt response to McMindfulness.

Husserl as read by Varela "claimed to be able to study the intentional contents of the mind purely internally," a method he called the "intuition of essences" (*Wesenschau*). However, Varela continues, Husserl's "intuition" to the meditator's gaze turns out to be "a sort of philosophical introspection." [40] Philosophical introspection is the semblance of contemplation in the West. However, note that Buddhists practice "analytical meditation"; they aren't necessarily in "analysis" as we Westerners conceive it. Philosophical introspection animated Husserl to take "the first step of the reflective scientist: he claimed that to understand cognition, we cannot take the world naively but must see it instead as having the mark of our own structure."[41] As "reflection," philosophical introspection remains inherently dualistic and dialogical. Reflection is observation of experience; philosophical introspection is discourse of experience. Neither is therefore properly "experience." Consequently, the co-authors of *The Embodied Mind* concluded that

> Husserl's turn toward experience and "the things themselves" was entirely *theoretical*, or, to make the point another way around, it completely lacked any *pragmatic* dimension. It is not surprising, therefore, that it could not overcome the rift between science and experience, for science, unlike phenomenological reflection, has a life beyond theory.[42]

All of Western thought is in the same gene pool. Reflecting and reflected mind reifies and objectifies mind. An image of mind is not mind. "Thinking" is conceptual, the truck and barter of an "I." Thinking is precisely the stuff that sustains illusions of "self," unwittingly or not a remnant of a dubious Cartesian ego. Negation won't get us out dualistic mind either. Nihilism is nourished by words, conceptions, ideas, and other mental objects nullified. No-thing is always some-thing. We know it is there when it struts around in Dionysian revelry. All Western thought projects, even those promising a return to the primal void, are

[40] Varela et al., *The Embodied Mind*, 16.

[41] Ibid.

[42] Ibid.

framed by the thoughts that thinking thinks, by a thinker thinking thought. The rationalist predicament, namely, dialogical discourses about experience outside of experience by a thinker thinking thought while assuming it is knowledge of experience extends into Martin "Heidegger's [1889–1976] existential phenomenology, as well as…Merleau-Ponty's phenomenology of lived experience."[43] Even Merleau-Ponty founders. All who follow Friedrich Nietzsche out of late modernity into postmodernity cannot "save the phenomena" by "unreason." Moving out of philosophy and into psychology, as Nietzsche anticipated we would, won't bring us to "experience." Positing "motives, fantasies, preferences, aversions, emotions, behaviors, and pathological symptoms—are explicable by means of the unconscious," psychoanalysts and psychotherapists objectify what is by their own definition outside of conscious awareness.[44] If the unconscious is unconscious then it is unconscious. "It" is not in or of "consciousness." Consciousness is already reified awareness that gives rise to a "subject." We cannot fail to mention but must avoid discussing unborn nature of mind. This reconstruction is cursory and provisional; it is a map to Adam Smith and a contemplative reading of the contemplative books *The Theory of Moral Sentiments* among the most important for our day and age.

VII.

Readers of Adam Smith's *The Theory of Moral Sentiments* (*TMS*) may recall that the author goes at some length to call the rational egoist "self" into doubt. Caricatures of the *Wealth of Nations* (*WN*) notwithstanding (the selfishness of butchers and such), the psychology of *TMS* describes operations of emotion, sense, and sensibility, filtered through a sympathetic imagination. We are social beings, according to Smith. My sense of self depends on the images of other selves. I regulate my emotions by watching them mirrored back to me through you. Your

[43] Ibid., 19.
[44] Ibid., 20.

sense of propriety and merit is constituted by exchanges of feelings, thoughts, and ideas; social context, social standing, time and place add texture to our moral sensibilities. Smith does not reduce commerce to buying and selling goods and services. You and I are "social networks," another way of saying that no man or woman is an island.

On the socially constituted and naturally endowed self, Smith ought to be heard at some length:

> Were it possible that a human creature could grow up to manhood in some solitary place, without any communication with his own species, he could no more think of his own character, of the propriety or demerit of his own sentiments and conduct, of the beauty or deformity of his own mind, than of the beauty or deformity of his own face. All these are objects which he cannot easily see, which naturally he does not look at, and with regard to which he is provided no mirror which can present them to his view. Bring him into society, and he is immediately provided with the mirror which he wanted before. It is placed in the countenance and behaviour of those he lives with, which always mark when they enter into, and when they disapprove of his sentiments; and it is here that he first views the propriety and impropriety of his own passions, the beauty and deformity of his own mind. To a man who from his birth was a stranger to society, the objects of his passions, the external bodies which either pleased or hurt him, would occupy his whole attention. The passions themselves, the desires or aversions, the joys or sorrows, which those objects excited, though of all things the most immediately present to him, could scarce ever be the objects of his thoughts. The idea of them could never interest him so much as to call upon his attentive consideration. The consideration of his joy could in him excite no new joy, nor that of his sorrow any new sorrow, though the consideration of the causes of those passions might often excite both. Bring him into society, and all his own passions will immediately become the causes of new passions. He will observe that mankind approve of some of them, and are disgusted by others. He will be elevated in the one case, and cast down in the other; his desires and aversions, his joys and sorrows, will now often become the causes of new desires and new aversions, new joys and new sorrows: they will now, therefore, interest him deeply, and often call upon his most attentive consideration. (*TMS*, III.i.3, 110)

The social currency of mirrored "selves" is compassion. The movement from social-constituted self to compassion is strikingly similar to versions of neural-Buddhism. Which brings us to the vexed matter called religion. Smith is ripe for appropriation by advocates of compassion without having to defend any particular tradition. Smith writes compassionately of compassion: "[p]ity and compassion are words appropriated to signify our fellow-feeling with the sorrow of others. Sympathy, though its meaning was, perhaps, originally the same, may now, without much impropriety, be made use of to denote our fellow-feeling with any passion whatever" (*TMS*, I.i.i.5, p. 10).

Were we to say that compassion moves from signification of fellow-feeling to a mechanism identifying any passion with fellow-feeling, some might wonder whether Smith has evacuated compassion of its traditional moorings and placed in the lap of contemplative neuroscientists looking at "processes." We could not attend to that question without considering the influence of Christianity on Western philosophy.[45] That promises another round of "selfish" and "selfless," "egoism" and "altruism," "believer" or "scientist," from which, in my estimation, does not shed light on what Smith or contemplative scientists are saying of "self." Consider just how vexed Smith's rendering of the "precept of nature" and the "the great law of Christianity" is:

> And hence it is, that to feel much for others and little for ourselves, that to restrain our selfish, and to indulge our benevolent affections, constitutes the perfection of human nature; and can alone produce among mankind that harmony of sentiments and passions in which consists their whole grace and propriety. As to love our neighbour as we love ourselves is the great law of Christianity, so it is the great precept of nature to love ourselves only as we love our neighbour, or what comes to the same thing, as our neighbour is capable of loving us. (*TMS*, I.i.5., p. 25)

[45] "Buddhism for the Spiritual But Not Religious," Special Section, *Shambala Sun* 22/2 (November 2013): 42–57.

Whether we love more than being loved or love being loved more than we love is a perilous question for readers of Smith. It is perilous because Smith has no reason for you and me to decide one way or another. He does not have to decide for himself because moral sensibilities are themselves constituted by self and other. It is my care for another that prompts me to act on their behalf. Bereft of all feelings of regard, how would that be compassion? To calculate my interest in the absence of fellow-feeling is the definition of a psychopath. You haven't "compromised" beneficence or benevolence or even your altruism when you feel for the plight or the happiness of a fellow human being. Even the staunchest champion of natural selection, E. O. Wilson, seems to agree. His latest book makes a concession to kin selection.[46]

Smith's references to contemplation are in his prickly chapter "Of the Effect of Utility upon the Sentiment of Approbation, Consisting of One Section." Contemplation is in the first paragraph of the first chapter of the one section; the chapter title is: "Of the beauty which the appearance of utility bestows upon all the productions of art, and of the extensive influence of this species of Beauty." The first paragraph reads,

> That utility is one of the principal sources of beauty has been observed by every body, who has considered with any attention what constitutes the nature of beauty. The conveniency of a house gives pleasure to the spectator as well as its regularity, and he is as much hurt when he observes the contrary defect, as when he sees the correspondent windows of different forms, or the door not placed exactly in the middle of the building. That the fitness of any system or machine to produce the end for which it was intended, bestows a certain propriety and beauty upon the whole, and renders the very thought and contemplation of it agreeable, is so very obvious that nobody has overlooked it. (*TMS*, IV.i.1., p. 176)

Two difficulties strike our sensibilities immediately: (1) utility is aesthetic pleasure; (2) beauty is placed alongside the observations of

[46] E. O. Wilson, *The Social Conquest of the Earth* (New York: Liveright, 2012).

machine or system, which is not mechanistic or systematic *per se* but rather of our thought or contemplation of the machine. In other words, Smith is aware of the distinction between what is within system or machine and that which observes system or machine. We aren't drawn to system so much by system as we are by sympathy. Sympathy is fellow-feeling, that is, interdependent, not individual. Another word is social:

> The same principle, the same love of system, the same regard to the beauty of order, of art and contrivance, frequently serves to recommend those institutions which tend to promote the public welfare. When a patriot exerts himself for the improvement of any part of the public police, his conduct does not always arise from pure sympathy with the happiness of those who are to reap the benefit of it. It is not commonly from a fellow-feeling with carriers and waggoners that a public-spirited man encourages the mending of high roads. When the legislature establishes premiums and other encouragements to advance the linen or woolen manufactures, its conduct seldom proceeds from pure sympathy with the wearer of cheap or fine cloth, and much less from that with the manufacturer or merchant. The perfection of police, the extension of trade and manufactures, are noble and magnificent objects. The contemplation of them pleases us, and we are interested in whatever can tend to advance them. They make part of the great system of government, and the wheels of the political machine seem to move with more harmony and ease by means of them. We take pleasure in beholding the perfection of so beautiful and grand a system, and we are uneasy till we remove any obstruction that can in the least disturb or encumber the regularity of its motions. All constitutions of government, however, are valued only in proportion as they tend to promote the happiness of those who live under them. This is their sole use and end. From a certain spirit of system, however, from a certain love of art and contrivance, we sometimes seem to value the means more than the end, and to be eager to promote the happiness of our fellow–creatures, rather from a view to perfect and improve a certain beautiful and orderly system, than from any immediate sense or feeling of what they either suffer or enjoy. (*TMS*, IV.i.11)

Speaking of the relative not absolute measure of things, the "I" and the "not I," we should consider a not so conditional statement of Smith's:

"If the chief part of human happiness arises from the consciousness of being beloved, as I believe it does, those sudden changes of fortune seldom contribute much to happiness" (*TMS*, I.11.5.2). Whether belief will suffice in a world of relative gains and losses is not settled. Smith would have us imagine a "consciousness" of joy that accompanies the feeling and belief that you and I are "the object of favourable regards." According to Smith, this is the way of "tranquility and self-satisfaction." He asks: "What so great happiness as to be beloved and to know that we deserve to be beloved?" (*TMS*, III.i.7).

A chasm opens up between theory and practice if you will, I would say between the requirements of a contemplative practice and contemplative inquiry. And there is no final "resolution" of this "problem" in Smith because there is no problem. Speech about "things" is not the "things" themselves or bodies. Yet we are creatures of speech and thus of mind. The "theory" is not the "sentiments." Theory informs sentiment, and sentiment habituates mind.

VIII.

Willoughby Britton is a contemplative neuroscientist studying sleep, emotions, and moods. She currently holds a five-year grant from the National Institutes of Health and is studying the effects of mindfulness and meditation in depression. She also holds dual appointments at Brown University; she is an assistant professor of psychiatry and human behavior in the Department of Public Health, and she is assistant professor of behavior and human behavior at the medical school. Britton is also co-director of the Contemplative Studies Initiative at Brown, one of the models for academic contemplative inquiry. On more than one occasion Britton earned the prestigious Mind and Life Summer Institute Research Fellowship and served as senior fellow at MLI. Her mindfulness instructor training was at UMass Medical School where Jon Kabat-Zinn made mindfulness famous. Britton did not abscond to some dark corner of the ivory tower. She studied mediation in Asia and she also practices meditation. At Mind and Life XXIV (in the sequence of dialogues that the 1987 meeting in Dharamsala set into motion), Britton was among six MLI Francisco Varela Award winners chosen to represent their research before the His Holiness, the fourteenth Dalai Lama.

At a 2012 meeting of Buddhist Geeks, one of the trendsetter groups in popular culture claiming to offer a combination of technological innovation and Buddhist spirituality, Britton took the mindfulness fad head-on. "Mindful Binge Drinking and Blobology: The Promises and Perils of Contemplative Neuroscience" is the title of her wickedly funny and rhetorically astute presentation.[47] Britton pointed out that pop-culture mindfulness is now a trait, a state, a practice, and the goal all wrapped into one. She borrows a catchy term already in circulation and calls this chimera "McMindfulness." Mindfulness as bandied about in popular culture is anything and everything. Mindfulness isn't always meditation. It is often conflated with mediation. Some speak of "mindful meditation" as if to suggest other forms of mindfulness or meditation. The popularity of meditation, embedded as it is in various forms of mindfulness, brought Britton to the table. One million new meditators in America alone each year, Britton said. With the mindfulness craze comes a "dogmatic distancing against anything that's considered religious." To appeal widely, meditation had to shake off its "religious" (even its less weighty "spiritual") baggage. "So it's probably not surprising," Britton said, "that karma and rebirth haven't made the cutoff in the scientific part of the dharma."

Wrenched from traditions of teaching, learning, and practice, meditation is likely to suffer the same fate as leisurely contemplation in its encounter with modernity. My analogy is not far removed from Britton's own words. "Now as Dharma and meditation has made its way into medicine and now is being applied to pretty much everything from back pain to writer's block," Britton said, "there has been another quiet casualty of modern dharma cherry picking." A funny and telling

[47] Willoughby Britton, "Mindful Binge Drinking and Blobology: The Promises and Perils of Contemplative Neuroscience," http://www.youtube.com/watch? v=RlmqoQVm-8nU (accessed 5 July 2013).

slideshow accompanies Britton's presentation. On one slide, two headings: "Old" and "New." At the bottom, a scale reminiscent of a childhood playground seesaw leaning to the audience's right weighted down by three words in blue boxes: "Science," "Modernity," and "Adapters." "Science" is tinged by a darker hue of blue. Elevated to Britton's left under "Old" two words boxed in red: "Tradition" and "Conservers." Beneath the scale italicized and boxed red: "Karma" and "Rebirth." Both are off the scale.

In their zeal for mindfulness now and by any means, and lest we forget an urge to cash in on its commercial success, champions of McMindfulness leave behind "the liberative teachings of the Dharma itself." It is no minor omission; that the liberative teachings of the Dharma are "Pretty much the center piece, if you want to call it that enlightenment, that's also been dismissed as really just folklore." Britton objected. If "you're going to dismiss liberation you might as well throw out Buddhism." And if you do that "how are you going to describe the point and goal of meditation if you're not allowed to use talks about enlightenment and Buddhism"?

Britton was not altogether unsympathetic. Scientists, contemplative scientists in particular, are in a "kind of a bind." Science is, if it is something, about precision and exactitude. Applying their methods and technologies to mindfulness, scientists have narrowed the meaning and scope of mindfulness. Without defining them, Britton said "we" now "have three practices in medicine and science" defined well enough to show we are "improved on the meditation front." Her praise of progress in meditation and mindfulness research is circumspect, however. Britton's criticisms are aimed at audience members, present and online. She criticizes scientists for tossing about words they ill-define referring to practices they do not know. The problem is not so much knowledge of science, although it is. The problem is what scientists claim for knowledge. Most do not know meditation from within. Varela's words were that the Western philosophical introspection has no pragmatic dimension.

The response is a new kind of contemplative science practiced by a new generation of contemplative inquirer. Britton envisions an inquirer practiced in the important disciplines of mind learned from meditation and the supporting disciplines of mind learned from science. "Contemplative Science 2.0 [is] the hybrid revolution and this is something that was masterminded by the Mind and Life Institute founded by the Dalai Lama, the neuroscientist Francisco Varela and entrepreneur Adam Engle." The new kind of scientist-meditator is "duly trained both in the traditional and sometimes *contemplative*, sorry, monastic aspects of the dharma but also the scientific and neuroscientific," Britton said (my emphasis). Britton's equivocation is not surprising; given what we've learned about the intellectual history of contemplation it is also understandable. Our confusion ends with the next generation of contemplative scientists who know "the inner technologies themselves," which is to say they are seasoned meditators with proper meditation training. Proper mind training is Buddhist mind training. These hybrids can say to academic contemplatives as Britton said to gurus and devotees of McMindfulness, "hey wait this [McMindfulness stuff] is a distraction."

Britton's concerns are those of all contemplatives, and if they aren't, they should be. They are in the legacy of Smith, who is in the image of a contemplative scientist. Science as science and contemplation as *academic* discipline vouchsafed by the neurosciences imposes obligations of rigor and precision on professional scholars that do not personally bind devotees of McMindfulness. Britton's "inner technologies" is a hopeful and foreboding placeholder for monastic mind training. Hopeful because "inner technologies" alleviate suffering, the results are compelling; foreboding because once harnessed algorithms of meditative states can be used as instruments of a vast, commercial, and medicinal pharmacology. Technology can be "liberating" and "democratic." The movement of aggregated data is tyrannical. By donning the robes of academic respectability, "Mc*Contemplatio*" may be less catchy but more insidious. Until we know otherwise, mind training includes a rigorous study of Buddhist traditions coupled with prolonged and disciplined meditation practice. On this score, most academics fail. Britton's current five-year research program funded by the National Institutes of Health is an example of the new hybrid. To her studies of the developmental stages of meditation she adds Buddhist meditation texts, among them the *Visuddhimagga*. "Path of Purification" as we may vaguely translate it, is one of the key texts of the Theravada Buddhist tradition. Scholars and monks alike regard it as one of the most important systematic treatises of Buddhist teachings and meditation techniques. "Outer technologies" is a copious term. It includes various related activities we lump together as "science." The machinery of brain and behavior imagery is decisive. Which is to say, we shall rely increasingly on the image.

Contemplative scientists, hybrids constituted by mastery of inner and outer technologies, emerge from this story as the proper mediators for research programs that will advance responsible contemplative inquiry. One example is "the Contemplative Development Mapping project" (CDM). Still in its early stages, CDM will eventually emerge with an authoritative guide to "contemplative development." Drawing as it does on various Buddhist traditions and contemporary contemplative science, it should provide a contemplative-meditation road map "sort of independent of religious traditions." The emphasis on secular and non-sectarian is Vincent Horn's interpretation of CDM during an interview with one of Britton's collaborators Judson Brewer, assistant professor of psychiatry at Yale University.[48]

XI.

Allow me to return to Pieper and to a question: how does one teach contemplation in the context of the Western tradition that honors and edifies what is so eminently the "West, " without having a life's work

[48] Judson Brewer, "BG 259: Mapping the Mindful Brain," Buddhist Geeks podcast, http://www.buddhistgeeks.com/2012/06/bg-259-mapping-the-mindful-brain/ (accessed 4 July 2013).

effaced by the specter of "religion"? How do we engage Smith's carefully crafted rhetoric without requiring students to choose between "science" and "non-science"? Pieper is a useful guide.

The Philosophical Act is an essay by Pieper; it is either read with or appended to *Leisure: The Basis of Culture*.[49] Not by accident, the former completes the latter. In *Leisure*, Pieper asked about alternatives to leisure in the way we ask for secular contemplation: "Can the realm of leisure be saved and its foundations upheld by an appeal to *humanism*?"[50] The emphasis is Pieper's. His answer is layered. "The soul of leisure, it can be said, lies in 'celebration.'" We cannot elaborate except to notice that joy is for Pieper the true mark of a contemplative soul. An analogy to compassion as the characteristic of an enlightened mind is a return to joyful teaching and learning. If nothing else, were the contemplative movement to do that, it would have done the greater part of a reformation much needed today.

Celebration is, Pieper continued, "the point at which the three elements of leisure come to a focus: relaxation, effortlessness, and superiority of 'active leisure' to all functions."[51] In turn, celebration as the core of leisure "can only be made possible and justifiable on the same basis as the celebration of a festival. *That basis is divine worship*."[52]

Readers seeking a purely philosophical and secular Pieper find his turn to worship disappointing. I discovered this among students reading Pieper in my undergraduate courses. When Pieper brings leisurely contemplation under the tutelage of Christianity, I invite students to inquire whether Pieper might not have compelling *reasons* to do so.

Begin, I say, by noticing that for all that supposedly Catholic in *Leisure* the Christian God is not marked by sectarian differences. Then I invite them to describe Pieper's God. Pieper's orthodoxy does not look

[49] See Josef Pieper, *Leisure: The Basis of Culture & The Philosophical Act* (San Francisco: Ignatius Press, 2009).

[50] Pieper, *Leisure: The Basis of Culture* (Reprint, 1952) 65.

[51] Ibid.

[52] Ibid. Pieper's emphasis.

like any orthodoxy they know. In *The Philosophical Act*, Pieper brings to the fore what has been present throughout *Leisure*, a quiet and subtle elision of philosophy and theology:

> The life and soul of philosophy, and the tension that goes with it, depend upon its retaining what I have called its contrapuntal relations to theology. That is where it strikes root and where it draws the salt of the existential. If Heidegger's philosophical work has had such a stimulating effect, it is because philosophy had become a shriveled-up, intellectual discipline, the preserve of specialists in the worst sense of the word, and had lost touch with theological themes (this was partially true even of so-called Christian philosophers). The explosive character of Heidegger's philosophy on the other hand is simply due to the fact that it asks challenging questions, and his questions are challenging because their source and impetus is theological, and so too should their answers be—though it is true that the theological answer is flatly rejected by Heidegger. But quite suddenly, once again, one could taste the salt of theology on one's tongue.[53]

Pieper writes of contemplation as he does and when he does, to pry it from the clutches of late modernity and post-modernity. We can only mention Heidegger's compromises with National Socialism and Nietzsche's anticipation of the Over-man. Late modernity's critique of rationalism is abysmal. It does reason a grave injustice and worse. Unthinkable cruelty and inhumanity donned the mantle of philosophical introspection, and this explains Pieper's repulsion to late modernity. We must sustain the disjunction between thought and action, while encouraging thoughtful action and active thought.

Smith wrote of the hyphen balance between mind-body, as if to warns of its erasure.

> Nature has not prescribed to us this sublime contemplation as the great business and occupation of our lives. She only points it out to us as the consolation of our misfortunes. The Stoical philosophy prescribes it as the great business and occupation of our lives. That philosophy teaches

[53] Pieper, *The Philosophical Act*, 134.

> us to interest ourselves earnestly and anxiously in no events, external to the good order of our own minds, to the propriety of our own choosing and rejecting, except in those which concern a department where we neither have nor ought to have any sort of management or direction, the department of the great Superintendent of the universe. By the perfect apathy which it prescribes to us, by endeavouring, not merely to moderate, but to eradicate all our private, partial, and selfish affections, by suffering us to feel for whatever can befall ourselves, our friends, our country, not even the sympathetic and reduced passions of the impartial spectator, it endeavours to render us altogether indifferent and unconcerned in the success or miscarriage of every thing which Nature has prescribed to us as the proper business and occupation of our lives. (*TMS*, VII.ii.1.46)

Contemplation provides no certainties, nor does it prescribe the management of universal compassion.

Fruitful tensions such as these are at home in contemplative neuroscience. I noticed this during a visit by Richard Davidson to the Washington and Lee University campus in early 2013. Davidson is familiar to contemplatives and is quickly becoming a household name. He was one of the first MLI scientists in dialogue with the Dalai Lama. Currently he is William James and Vilas Professor of Psychology and Psychiatry, director of the Waisman Laboratory for Brain Imaging and Behavior, the Laboratory for Affective Neuroscience, and founder and chair of the Center for Investigating Healthy Minds, also at the Waisman Center, University of Wisconsin-Madison. *The Emotional Life of the Brain* is his latest book, co-authored with Sharon Begley. If Davidson is contemplative science 1.0, hold the updates. Call me a Luddite if you must, but the first version looks pretty darn good.

During Q&A, Davidson took a characteristically convoluted academic question and reduced it to its essence: Is mind brain? Davidson answered his question with a story. His students and research assistants, he said, are often asked about the so-called "mind-body problem." Davidson counsels them to practice ignorance. "Practice not-knowing," he said unabashedly to the Washington and Lee audience. I doubt most were reassured. Is this not evasion? Irresponsibility? Or worse, a dereliction of his duties as a scientist? I was reassured. To hear a contemplative scientist say that he knows that he does not know is a testament that Socratic wisdom is alive and well in the heart of contemplative inquiry.

10 | A Note on Prudence, Practical Wisdom, and Commerce in Adam Smith

Douglas Den Uyl

Perhaps no other virtue has had such a varied assessment of its value as the virtue of prudence. As I documented some years ago,[1] what began with Aristotle's *phronesis* as the pinnacle of all the virtues, to be carried over later by authors writing in Latin as *prudentia*, became by the modern era essentially no virtue at all. The reasons for this transformation are manifold, but one figure who might be said to run somewhat counter to this trend is Adam Smith. In Part VI of his *Theory of Moral Sentiments* (*TMS*),[2] Smith gives prudence a central place in his moral philosophy alongside the virtues typically admired by eighteenth-century British writers, namely justice and benevolence. It is, furthermore, possible to speculate that prudence is the virtue that links Smith's interest in commerce with his interest in ethics, since the connection between *TMS* and the *Wealth of Nations* (*WN*) has long been an issue of scholarly interest, and prudence would seem to be a natural candidate for their connection. Although I will have my eye on commerce[3] in this brief note, the main point here is simply to identify an important difference between Smithean prudence and the classical variety most closely identified with

[1] See Douglas J. Den Uyl, *The Virtue of Prudence* (New York: Peter Lang Publishing 1991).

[2] References are taken from Adam Smith, *The Theory of Moral Sentiments* (Oxford: Oxford University Press/Liberty Fund 1982) and designated by "*TMS*". In addition, we shall refer to Adam Smith, *An Inquiry into the Nature and Causes of the Wealth of Nations* (Oxford: Oxford University Press/Liberty Fund, 1981) designated at "*WN*."

[3] I discuss the connection between prudence and commerce more fully in "The Fortune of Others" forthcoming in *Foundational Thinkers and Business Ethics* (University of Chicago Press, 2014). A few of the following paragraphs come from that essay with slight modifications.

Aristotle. Doing so may have some bearing on the importance of this virtue for commerce.

Smith defines prudence in *TMS*, VI.i in the following way: "The care of the health, of the fortune, of the rank and reputation of the individual, the objects upon which his comfort and happiness in this life are supposed principally to depend, is considered as the proper business of that virtue which is commonly called prudence" (*TMS*, VI.i.5). The general point of this section of *TMS* is to discuss how one's character can affect one's own happiness and what quality of character is needed to accomplish that end. This personal quality, as we see from the foregoing passage, Smith defines as prudence. Despite the fact that prudence is a virtue focused on one's own happiness or well-being rather than that of others (Smith also discusses traits of character that affect the happiness of others in the following section of *TMS*), it does not follow that such a focus means a lack of consideration for others. Indeed, Smith explicitly tells us the following:

> The desire of becoming the proper object of this respect, of deserving and obtaining this credit and rank among our equals, is, perhaps, the strongest of all our desires, and our anxiety to obtain the advantages of fortune is accordingly much more excited and irritated by this desire, than by that of supplying all the necessities and conveniences of the body, which are always very easily supplied. (*TMS*, VI.i.3)

Our own happiness is thus inextricably other-oriented, being bound up in gaining the respect of others as we go about doing the things necessary to advance our well-being. Indeed, one would expect that our "anxiety" over obtaining such respect would no doubt influence the very ways we choose to effect our own fortunes. In any case, it is clear that this desire for respect is also a central feature of the constraints upon our conduct and the source of the norms that come to guide that conduct. Thus we cannot equate prudence in Smith with self-interest as it is so often understood today, if by "self-interest" one means what would benefit one irrespective of a consideration of others. The goal of prudence may indeed be what is conducive to one's well-being, but there is nothing necessarily selfish about it. Prudence can involve strong degrees of other-orientedness, for others are certainly components of our well-being.

Prudence typically begins with a concern for security, which for Smith means minimizing the risks to our health, reputation, and fortune. As one looks into the matter further, however, one discovers that prudence for Smith is not simply a negative or cautious attitude, but actually calls us to positive self-improvement and the development of our reason and talents.[4] In caring about our well-being by being careful with our risks and by improving ourselves both with respect to our talents and our standing in the community, we learn that "the prudent man is always both supported and rewarded by the entire approbation of the impartial spectator" (*TMS*, VI.i.11). Smith's "impartial spectator" is, in essence, the standard used for judging moral conduct. Approval by the impartial spectator indicates worthy moral action; disapproval unworthy. As it turns out, the use of the impartial spectator marks one of the key differences between Smithean prudence and classical Aristotelian phronesis.

Why would the impartial spectator find some actions worthy and others not? In the case of prudence and the actions associated with it, the bulk of Smith's focus in *TMS*, VI is upon the state of character prudence represents, and less upon its source and justification. In general, Smith simply begins by describing the sort of character a prudent individual would possess, its various strengths and limitations, and its degree of appeal to the impartial spectator. Other than the connection with what he later calls "superior prudence," little is said here about the justification for such a character and its connection to something like "practical wisdom," which is the term often used to translate Aristotle's *phronesis*. There is, more specifically, no discussion of the role of the intellect or reason in the discernment of the differences between right and wrong, propriety and impropriety, when discussing prudence, as one would expect in virtually any classical discussion. Indeed prudence, which was in

[4] See *TMS*, IV.2.6-7 for example.

classical times a virtue of the intellect, becomes primarily a disposition of character in Smith's hands.[5] This was not, I believe, by accident. Smith was fully aware of the classical notion.

> In the strength, acuteness, and perfection of the governing principle [reason—the governing principle of the soul for Plato] was placed the essential virtue of prudence, which, according to Plato, consisted in a just and clear discernment, founded upon general and scientific ideas, of the ends which are proper to be pursued, and of the means which were proper for attaining them. (*TMS*, VII.ii.6)

One is struck in reflecting on the foregoing passage how different a discussion along the lines of this passage would have been from the one actually found in Part VI of *TMS*.[6] Instead of describing the qualities of character which influence behavior and the responses to that behavior by others, a discussion based on the ideas of the preceding passage would have explored how reason discerns what is proper and improper and the goods implied by that discernment, followed by a discussion of how to put that knowledge to practice. In Smith's own discussion of prudence, however, the intellect plays virtually no role at all. Classical "practical wisdom" comes to be replaced by what might be called the "practical character."

[5] A typical description might be the following: "prudence or practical wisdom involves primarily the ability to use one's intellect to appreciate that the human goods *are indeed goods* and hence to be pursued. Only secondarily does it involve the ability to work out the best *means* to achieve those goods." David S. Oderberg, *Moral Theory: A Non-consequentialist Approach* (Oxford: Blackwell Publishers, 2000) 51.

[6] Smith says of the faculty of reason in reference to Plato that it is "not only that faculty by which we judge of truth and falsehood, but that by which we judge of the propriety or impropriety of desires and affections" (*TMS*, VII.ii.1.3). While certainly true of the classical understanding, this description does not specify the *basis* for distinguishing propriety from impropriety, just as "proper" in the passage cited in the body of the text above leaves open what determines that. It does seem, however, that the very terms "propriety" and "proper" give the sense that what is fitting is more significant than what is good, somewhat contrary to the classical conception.

Practical character is moved more by sentiment than reason, which is consistent with the centrality Smith gives generally to the imagination over reason.[7] Indeed, philosophy, which for Aristotle is quintessentially devoted to reason, for Smith should be "regarded as one of those arts which address themselves to the imagination" (*Essays on Philosophical Subjects* [*EPS*], II.12). That perspective on philosophy is itself quite consistent with a tendency to give primacy to the aesthetic, where the compelling qualities of fittingness or coherency are given such centrality. Indeed, as it turns out imagination is fundamental at the deepest levels of scientific inquiry:

> Let us consider them ["systems of nature"] only in that particular point of view which belongs to our subject; and content ourselves with inquiring how far each of them was fitted to sooth the imagination, and to render the theatre of nature a more coherent, and therefore a more magnificent spectacle, than otherwise it would have appeared to be. (*EPS*, II.12)

We are, thus, inevitably and ineluctably drawn to coherence and unity, and we come to regard that very coherence as being the structure of reality.

> Even we, while we have been endeavoring to represent all philosophical systems as mere inventions of the imagination, to connect together the otherwise disjointed and discordant phaenomena of nature, have insensibly been drawn in, to make use of language expressing the connecting principles of this one, as if they were the real chains which Nature makes use of to bind together her several operations. (*EPS*, IV.76)

With this centralizing of the imagination, we would thus have to expect a different sort of treatment regarding the development of a virtuous practical character than we would find in a framework of classical practical wisdom. Coherency on this model would have more

[7] See, for example, Smith's "History of Astronomy" cited in the passages below in the volume of Adam Smith, *Essays on Philosophical Subjects* (Oxford: Oxford University Press/Liberty Classics, 1980).

significance than, say, insight. In the case of practical action, what is being "cohered" is social cooperation or social harmony.

The practical character of the prudent man is, in other words, a function of his fittingness for society as measured by the impartial spectator's sense of fittingness and as motivated by the agent's own desire for social respect and his vision of the appropriate life. It is with respect to the "humble" and "private" person that Smith is especially concerned when thinking about the extended form of prudence that goes beyond mere caution and security and seeks a more complete form of well-being and social integration.

> Temperance, decency, modesty, and moderation, are always amiable, and can seldom be directed to any bad end. It is from the unremitting steadiness of those gentler exertions of self-command, and the amiable virtue of chastity, that the respectable virtues of industry and frugality, derive all that sober lustre which attends them. The conduct of all those who are contented to walk in the humble paths of private and peaceable life, derives from the same principle the greater part of the beauty and grace which belong to it; a beauty and grace, which, though much less dazzling, is not always less pleasing than those which accompany the more splendid actions of the hero, the statesman, or the legislator. (*TMS*, VI.iii.13)

Smith contrasts what I am calling "extended" prudence as exemplified in this last passage with what he calls a "superior prudence."

> wise and judicious conduct, when directed to greater and nobler purposes than the care of the health, the fortune, the rank and reputation of the individual, is frequently and very properly called prudence. We talk of the prudence of the great general, of the great statesman, of the great legislator. Prudence is, in all these cases, combined with many greater and more splendid virtues, with valour, with extensive and strong benevolence, with a sacred regard to the rules of justice, and all these supported by a proper degree of self-command. (*TMS*, VI.i.15)

The sort of superior prudence just mentioned goes well beyond the concerns of our present discussion, and yet it is important to appreciate that Smith does recognize dimensions of human perfection that may have little connection to "ordinary" human life. The form of extended prudence with which we are concerned by contrast, though certainly a form of superior prudence, is one that has general applicability. By the time Smith gets to the lines just cited in the last passage, he has moved well beyond what has any general applicability. We know this interestingly enough because immediately after he tells us about the "wise and judicious" conduct that goes beyond rank, reputation, and fortune when forming superior prudence, he gives as examples "the prudence of the great general, of the great statesman, or the great legislator." One might recall from the passage cited just prior to this last one that the sort of general extended prudence exhibited there was contrasted with the "hero, the statesman, and the legislator." And, of course, the first virtues mentioned in connection with a superior prudence above were valor, benevolence, and justice—virtues that correspond exactly with the general, the statesman, and the legislator.[8]

The foregoing is meant to illustrate that what we are calling extended prudence, while certainly a version of superior prudence, is the prudence most suited to ordinary living in a commercial order.[9] It occupies the middle ground between the superior prudence described in

[8] Alexis de Tocqueville echos much of our point about Smith in saying the following: "But if it seems useful to you to divert the intellectual and moral activity of man toward the necessities of material life, and to use it to produce well-being; if reason appears to you more profitable than genius; if your object is not to create heroic virtues, but peaceful habits...if instead of acting within the bosom of a brilliant society, it is enough for you to live in the midst of a prosperous society; if, finally, in your view, the principal object of a government is not to give the entire body of the nation the most strength or the most glory possible, but to provide for each of the individuals that make up the society the most well-being and to avoid the most misery; then equalize conditions and constitute the government of democracy." *Democracy in America* (Historical Critical Edition) vol. 2, ch. 6, "Activity That Reigns In All Part of the Political Body in the United States, etc." p. 85.

[9] It may seem arbitrary that we have invented dual terms for prudence that is not yet of the superior variety, but Smith does give us leave himself to make this type of move with his own distinction between "vulgar" or "mere" prudence and prudence. See *TMS*, VI.concl.5.

the preceding passages and the narrow prudence depicted in the opening sections of Book VI of *TMS*. We find in extended prudence both the discipline of our self-interested passions as well as the development of our social and intellectual capacities to the point where we have the full approval of the impartial spectator. Moreover, extended prudence is generally outwardly directed, because a strong dimension of concern for the fortunes of others is added to narrow prudence, not to mention that the increased development of our skills and intellect is also often accompanied by a broadened perspective. We can certainly make our own characters the object of refinement and thus move ourselves towards extraordinary forms of superior prudence (*TMS*, VI.iii.25). We thus might find ourselves in circumstances where the responsibilities of the general, statesman, or legislator are upon us. In these cases, we would have ideals in mind different from what is applicable to the vast majority of actors fitting themselves into a commercial society.

There is, in a way, no such fittingness for what might be called the heroic prudence of the general, statesman, or legislator or for the prudence of the peripatetic sage mentioned in another passage.[10] These are individuals who more or less stand outside of society or who stand above it and fashion it in significant ways. They are subject to the judgments of the impartial spectator but not always so influenced by it, especially when it comes to their own self-assessments.[11] By contrast, the ordinary person has the "natural disposition to accommodate and to assimilate, as much as [he] can, [his] own sentiments, principles, and feelings, to those which we see fixed and rooted in the persons whom we are obliged to live and converse a great deal with" (*TMS*, VI.ii.I.17). This, in essence, is the basis from which our characters are formed. The problem of practical wisdom in Smith then is this: where is the wisdom? The exhibition of a given character trait is not a function of any special

[10] See *TMS*, VI.i.15 and also *TMS*, VI.ii.3.6.

[11] Indeed Smith suggests that it might even go the other way, with the good or bad fortunes influencing the impartial spectator. See, for example, *TMS*, VI.iii.30.

insight into, or deliberation about, the good, but rather the result of having one's character polished through social interaction.[12] Smith is not particularly concerned with practical wisdom in the classical sense of deliberative insight because virtuous characters, at least at some level, can be the product of the endeavor to fit oneself into society through the constraints that doing so puts upon one's actions and sentiments.[13]

We might express the point in another way. In the classical—that is Aristotelian—conception of practical reasoning there is a practical syllogism whereby the major premise is a universal and the minor premise is the perception of a particular covered by that universal which then issues in a conclusion about action. Thus to oversimplify a bit, an example of such a syllogism might be something like, "eating vegetables promotes health," "this is a vegetable," therefore, "I should eat this." In the first premise we have a universal expressing an insight into the good; in the second there is a "perception" of a particular that seems to exemplify the universal, and in the conclusion there is a call to action based upon the logic of integrating the first two premises. The major (first) premise is thought by Aristotle to be a function of an intellectual insight by the actor into the nature or character of a human good expressed in universal terms.[14] For Smith's practical character, however, we might say that the major premise is supplied by social norms generally and the impartial spectator in particular who give to the agent the necessary universal. The agent thus need not possess wisdom but rather need only take an interest in the views and "the fortunes of others" and

[12] This is a standard metaphor of the time originating from Anthony Ashley Cooper, the Third Earl of Shaftesbury. For a discussion of Shaftesbury's connection to Smith, see Den Uyl, Hanley, and Otteson in *The Adam Smith Review* 6 (Routledge: London 2011): 209–32.

[13] We are reminded here of the passage in *WN*, V.i.g.12-13 where our environment does affect the kind of person we can become.

[14] *Nicomachean Ethics* 1141a16-20. Aristotle speaks of virtue in the "strict sense" (1144b10ff) versus natural virtue where one is referring to a kind of natural disposition towards the good. Strict virtue flows from reason. In a sense, Smith's practical character is more "natural" relying as it does upon sentiment to generate the virtue.

possess the ability to understand what is socially respectable and integrative. The minor premises and conclusions would still be processed the same way, as examples of the universal needing to be deployed into action. Rather than having to depend upon some internalization of the good on the part of the agent, the Smithean approach allows the major premise to be supplied by a kind of externalization. All that is required is the freedom to adapt to those social norms and the disposition to do so.

The advantage of Smith's approach is that more people are potentially able to exhibit behavior that accords with "practical wisdom" than with those who must meet the standards of Aristotelian practical wisdom. Rather than needing a special insight into the good, all that is required in Smith's system is the unleashing of our natural disposition to take an interest in others coupled to the freedom to adapt to their reactions and sentiments according to the norms that evolve out of them. Such mutual polishing is presumably open to all. Strongly hierarchical or authoritarian orders, to give another type of example, would have other ways of supplying that major premise than what is envisioned here by Smith—namely, through commands and generalized forms of supplication. These modalities are inconsistent with the liberty needed to claim that an individual possesses virtue. It is clear, in any case, that Smith believes that commercial orders tend to undermine such hierarchical structures leaving commercial orders as the only real alternative for generalized possibilities of virtue in this adaptive framework of action.

> The gradual improvements of arts, manufactures, and commerce, the same causes which destroyed the power of the great barons, destroyed in the same manner, through the greater part of Europe, the whole temporal power of the clergy.... The ties of interest, which bound the inferior ranks of people to the clergy, were in this manner gradually broken and dissolved. (*WN*, V.i.g.25)

Fittingness through adaptation undercuts hierarchy and creates its own generalized sentiments and norms.

In a world where the norms exhibited in action are not supplied by authority and hierarchy, nor where they require the wisdom of the *phronimos* (Aristotle's man of practical wisdom), it is important to emphasize that it would not follow that one of Aristotle's other important distinctions in this context would be any less relevant. Aristotle distinguishes between what he calls practical wisdom and cleverness.[15] Cleverness is the ability to "do things that tend towards the mark we have set for ourselves, and to hit it."[16] Practical wisdom depends upon this ability. Without the ability to achieve one's ends, one's actions would be ineffective and there would be virtually no practice. But the ability to achieve one's ends says nothing about the value or appropriateness of those ends, or that one is doing anything more than satisfying one's desires. Aristotle's *phronimos* organizes his desires according to the principles exhibited by the major premise of a practical syllogism, as grasped by his insight into the nature of the good, thereby knowing what is appropriate. Using our parallel Smithean conception, the person of practical character would also be one to organize her desires according to norms appropriate to her situation and aspirations. The mere ability to achieve one's ends is quite distinct from achieving them appropriately.

In saying all this, one of the problems of practical wisdom for Smith, and commercial societies generally, only becomes more evident, and that is how precisely to distinguish cleverness from prudence, given that success matters so significantly? Success is certainly the most visible measure. Success may sometimes come, however, through cleverness as well as prudence. The passage cited above, as well as others we have considered, gives us a clue to "solving" this problem, namely that character itself matters to us. Even if we are not always accurate, we can always attempt to discern the character who stands behind an action and know with some measure of reliability that those characters who match the descriptions given by Smith above will tend also to produce the consequences he describes, both for the individuals themselves and society at large. The "beauty" of those characters compels us to admire

[15] *NE*, 1144a25-36.

[16] *NE*, 1144a26.

them, and Smith's hope is that the incumbent approval of such characters will thereby reinforce their presence.

Hence character matters, and the practical character exhibited by Smithean extended prudence is the sort of character not only suitable to commercial orders, but a function of those orders. Once we realize both how markets operate and how Smith conceives of prudence, we see a remarkable parallel. Markets are themselves an interactive series of exchanges and offerings where one must fit oneself into the patterns it generates in order to remain a player. Markets tend towards equilibrium, and their beauty lies precisely in their ability to fit every rational actor into its equation through mechanisms such as pricing which provide incentives to conform. Prices are, in fact, analogous to the impartial spectator in that both are general impersonal guides that nonetheless engage one's personal interest. It is perhaps no accident, then, that prudence reemerges in Smith as an important virtue, for its orientation to context and surroundings is not only suitable for, but expressive of, the successful commercial actor. Justice and benevolence are perhaps to be found in any type of social order, but Smithean prudence requires a degree of personal freedom within a context where one is responsible for one's own actions by means of free interaction with others. To make this move towards centralizing the virtue of prudence, the classical understanding of it had to be modified in the way we have suggested above. It is not so much a type of wisdom that marks the prudent individual as it is the formation of a character able to adapt to the social conditions in which she must act. Sensitivity rather than insight is the more useful mental demeanor.

Although prudence may arise as an important virtue in a commercial culture in a way that may not be true in other orders, it is important to conclude that the extended prudence we have been describing here supposes that one have a conception of one's well being that includes more than simply commercial transactions or success. Prudence narrowed largely to a commercial context alone is "regarded as a most respectable and even, in some degree, as an amiable and agreeable quality, yet is never is considered as one, either of the most endearing, or of the most ennobling of the virtues" (*TMS*, VI.i.14). When prudence is extended to include decency, moderation, self-command and the like—as noted earlier—in the life of "private and peaceable" persons, we end up with the happy coincidence of what serves both the well-being of the individual as well as that of society.